SPOTLIGHT ON WORLD POLITICAL SYSTEMS

AN INTRODUCTION TO COMPARATIVE GOVERNMENT

World Political Systems

Dr J. Denis Derbyshire is a political and communications consultant.
His varied career has embraced senior posts in public administration
and teaching and management in further and higher education. He
has long experience as an external examiner in political studies.

Dr Ian Derbyshire was formerly a British Academy Post Doctoral
Research Fellow at Cambridge University. He specialises in
contemporary international politics and is currently teaching at the
University of York.

SPOTLIGHT ON

WORLD POLITICAL SYSTEMS

AN INTRODUCTION TO COMPARATIVE GOVERNMENT

J DENIS DERBYSHIRE
AND
IAN DERBYSHIRE

Chambers

Published 1991 by W & R Chambers Ltd,
43–45 Annandale Street, Edinburgh EH7 4AZ

British Library Cataloguing in Publication Data
Derbyshire, Ian
    World political systems: an introduction to comparative government.
    1. Political systems
    I. Title II. Derbyshire, J. Denis
    320

ISBN 0-550-20753-8

Cover design by James Hutcheson

Typeset by Pillans & Wilson Ltd. Edinburgh and London
Printed in England by Clays Ltd, St Ives plc

Preface

There are between 150 and 200 sovereign states in the world today, the number varying according to how the word sovereign is defined. Each has its own unique ethnic and social composition and its own unique history. The interplay of these, and other, factors has created, in turn, a unique system of government. There will be similarities between different systems but, in the final analysis, each is distinctively unique. Nevertheless, we have identified particular features which are common to all, or most, of them and have classified them in an attempt to make objective comparisons.

In our classifications we have looked at countries where citizens have a comparatively free choice of which group of people should control the levers of political power and those where that choice is limited. The first we have called multi-party, or pluralistic, states and the second one-party, or monistic. This is an important distinction but it is not the only criterion for deciding whether or not a political system can be said to be democratic.

As we enter the last decade of the present century we are confronted with momentous changes in all parts of the world and it is impossible to predict with certainty the extent to which they will develop. The accession to power in the Soviet Union of Mikhail Gorbachev has already had the effect of casting a stone into the apparently static pool of Eastern European politics and its ripples are spreading to other regions.

There are clear signs that politicians throughout the world are becoming aware that economic systems cannot be changed without affecting political systems. In the Soviet Union, for example, political changes have been made to facilitate economic reform. In China, on the other hand, economic change has preceded political reform with dire, if predictable, consequences. It seems certain that if people are given greater economic choice then, sooner or later, they will demand political choice as well.

In the pages that follow we have tried to provide a better understanding of political institutions and events in the contemporary world and have addressed ourselves not just to academics and professional observers of the political landscape but also to the more general reader who is looking for a serious, but not over-technical, account of global politics.

Contents

List of Tables

Chapter 1

UNDERSTANDING POLITICAL SYSTEMS

1.1 Political Man

The Greek philosopher, Aristotle (384–322 BC), said that man was by nature a political animal. He argued that it was within man's natural development to live in some sort of ordered society under a system of government. In the times in which he lived the kind of community he saw as natural was the comparatively small city-state of Ancient Greece, with thousands, rather than millions, of citizens able to practise direct democracy.

In the world of today there are few communities that resemble those small communities. The Most Serene Republic of San Marino in Italy is probably the best example. It is the sole city state which survived after the unification of Italy in the nineteenth century and has the distinction of being the world's oldest republic, its independence recognised and its protection guaranteed by Italy. Because of its small population, about 20,000, San Marino is able to enjoy a uniquely intimate kind of government.

The majority of countries have considerably larger populations, of course, and their governments are more remote from the average citizen. Nevertheless, Aristotle's belief that mankind achieves natural fulfilment by living in a political community seems to have been borne out by subsequent events, as this account of the political systems of the world will try to show.

1.2 What is a Political System?

So that we can better understand the nature of a political system it will be helpful if we first attempt to define certain words which are frequently used in everyday speech but whose meanings are not always clear.

We use the word government in a variety of ways. In a general sense we use it to mean an orderly way of running a community's affairs and it is possible to distinguish between local government, perhaps regional government, and national government. The absence of government is anarchy, with everyone looking after him or herself: the law of the jungle. In a more specific sense we speak of the government as a body of people who have power to make us behave in certain ways. Because they are the government they have authority as well as power. In other words, their power is legitimate. We will not concern ourselves for the moment about how this power is achieved. That is something we shall discover as we look at each country more closely.

Another word frequently used in this context is the state. Often we see it as synonymous with government, with the two words interchangeable. To some extent this is quite valid: a government department might also be called a department of state. The word should be used a little more precisely, however. Governments come and go, as we all know, but the state may be said to be permanent, comprising the whole apparatus by which a community is governed: the armed forces, the police, the civil service, the judicial system and so on.

The word can also be used to describe a country which has an independent, internationally recognised, government, such as the state of Israel or the state of Egypt. What then should we say of the United States of America? Is this another use of the word state? No, the word is applicable to nations or parts of nations. It just happens that the contemporary world consists largely of nation-states and the United States is simply a nation-state comprising fifty sub-national states. We will look at the concept of the nation-state more closely a little later.

Within the same broad context we speak of politicians. They are the people who achieve, or hope to achieve, power and, in simple terms, run the government. How do they fit into the scheme of things? Civil servants, members of the armed forces, judges and similar public servants are the permanent personnel of the state while the politicians provide the temporary element. Politicians are the people who occupy positions of power as long as they have the support of the community, or they may be the people who aspire to power but are temporarily out of office. Exactly how politicians achieve power need not concern us at the moment; this will become evident as our study proceeds. We will see that power is obtained sometimes on the basis of consent, the democratic approach, and sometimes on the basis of force, the autocratic approach.

Both the words government and state are rather static terms but if we add to them the political dimension, provided by politicians and their activities, we have something much more dynamic: a political system.

A political system can probably best be understood in demand-response terms. In the majority of countries politicians are elected to positions of power and authority, the ballot box giving the ordinary citizen an opportunity to make his or her demands known. Politicians will try to anticipate these demands by offering a 'prospectus' of what they will provide if elected – a manifesto of promises – and the elector can then choose between different manifestoes on offer. Once a political party has been elected to office it will be judged by its performance and the electorate's response to that performance will again be demonstrated through the ballot box at subsequent elections.

Not all political systems provide such an open choice through the ballot box. There are still a number where a government is imposed by force or where the opportunity to vote politicians into office is limited to a section of the population. The South African political system, for example, provides opportunities for people to elect a government of their choice provided the colour of their skin is white. If it is a little darker, their opportunities to be governed by politicians of their own choosing are more limited. If they are black then a government is imposed on them and there is nothing in the political process which allows them to express their views.

A country's political system, then, is more than its institutions and more than the formal processes of government. It includes the dynamic interplay of people's ideas and interests: the whole process of demand and response which politics represents. Even if a government is highly authoritarian, giving little room for the political process to work, there will always be at least an undercurrent of activity which expresses the true aspirations of people, however subordinated they may be by those with power and authority.

1.3 The Advantages of Comparing Systems

The comparative approach is a particularly advantageous way of arriving at a better understanding of political systems. Not just systems in general, but also a specific one about which you may consider yourself to be very knowledgeable.

First, the comparative approach forces you to stand back and look objectively at a particular system. It should be no surprise that some of the best studies of the American system of government, for instance, have been made by people whose personal experience has been gained in a different political environment.

Second, the comparative approach alerts you to similarities in institutions and processes which make your own system more understandable.

Third, the experience of one country can be used to anticipate the effects of change in the political system of another. For example, a knowledge of the voting system in the Republic of Ireland, where a form of proportional representation operates, will enable some sort of prediction to be made of the likely impact if it were introduced into the United Kingdom.

Finally, and this is probably the greatest advantage of all, a wider understanding of how countries with different histories, different ethnic compositions, different social problems and different philosophical backgrounds have approached the basic problem of creating and sustaining satisfactory institutions and processes of government is an excellent way of stimulating interest in the political process and a greater degree of participation. It is surely a sad reflection on the state of contemporary democracies that, at best, fewer than 5 per cent of their populations can be classed as being 'regularly' active in a political sense.

1.4 The Nation-State

The comparisons of political systems which will be made are based on the concept of the nation-state and Table 1 lists those which will be considered. Although today it is seen as the 'natural' political unit for most areas of the world the nation-state is a comparatively new concept. No fewer than 123 of the 165 states which will be examined are products of the present century, 74 being post-1959 creations. In the Middle East and Africa only three of the 65 were in existence before 1910 and even in Europe, where a majority of 'old' states might be expected, more than 40 per cent of them achieved full independent nationhood after the First World War.

Before the twentieth century most of the world's inhabitants were, in one way or another, in the thrall of the established Western European powers and if a datum point of, say, 1810 is taken, only 15 of today's 165 states existed in a form that might be readily recognisable today.

A nation may be described as a group of people, often from

different backgrounds, and sometimes from different races, who have come to live together and have adopted a common identity. The unity of a nation is usually reinforced by a common language and sometimes a common religion. A state is the name given to the whole apparatus of government which a nation creates as the machine for operating its political system.

The nation-state is then enshrined and perpetuated by the adoption of symbols such as a national flag and a national anthem. The human apex of the nation-state is the individual designated as head of state, in the person of a king, queen or president. Sometimes the head of state is little more than a symbol of national unity, with few or no political powers. Sometimes the roles of head of state and head of government are combined but, in such cases, an attempt is usually made to differentiate between the two roles. In the United States, for example, the office of president generally attracts the respect of most citizens regardless of the personality or political views of the holder.

The nation-state manifests itself in a wide variety of different forms, ranging from the democratic to the highly authoritarian. It is this rich variety which provides the material for what will follow.

1.5 The Comparative Approach

The comparative approach looks first at the various constitutional forms which can be adopted for political systems and then at the philosophies or ideologies which underlie the constitutional structures. Then executives, heads of state and heads of government, and assemblies or parliaments in different countries are compared. Then, moving on to the more dynamic elements of political systems, voting methods and parties are examined.

Altogether 164 states are covered. They include 156 of the current 158 full members of the United Nations plus the eight independent states of Kiribati, North and South Korea, Nauru, Switzerland, Taiwan, Tonga and Tuvalu. The Byelorussian and Ukrainian Socialist Soviet Republics have been excluded since, although they are both individual members of the United Nations, they are, in reality and in a political sense, part of the Soviet Union.

The eight non-UN states have been added because all have full national sovereignties and their presence outside the United

Nations organisation has no useful bearing on the subject matter of our present examination of political systems. Switzerland, for example, has chosen, on the basis of its long history of neutrality, not to be a UN member and Taiwan was a member, under the title of the Republic of China, from 1945 to 1971, when the People's Republic of China received full international recognition. South Korea has repeatedly sought UN membership since 1949, but has been rebuffed by Soviet vetoes. The four South Pacific states of Kiribati, Nauru, Tonga and Tuvalu, which attained independence only relatively recently, have determined on a neutralist course and have not yet applied for direct UN representation.

TABLE 1   NATION-STATES OF THE WORLD

Afghanistan	1747	Côte d'Ivoire	1960	Jamaica	1962
Albania	1912	Cuba	1899	Japan	5th C
Algeria	1962	Cyprus	1960	Jordan	1946
Angola	1975	Czechoslovakia	1918	Kenya	1963
Antigua and Barbuda	1981	Denmark	c940	Kiribati*	1979
Argentina	1816	Djibouti	1977	Korea North*	1948
Australia	1901	Dominica	1978	Korea South*	1948
Austria	1918	Dominican Rep	1844	Kuwait	1961
Bahamas	1973	Ecuador	1830	Laos	1954
Bahrain	1971	Egypt	1922	Lebanon	1944
Bangladesh	1971	El Salvador	1838	Lesotho	1966
Barbados	1966	Equatorial Guinea	1968	Liberia	1847
Belgium	1830	Ethiopia	11th C	Libya	1951
Belize	1981	Fiji	1970	Luxembourg	1848
Benin	1960	Finland	1917	Madagascar	1960
Bhutan	1907	France	741	Malawi	1964
Bolivia	1825	Gabon	1960	Malaysia	1957
Botswana	1966	Gambia	1965	Maldives	1965
Brazil	1822	Germany	1949/1990	Mali	1960
Brunei	1984	Ghana	1957	Malta	1964
Bulgaria	1908	Greece	1829	Mauritania	1960
Burkina Faso	1960	Grenada	1974	Mauritius	1968
Burma	1948	Guatemala	1839	Mexico	1821
Burundi	1962	Guinea	1958	Mongolia	1921/1946
Cambodia	1953	Guinea-Bissau	1974	Morocco	1956
Cameroon	1960	Guyana	1966	Mozambique	1975
Canada	1867	Haiti	1804	Namibia	1989
Cape Verde	1975	Honduras	1838	Nauru*	1968
Central African		Hungary	1918	Nepal	1768
Republic	1960	Iceland	1944	Netherlands	1648
Chad	1960	India	1947	New Zealand	1853/1947
Chile	1818	Indonesia	1949	Nicaragua	1838
China	2nd C BC	Iran	1499	Niger	1960
Colombia	1830	Iraq	1932	Nigeria	1960
The Comoros	1975	Ireland, Republic of	1937	Norway	1905
Congo	1960	Israel	1948	Oman	1951
Costa Rica	1821	Italy	1861	Pakistan	1947

Table 1—Nation-States of the World (contd)

Panama	1903	South Africa	1910	Tunisia	1956
Papua New Guinea	1975	Spain	1492	Turkey	1923
Paraguay	1811	Sri Lanka	1948	Tuvalu*	1978
Peru	1824	St Kitts-Nevis	1983	Uganda	1962
Philippines	1946	St Lucia	1979	United Arab Emirates	1971
Poland	1918	St Vincent and the		United Kingdom	1707/1921
Portugal	1128	Grenadines	1979	United States	1776
Qatar	1971	Sudan	1956	Uruguay	1825
Romania	1881	Suriname	1975	USSR	1917–22
Rwanda	1962	Swaziland	1968	Vanuatu	1980
Sao Tome and		Sweden	1523	Venezuela	1830
Principe	1975	Switzerland*	1648	Vietnam	1954/1976
Saudi Arabia	1932	Syria	1946	Western Samoa	1962
Senegal	1960	Taiwan*	1949	Yemeni	
Seychelles	1976	Tanzania	1961	Republic	1967/1990
Sierra Leone	1961	Thailand	1350	Yugoslavia	1918
Singapore	1965	Togo	1960	Zaire	1960
Solomon Isles	1978	Tonga*	1970	Zambia	1964
Somalia	1960	Trinidad and Tobago	1962	Zimbabwe	1980

All the states in this table, except for those asterisked, are current members of the United Nations. The dates indicate the year of each country's inception as a nation-state. This date will normally be the year in which its first constitution was adopted, which may or may not be the one currently in force. In the case of a minority of countries, particularly those with dates prior to the nineteenth century, the inception of nationhood will pre-date the adoption of the first constitution or a codified constitution may never have been adopted.

The 164 states have been grouped into nine geographical regions: Western Europe; Eastern Europe; the Middle East and North Africa; Central and Southern Africa; North America; Central America and the Caribbean; South America; Asia; and Oceania. This classification has been chosen in preference to one based purely on philosophical values, such as liberal-democratic, totalitarian and so on. Such an approach is superficially attractive but fraught with difficulties. It is, inevitably, subjective and can have the effect of distorting the profile of a political system so as to force it into one of the chosen categories. On the other hand there are, apart from convenience, some good reasons for adopting the regional approach.

First, there is an undoubted link, as will be demonstrated, between a country's geography and history and the political system it develops. A look at the continent of America, and its associated islands, will illustrate this point.

The whole of North America was at one time a British colony. The fact that Canada, which retained its connection with Britain, also retained aspects of the British constitution in its political system is understandable. Equally understandable is the recognition that the United States, which broke its link with Britain 200 years ago, chose to develop a different system which looks more guardedly at the dangers of unfettered executive power and seeks to control and restrain it. The United States constitution, therefore, reflects other influences, such as the political climate in eighteenth-century France.

The geography and social composition of North America have also had effects on the political systems of both Canada and the United States, resulting in federal structures of government which take into account the size and diversities of both countries.

Moving south down the continent, the fact that much of Central and South America were once part of a Spanish empire whereas the islands of the Caribbean came under British and French influence is, again, reflected in their political systems.

Second, there is a discernible link between a country's ethnic characteristics and the political system it develops, and these characteristics tend to be regionalised in many cases. For example, it is not surprising that the majority of Islamic states are to be found in the Middle East and North Africa.

An attempt to classify states geographically or politically is, inevitably, a somewhat arbitrary process. Where does Western Europe end and Eastern Europe begin? Should Turkey, which bestrides both Europe and Asia, be included in Europe? If in Europe, why the Western, rather than the Eastern, part?

Similar problems occur when classifications are attempted in other parts of the world. What exactly is meant by the Middle East? Should not the continent of Africa be regarded as a whole? If not, how should it be divided? Asia produces similar, and perhaps even more intractable, problems, such as that of defining boundaries. Another arises from the sheer size and complexity of the area, extending from Afghanistan in the west to Japan in the east.

One region which has been used for classification purposes is Oceania. Where exactly are its boundaries? Indeed, can it be said to exist at all? For the purposes of this book it is regarded as including Australasia and those island territories in the Pacific which do not fit easily into any other of the regional groupings which have been chosen.

The arbitrary nature of the classification is freely admitted and no apologies are offered. Without such an approach much of the material would have been less manageable and, in any event, for the majority of states alternative groupings would not have brought out so clearly the influences of history, geography and social development.

Chapter 8 deals with residual territories in the world which cannot be viewed as fully fledged independent states. Into this category fall five tiny West European principalities, city and theocratic states, Andorra, Liechtenstein, Monaco, San Marino, and the Vatican City, which are closely linked to and heavily dependent for their external security upon their much larger neighbours. These have been termed semi-sovereign states. Also into this category fall the 50 overseas colonies and external dependent territories that still exist in the world of today.

Chapter 9 also looks beyond nation-states and their dependencies to regional and global groupings, recognising that the accelerated improvements in communications of all kinds, and the growing economic interdependence of countries, will inevitably cause the world to shrink in political as well as physical terms.

Chapter 10 assesses the impact of the momentous changes of 1989 and 1990 on world political systems.

Recommended Reading

Charlton, R., *Comparative Government*, Longman, 1986, Ch 1.

Crick, B., *In Defence of Politics*, 2nd edn., Penguin, 1982.

Dogan, M. and Pelassy, G., *How to Compare Nations*, Chatham House, 1984.

Evans, P. B., Rueschemeyer, D. and Skocpol, T. (eds), *Bringing the State Back In*, Cambridge University Press, 1985.

Hague, R. and Harrop, M., *Comparative Government and Politics: An Introduction*, 2nd edn., Macmillan, 1987, Chs 1–3.

Harding, N. (ed), *The State in Socialist Society*, Macmillan, 1984.

King, R., *The State in Modern Society: New Directions in Political Sociology*, Macmillan, 1986.

Leftwich, A. (ed), *What is Politics? The Activity and its Study*, Basil Blackwell, 1984.

Lukes, S. (ed), *Power*, Basil Blackwell, 1986.

Macridis, R. and Brown, B. (eds), *Comparative Politics: Notes and Readings*, 5th edn., Dorsey, Homewood, Illinois, 1977.

Roberts, G. K., *An Introduction to Comparative Politics*, Edward Arnold, 1986, Ch 1.

Chapter 2

CONSTITUTIONS

2.1 What a Constitution is

A constitution can be regarded in two ways. First, it is a general statement of how a country is governed. For example, the United States constitution could be described as republican, federal and presidential, whereas that of the United Kingdom would be monarchical, unitary and parliamentary. For someone familiar with 'constitutional language' but who knew nothing about the political systems of the United States and the United Kingdom these two statements would say something, but not much.

On the other hand, for someone completely unversed in constitutional and political terminology the two descriptions would do little or nothing to advance a knowledge of the two countries. Republican, monarchical, federal, unitary, presidential, parliamentary are all words which are intended to have precise meanings within the context of an exposition of a political system.

In an even more general sense a constitution may be said to be liberal or authoritarian, using two contrasting words which can be found in any non-technical dictionary. These distinctions would probably conjure up a picture of two political systems that a layman would understand. If you had the choice, which would you prefer: liberal or authoritarian? Most people would choose the former, if only because it had a more 'comfortable' sound. But if one constitution was said to be more liberal than another or more authoritarian than another difficulties would immediately be created.

To use the word constitution in a general sense, therefore, is not particularly helpful. It is rather like saying that France has better weather than Britain. What parts of France and Britain? What times of the year? Is the weather consistent, year in and year out? Obviously, more questions are raised than answered.

In a more specific sense, a constitution is a document or set of documents describing the framework of a political system. It stipulates where power lies within a state, what the institutions of government are, how they are constructed and how they are intended to operate. In doing so, it provides what might be said to be a set of rules for politicians in a particular country to follow: what offices they can hold, how they get to office, what they can do and not do in office, how laws are made, how they are enforced, how disputes between citizens and the state are resolved.

2.2 What a Constitution is not

A constitution falls far short of being an accurate description of a political system. For example, it is unlikely even to mention political parties or any other forms of organised interests. It will say how power is distributed but not how it is used.

There are several possible analogies which could be used to point out differences between a constitution and a political system but the most accurate is probably a theatrical one. A constitution can be said to be the text of a play whereas the political system is its enactment. Often a constitution even falls short of being a complete text and is rather more a plot with a cast of characters. There are two missing elements which are needed if a constitution is to become alive and translated from a written text into a live production.

The first is political activity or the interplay of power: in other words, how a head of government arrives at a position of power, how that power is used, how he and his supporters try to retain power and how their opponents try to divest them of it. This is where the activities of parties and interest groups are all important.

The second missing element is what are called constitutional conventions. These are the understandings which politicians accept as being the unwritten rules of how a constitution should work in practice. Conventions bring flexibility and reality into the political process. They allow a constitution to remain firm in its fundamentals but flexible enough to adapt to changing political circumstances.

The use of the word convention is, perhaps, unfortunate because it can have a very different meaning, particularly in the United States where it is the name given to conferences or rallies of political parties. Furthermore the combined term, constitutional convention, refers in the United States to a special meeting of state government representatives, called at the request of two-thirds of state legislatures, to draft new amendments to the constitution. A better approach would be to speak of conventional behaviour, in other words customary practices which politicians adopt because experience has shown that they make the governmental process work more smoothly. This conventional behaviour acts as a lubricant to the political system.

A constitutional convention begins life as an attempt to solve a problem or potential problem. If it is successful then it may be accepted by politicians as an agreed way of approaching a similar problem in the future. If it works successfully on a number of occasions there will be tacit agreement that it has achieved the status of a constitutional convention. It may even be written into a constitution as a formal amendment so that there will be no confusion about whether or not this, originally conventional, procedure should always be followed.

In the United Kingdom there is no legislation which says that the Prime Minister must be a member of the House of Commons but, although in the second half of the nineteenth century no fewer than six of the twelve governments were headed by peers, there has been no Prime Minister sitting in the House of Lords since 1895. A constitutional convention has established this practice. A similar convention ensures that government ministers must be members of one or other of the Houses of Parliament.

To recapitulate, a constitution provides the framework for a political system. It does not give a full, or even accurate, picture of how the system works in practice.

2.3 Written and Unwritten Constitutions

Most states have a basic, written document which is called its constitution. It may not be the same one which was adopted when the state first came into existence. Even if it is, it is likely to have been amended several times since its original adoption.

A minority of states do not have such a basic document. Excepting those in which the existing constitution has been temporarily suspended, of the 165 states listed in Table 1 only six fall into this category: Bhutan, Israel, New Zealand, Oman, Saudi Arabia and the United Kingdom. Because of this they are often said to have unwritten constitutions. This is not strictly true.

Although the King of Bhutan would appear to have unlimited powers, with no constitution to restrain him, there are written rules which govern procedures for elections to the Royal Advisory Council and the National Assembly and say how they operate, and the King is expected to ensure they are observed.

In the cases of the other two absolute monarchies of Oman and

Saudi Arabia, fewer informal quasi-constitutional checks exist. In both countries, however, the head of state is expected to govern in conformity with the Sharia, the sacred law of Islam. In addition, in Saudi Arabia the King must retain the consensus of the rest of the extensive royal family as well as the ulema (Muslim religious jurists) and sheikhs.

Israel has no single document which it calls a constitution but in 1950 the state parliament voted to adopt one by evolution over an unspecified period of time and since then a number of laws have been passed which are regarded as being part of the constitution. The Jewish holy book, the Torah, also remains an ancient source of political authority.

When it became a fully independent state New Zealand decided to model its political system on that of the United Kingdom even to the extent of not adopting a formal written constitution. Nevertheless, there are certain pieces of legislation which are seen to have a particular constitutional significance, such as the Acts which determine the eligibility of voters and their representatives.

The United Kingdom is usually cited as the classic example of a state without a written constitution but again, as in the other three countries, there are Acts of Parliament which are regarded as being constitutionally important. The most notable is probably the 1689 Bill of Rights which established the legislative supremacy of parliament and from which the rest of the evolutionary constitution developed. In more recent years the legislation restricting the powers of the House of Lords (the Parliament Acts of 1911 and 1949), and widening the franchise (the Reform Acts of 1832, 1867, 1884, 1918, 1928, 1948 and 1970), must be regarded as being a form of constitutional amendment.

Thus it is not really accurate to distinguish between written and unwritten constitutions. A better distinction would be between codified and uncodified documents for it is certain that, although it would probably be a long and tortuous process, it would be quite possible to draw up a written, codified constitution for the United Kingdom, and for the other five countries, if it were thought useful and necessary.

2.4 What a Constitution Contains

Individual constitutions do vary but most contain certain basic statements about the institutions which have been created to

13

govern a state and how they are expected to operate. Some constitutions go further and, being framed either at a state's inception or following a major political upheaval resulting in a change of regime, identify the kind of society a political system is trying to create and maintain.

The main thrust of most constitutions is to distinguish between the three basic powers of government: the power to make laws, the *legislative* function; the power to enforce laws, the *executive* function; and the power to interpret laws and adjudicate in disputes between the citizen and the state, the *judicial* function.

The United States constitution, for example, has seven main Articles:

Article 1	defines the legislative powers;
Article 2	deals with the office of President, as the nation's chief executive;
Article 3	sets out the powers of the courts, including the Supreme Court;
Article 4	deals with relations between the individual states;
Article 5	describes how the constitution can be amended;
Articles 6 and 7	deal mainly with arrangements for transforming a loose federation of states into a full union.

The constitution of the French Fifth Republic has fourteen main Titles:

Title 1	deals with the sovereignty of the Republic;
Title 2	sets out the powers and duties of the President;
Title 3	describes the role of the Prime Minister and the rest of the government;
Title 4	sets out the structure and functions of parliament;
Title 5	deals with the relationship between parliament and the government;
Title 7	sets out the composition and role of the Constitutional Council;
Title 8	describes judicial powers;
Title 10	sets out the composition and role of the Economic and Social Council;
Title 14	describes how the constitution can be amended.

The other titles deal with detailed, specific matters.

Many constitutions begin with a broad statement of the aims which they hope to achieve.

The preamble to the United States constitution of 1787 reads:

> We, the people of the United States, in order to form a more perfect Union, establish Justice, insure domestic Tranquillity, provide for the common Defense, promote the general Welfare, and secure the Blessings of Liberty to ourselves and our Posterity, do ordain and establish this Constitution for the United States of America.

The preamble to the French constitution of 1958 reads:

> The French people hereby solemnly proclaim their attachment to the Rights of Man and the principles of national sovereignty as defined by the Declaration of 1789, reaffirmed and completed by the Preamble to the Constitution of 1946.

Most states have a Bill of Rights, guaranteeing certain basic individual rights, such as freedom of speech and freedom of assembly, either incorporated in or associated with a codified constitution. It would be possible for any state to adopt such a charter even without a codified constitution and whether or not to have a Bill of Rights has been a matter of debate for some years within the United Kingdom.

Although the great majority of states have a guarantee of individual rights either built into their constitutions or associated with them, the mere fact of there being such a written guarantee should not be assumed to mean that such rights really exist and are protected. Some of these apparent guarantees are couched in rather limited terms. The Iranian constitution, for example, states that the press is free but adds: 'except in matters that are contrary to public morality or insult religious belief'. In similar vein, Article 50 of the Soviet Union's 1977 state constitution (Fundamental Law) grants freedom of speech, of the press and of assembly, so long as it is 'in accordance with the interests of the people' and is used 'to strengthen and develop the socialist system'.

Whether or not individual rights are really guaranteed and protected needs therefore to be determined by rather more objective means than just the reading of such a guarantee in a constitution.

2.5 Rigidity and Flexibility

Sometimes attempts are made to distinguish between what are seen as rigid and flexible constitutions, usually on the basis of how easily a constitution adapts to changing circumstances. If it adapts readily it is said to be flexible and if it does not it is rigid.

Perhaps understandably, an unwritten constitution suggests great flexibility. After all, there is no formal, legalistic procedure for making a change. If the political will is there then a change will take place, probably by introducing a new constitutional convention or usage, or discarding an old one. But the assumption that a codified constitution is less flexible than an uncodified one is often misleading. When a usage can be changed or discarded without any technical obstacles it seems reasonable to conclude that the politicians who might make a change will approach a proposal very warily.

If a change has to go through some elaborate, formal procedure, such as in the United States, where an amendment to the constitution has to be proposed by a two-thirds vote of both houses of Congress and then ratified by the legislatures of three-quarters of the states, it seems reasonable to assume that a lightly or poorly conceived change will get a thorough consideration before it is finally accepted. However, in a state where such a weighty, formal procedure is absent the onus is placed on proposers of change to be absolutely certain in their own minds that there will no lasting, damaging consequences. Confronted with this responsibility, it is understandable that, in more cases than not, the *status quo* will be retained and the change cautiously avoided.

This is especially the case in liberal democracies, where constitutional government, in accordance with formal rules, is most deeply embedded in the public and political psyche. An exception has been France, which has framed 17 constitutions since 1789. In newer, emergent, or one-party, regimes the process of constitution re-drafting has often been frequent, with fresh codes being introduced to meet the changed circumstances of the day. The South American states, independent since the early nineteenth century, have been particularly prominent in this respect. Venezuela, for example, has had 26 constitutions, though the present one dates back almost 30 years. The Dominican Republic has had 25; Haiti more than 20; Ecuador 17; El Salvador, Bolivia, and Colombia 16 apiece; Honduras twelve; and Brazil eight. Similarly, in communist or former communist regimes new constitutions have regularly been framed as a means of giving recognition to the advancing stages of 'socialist development' that have been attained. The Soviet Union had four such documents, in 1918, 1922, 1936 and 1977, since the revolution of 1917. Yugoslavia had a similar number since the federal republic was first established in 1945, while Czechoslovakia and Romania each had three.

2.6 Separation or Fusion of Powers

We have already said that the main area of concern of a codified constitution will be the three main institutions of government: the legislature, the executive and the judiciary. A comparison of constitutions could attempt to discover whether these institutions are kept separate or are fused.

The best known proponent of the doctrine of the separation of powers was the French philosopher, Baron Montesquieu (1689–1755), who set out the theory in *De L'Esprit des Lois* (1748). He argued that by keeping the three institutions separate and balanced the possibility of one of them, and particularly the executive, accruing undue power, and then exploiting it to the detriment of the citizenry, would be avoided.

His views made a considerable impact and were clearly taken into account by the framers of the United States constitution. As one of them, James Madison (1751–1836), said: 'the accumulation of all powers, legislative, executive and judiciary, in the same hands . . . may justly be pronounced the very definition of tyranny.' Oddly enough, Montesquieu cited England as a country enjoying relatively great liberty because the powers of government were distributed between the legislative, executive and judicial institutions and had the effect of balancing each other. In reality, as will be seen later, a political system based on a parliamentary executive, as in the United Kingdom, creates a fusion, rather than a separation, of the legislative and executive functions.

The concept of a separation or balancing of powers is still a useful test of the degree of freedom from autocratic rule within a political system but on its own is an insufficient, and sometimes unreliable, criterion.

2.7 Unitary or Federal States

A constitution invariably seeks to clarify the relationship between the government with the responsibility for the whole of a state's territory and that concerned with only part of it: in other words, central government and localised government.

Democratic government is believed to have begun in the city states of ancient Greece, and particularly the city of Athens, which, with a total population of less than 50,000, was able to practise direct and universal participation in government. In fact the very word democracy (*demokratia*), roughly meaning rule (*kratos*) by the people (*demos*), is derived from ancient Greece. In that situation democracy was direct, involving the active and personal participation in government of all adult 'full-citizens' at some time in their lives, by accepting office on a rota basis. There are still vestiges of direct democracy in those contemporary states which make use of juries in their judicial systems.

Today, of course, there are few, and no major, states small enough to enjoy direct democracy. The unusual, perhaps unique, example of the tiny Most Serene Republic of San Marino in Italy has already been noted. Elements of direct democracy also survive in several of the smaller cantons (states) in the Swiss Confederation, with the electorate, numbering at most 10,000, meeting in a public place on one day each year to select officials and vote on issues. These cases are anachronisms and the vast majority of states which claim to be democratic do so on the basis of representative, rather than direct, democracy.

Putting exceptions such as San Marino and the Swiss cantons aside, all modern states find it necessary to have institutions to administer the needs of particular localities as well as the whole population. The larger the area the more obvious the need to cater for local, or regional, as well as national interests. The extent to which power is devolved by the government in the centre to the localities and the nature of the power devolved indicate whether or not a genuinely federal system is operating.

A nation-state is one which claims sovereignty over the whole of its territory. In other words, everyone within its boundaries is subject to its laws. If a government decides to divide its sovereignty within its boundaries and pass some of it to local bodies it means the devolution of some of its law-making powers. If the central government retains the right to override these devolved powers at any time then the state cannot be said to be truly federal.

If a federal system is adopted the respective legislative powers of the governments in the centre and the localities must be clearly defined and the local governments must be protected against the erosion of those powers by central government. This can only be done successfully through the medium of a written, codified constitution. Because circumstances change, there must be provision for this distribution of legislative power to be reviewed but in a truly federal system that review cannot be undertaken arbitrarily by the central government and the process must involve the localities, either by giving them 'blocking' powers with respect to proposed constitutional amendments in their areas of concern or through the adjudicatory medium of an impartial constitutional court.

The supreme example of a genuinely federal system of government is found in the United States constitution. Section 8 of Article I sets out the powers of the central legislature, Congress, and, by implication, leaves the residue of powers to the state legislatures. Article V prescribes how the constitution can be amended, such amendments requiring the approval of three-quarters of the state legislatures, and Article III the adjudicatory authority of the Supreme Court.

This form of devolution is effected by prescribing the legislative powers of the centre and leaving the residue with the localities. Another method is to prescribe the powers of the localities and leave the residue to the centre. Virtually all the world's federal systems adopt the former approach although the Canadian constitution comes nearer to the latter, defining precisely the powers of both the federal and state governments.

When executive, rather than legislative, powers are decentralised a state is said to have a unitary constitution and of the 165 states in Table 1 the great majority are unitary, only 20 having federal structures. As with most other aspects of political systems, history, geography and culture are the strongest factors behind the choice of a federal system of government. Of particular importance, not surprisingly, is country size, with seven of the eight largest nations in the world having federal structures. Moreover, the one exception within this grouping, China, has established five 'autonomous regions', for its non-Han minority border communities, which are of a quasi-federal nature. It is for this reason that, despite their small numbers, 40 per cent of the world's population live in states with federal constitutions. The broad range of factors that have determined the existence of federal structures in these and the remaining 13 states are presented in Table 2 together with a brief exposition of the types of federal system in operation.

TABLE 2   FEDERAL STATES IN THE CONTEMPORARY WORLD

In brackets are the world rankings (WR) of these states in terms of population (c 1985) and areal size; the chief determinants of federalism and its form then follow.

Argentina: pop: 31.20m (WR 28); area: 2.78m km^2 (WR 8).

Historical, cultural and geographical: early history was dominated by a conflict between town and country, particularly the European-style sophistication of Buenos Aires and the rough, uncivilised style of the gaucho. An attempt to impose a unitary system in 1829 failed. There are today 22 provinces, each with its own assembly, governor and constitution. The five-member Supreme Court adjudges federal-state constitutional conflicts.

Australia: pop: 15.76m (WR 48); area: 7.69m km^2 (WR 6).

Geographical and historical: the size of the country and distribution of the population have created distinctive, separate communities. For example, both Darwin, in the north, and Perth, in the west, are more than 3,000 kilometres from the capital, Canberra, whereas the two largest cities, Sydney and Melbourne, are, respectively, less than 300 and 500 kilometres. Historically, throughout the 19th century the country was divided into six distinct colonies, founded separately, governed separately and bounded by largely uninhabited land. Not until 1901 did the colonies unite in the Commonwealth of Australia. The six states have their own legislatures and constitutions, with, still today, 60 per cent of the nation's population residing in their capitals. They receive the bulk of their funds in the form of annually negotiated grants from the centre, which has authority to levy income tax. Federal-state conflicts are ruled upon by the seven-member Australian High Court.

Austria: pop: 7.55m (WR 73); area: 0.08m km^2 (WR 109).

Partly historical and partly artificial: a weak federal system which had operated between the two world wars was revived, under United States influence, in 1945. There are nine states (*Länder*), each with its own assembly. The policy-framing powers residing with the state governments are however limited to the spheres of regional planning, agriculture, hospitals and electricity. Federal-state disputes are adjudged by the 14-member Constitutional Court.

Brazil: pop: 143.30m (WR 6); area: 8.51m km^2 (WR 5).

Geographical and cultural: the size of the country and distribution of the population favoured federalism. The land mass is greater than continental United States, minus Alaska. Each of the 23 states has a single-chamber assembly, elected governor and constitution. There is a 16-member Supreme Court to decide on federal-state conflicts though it is viewed as strongly susceptible to presidential influence. The new constitution adopted in 1988 will enhance states' powers and their tax-raising capabilities *vis-à-vis* the federal government, strengthening what was previously a comparatively weak federal system.

Table 2—Federal States in the Contemporary World (contd)

Canada: pop: 25.63m (WR 31); area: 9.98m km² (WR 2).
Geographical, historical and cultural: the size of the country and the wide cultural mix created strong regional differences. Historically, the nation was created by the confederation of four British colonies in 1867. Six other former colonies joined the Dominion between 1870 and 1949. The ten resulting provinces have their own assemblies and elected premiers. They can frame their own civil laws and have control of education policy. The nine-member Supreme Court rules on federal-state constitutional disputes.

The Comoros: pop: 0.47m (WR 147); area: 0.002m km² (WR 160).
Geographical and historical: this state is a group of three islands. Each island has its own elected governor and island assembly, with partial administrative and legislative autonomy.

Czechoslovakia: pop: 15.50m (WR 50); area: 0.13m km² (WR 93).
Historical and cultural: a federal system, adopted in 1968, is a means of giving recognition to the nation's Slovak minority. The country is now divided into two equal, Czech and Slovak, republics, each with its own assembly, cabinet and Prime Minister. The republics have legislative competence in the spheres of education, health, culture and local justice.

Germany: pop: 78.40m (WR 12); area: 0.36m km² (WR 56).
Historical and partly artificial: the Weimar Republic, carrying on earlier German Empire traditions, had a weak form of federalism which was destroyed by the Hitler regime. Under United States influence it was revived in 1945 as a means of providing a check against the possible future abuse of central authority. Since unification, in 1990, there are 16 states (*Länder*) each with its own constitution, elected assembly and government, headed by a minister-president, and substantial civil service. The states have powers in education, police and local government matters and have local taxation powers, raising and collecting property, motor-vehicle and inheritance taxes. In addition, they receive an assigned equal share of federal revenue accruing from VAT, income tax and corporation tax and are responsible for carrying out the administration of federal matters. The *Länder* are, as a consequence, today, responsible for half of total government spending in Germany and rely on the federal exchequer for only a quarter of their revenue needs. Federal-state disputes are policed by an independent 16-member Federal Constitutional Court. In practice, however, German federalism is largely consensual in character, based on the striking of pragmatic committee-room deals between senior federal and state politicians and civil servants in Bonn or Berlin, whichever eventually becomes the administrative capital. For this reason, the term 'bureaucratic federalism' is frequently employed to describe the German federal system.

India: pop: 785.00m (WR 2); area: 3.29m km² (WR 7).
Geographical, historical and cultural: the land mass makes it the second-largest state in Asia and historically the country was apportioned

Table 2—Federal States in the Contemporary World (contd)

during the British period into separate provinces, with specified areas of legislative and fiscal autonomy, and princely states, each owing separate allegiance to the crown. Today there are 25 self-governing states, organised primarily on language lines. Each has its own elected assembly, council of ministers and chief minister. There is also a figurehead governor appointed by the federal President. The states have primary control over health, agriculture, education, police and local government. Overall, however, although relatively strong in comparative terms, particularly when non-Congress parties control state assemblies, Indian federalism remains weighted towards the federal government, which has sole control of income tax, the states relying on land and sale taxes and federal grants for their revenue. The government at the centre also has the power to impose direct 'President's Rule' in any state during a period of turmoil. A substantially independent 18-member Supreme Court adjudges federal-state constitutional conflicts.

Malaysia: pop: 15.82m (WR 49); area: 0.33m km^2 (WR 60).
Historical and cultural: the state is a federation of eleven separate states and two British colonies which were brought together into a federation between 1963–65. Each state has its own constitution, elected assembly, led by a chief minister and cabinet, and head of state. The states, however, have only limited original powers in the spheres of land and natural resource management and are reliant upon the federal government for almost all of their funds. Federal-state constitutional disputes are ruled upon by a traditionally independent Supreme Court. This has, however, been subject to mounting central political pressure, exerted by the Prime Minister and monarch, during recent years.

Mexico: pop: 81.70m (WR 11); area: 1.97m km^2 (WR 14).
Geographical and partly imitative: the size of the country made a federal system sensible in geographical terms and also the United States constitution was seen as an attractive model to copy. The 31 states have their own elected assemblies, governors and constitutions. Most powers reside with the governor who is pre-selected by the dominant Institutional Revolutionary Party's (PRI) inner council. For this reason, Mexico remains, in practical terms, a significantly centralised state. For similar reasons, the Supreme Court is subject to effective PRI control.

Nigeria: pop: 105.45m (WR 9); area: 0.924m km^2 (WR 31).
Geographical, historical and cultural: the recognition of tribal and religious differences, particularly between the north and south-east, which culminated in civil war between 1967–70, has been made in a federal system. Prior to independence, Nigeria was divided, in accordance with the 1946 'Richards Constitution', into three semi-autonomous regions. These became four in 1963, twelve in 1967 and 19 in 1979. At present, each state is under the control of a military governor appointed by the central Armed Forces Ruling Council.

Pakistan: pop: 101.90m (WR 10); area: 0.80m km^2 (WR 35).
Historical and cultural: the absorption of twelve princely states into

independent Pakistan in 1948 was achieved by recognising their earlier history and creating a federal structure of four provinces. These provinces exhibit strong cultural and ethnic distinctions and rivalries. The provinces are administered by centrally appointed governors and local governments drawn from elected provincial assemblies.

St Kitts-Nevis: pop: 0.04m (WR 163); area: 0.0002m km² (WR 163).
Geographical and historical: the state is a unique union of two islands which are the residue of what was to have been a wider West Indies federation. Nevis Island, with its own elected assembly, Prime Minister and cabinet, retains the option to secede.

Soviet Union: pop: 280.00m (WR 3); area: 22.40m km² (WR 1).
Historical, geographical and cultural: the federal system, which was established in 1922, allows the national minorities to be recognised while maintaining the unity of the state through the party machine. For this reason it is officially described (Article 70) as a 'unitary, federal, multinational state'. There are 15 Union Republics, each of which has its own assembly and council of ministers. The Union Republics have, in theory, a free hand in the welfare and social spheres, as well as the right of secession. The former has traditionally been overridden, however, by the centrally planned nature of the Soviet economy and the principle of democratic centralism. The latter is, in practice, made impossible by the terms of Article 75 of the constitution. The Union Republics, as well as the 20 Autonomous Republics and eight Autonomous Regions which also exist, are thus principally of value in enabling slight adjustments to be made to centrally devised policies to suit local circumstances and of preserving local languages and cultural practices.

Switzerland: pop: 6.47m (WR 80); area: 0.04m km² (WR 121).
Historical and cultural: the state is a weak federation of 26 cantons (including six half-cantons), or political units, dating back to the late thirteenth century. The cantons also reflect the cultural diversity of a country divided among German-, French-, Italian- and Romansch-speaking communities and between Catholic majority and Protestant majority areas. Each canton has its own constitution, legislative assembly and government, with substantial powers in socio-economic spheres such as education, environmental issues, tourism, transport, and police affairs. Cantons also have protected sources of finance and the ability, through the successful use of referenda, effectively to veto federal policies.

United Arab Emirates: pop: 1.33m (WR 127); area: 0.08m km² (WR 110).
Historical: this is a loose federation of seven sheikhdoms which were under British protection between 1892 and 1971. Each of the sheikhs is an hereditary and absolute ruler in his own emirate.

United States: pop: 241.00m (WR 4); area: 9.37m km² (WR 4).
Historical and geographical: the federal system resulted from the voluntary coming together of the original 13 British colonies after the

Table 2—Federal States in the Contemporary World (contd)

War of Independence. The state developed by expanding its federal membership and the structure also usefully recognises the geographical and cultural diversity of the country. Each of the 50 states that presently exist has its own constitution, assembly, elected governor and Supreme Court. The federal government has responsibilty for defence and foreign affairs and the authority to co-ordinate 'inter-state concerns'. A liberal interpretation of what the latter phrase might constitute has resulted in a steady expansion in federal government interests. State governments remain influential bodies, framing much of their own civil and criminal law; being substantially involved in health, educational and welfare affairs; and raising more than three-quarters of their funds from state property, sales and, in some cases, local income taxes. Federal-state constitutional disputes are adjudged by the independent nine-member Supreme Court.

Venezuela: pop: 17.80m (WR 43); area: 0.91m km² (WR 32).
Historical, cultural and imitative: the federal system recognises the historical and cultural differences in the country but also reflects admiration for the US model, the country having been called the United States of Venezuela until 1953. It is divided into 20 states, each with its own elected assembly and executive governor. Since, however, the governor is appointed by the federal President and the states are heavily dependent upon the centre for revenue resources, the federal system remains weak in practice. The adjudicatory Supreme Court is heavily susceptible to political influence.

Yugoslavia: pop: 23.20m (WR 32); area: 0.26m km² (WR 72).
Historical and cultural: the federal structure recognises the historical independence of the different national minorities and religious groupings which exist in this heterogeneous nation. Six Republics and two Autonomous Regions have thus been formed, each with its own elected assembly, council of ministers and collective presidency. The republics have exclusive jurisdiction in the social welfare, health and educational spheres and also considerable authority over local economic affairs. As a result of heightened inter-regional tensions and party rivalries, the Republics and Autonomous Regions have been able to force the steadily increased devolution of federal powers during recent years, moving the Yugoslavian political system, in a number of respects, towards that of a confederation. There is a Constitutional Court to adjudge federal-state disputes.

As Table 2 suggests, federalism is stronger in some countries than others, the most vigorous being Australia, Canada, Switzerland and the United States, with India and Germany following closely behind. The weakest example is probably the Comoros, where most legislative power is retained by the federal assembly. The Mexican, Soviet Union and Venezuelan federal systems are also weak in practice as a result of the *de facto* control exerted over state/regional associates by the federal party leadership and machine.

2.8 The Distribution of Power

Whatever safeguards may be written into a constitution, political realities will ultimately determine the distribution of power between the centre and the localities and the most significant reality is, invariably, a financial one.

In Australia, for example, the states are dependent on the federal government for about 60 per cent of their revenue and even in the United States, where the clearest distinction between central and local power is made, most states rely on indirect sales taxes which are much less buoyant and stable than the direct income tax which forms the bulk of federal government revenue.

At the other extreme, in a unitary state such as the United Kingdom local authorities are entirely the creatures of parliament, which is controlled by the party in power, and dependent on central government not only for the bulk of their income but for their very existence. The abolition, in 1986, of a whole tier of local government, the metropolitan county councils, including the Greater London Council, is evidence of the disproportionate distribution of power in the United Kingdom.

2.9 The Role of the Judiciary

Most constitutions speak, directly or indirectly, about the supremacy of law. This is generally seen as the guarantee of personal liberty and the chief protection against the overweening power of the state. Clearly the law of the land is the law enacted and whether or not the laws which are passed are fair is a matter which the political system, as a dynamic entity, must determine.

However, once a law has been enacted it is the role of the judiciary to ensure that it is fairly enforced and in practice this means more than just adjudicating in disputes between individuals and groups or between them and the state. It also involves interpreting the law. Since it is virtually impossible to construct a law which is completely unequivocal the task of judicial interpretation is a continual process and of considerable importance. To have an independent and unbiased judiciary is, therefore, vital if personal liberty is to be protected.

Judges are generally guaranteed their independence in a constitution by a provision which ensures their continuance in office during 'good behaviour'. Although independence and security of tenure usually apply to judges in the higher courts, in lower courts this is not always true. In many states in the United States, for example, members of the state judiciary are elected and may be dismissed by the people who elected them: a notable recent example being the California voters' sacking of Chief Justice Rose Bird in November 1986 for alleged 'liberalism' in her conduct of affairs. This makes judicial office holders responsive to public opinion, but is not always the best prescription for justice. In most one-party states, as well as in many Latin American countries, it is the party which chooses the judges for election by the assembly, another process clearly open to abuse.

In the United Kingdom the judiciary are appointed by the government of the day and although the Lord Chancellor, as the head of the judiciary, provides advice, to ensure the quality of the appointees and in theory at least to avoid political bias, it should not be forgotten that he is himself a politician and a leading member of the government. In the United States, Supreme Court judges are appointed by the President, subject to Senate approval, which in recent years has been by no means automatic, so appointment is, inevitably, subject to some political influence. Nor is it possible to say that any judge, however qualified and experienced, can be completely free from the bias which stems from his own social background and political inclinations.

A constitution can therefore go some way towards ensuring an independent judiciary but it can never guarantee complete impartiality. In practice most constitutions go little further than setting out the structure of the judicial system, with a few adding something a little more specific. The constitution of the Republic of Algeria states: 'Judges obey only the law. They defend the socialist revolution', and in Cameroon and Gabon the President is given the task of ensuring the independence of the judiciary.

An important role of judges is, of course, to protect the constitution itself and, even in a state such as the United Kingdom which has no codified constitution, they are required and expected to uphold the rule of law. In federal states, as has been noted, the judiciary's task of upholding the constitution is particularly significant in that they have to interpret as well as enforce, so as to preserve the intended balance between the centre and the localities. In quasi-federal Spain there is a Constitutional

Court with this specific task, as there is in Italy and, though the body is somewhat less influential, in France also. The similar apical judicial bodies which exist in fully federal states are set out in Table 2.

2.10 Religion and the State

Some states have adopted a particular belief as the national religion and enshrined this in their constitutions. Table 3 sets out the current established or state religions.

TABLE 3   STATE OR ESTABLISHED RELIGIONS

ISLAM (25) Afghanistan, Algeria, Bahrain, Bangladesh, The Comoros, Egypt, Iran, Iraq, Jordan, Kuwait, Malaysia, The Maldives, Mauritania, Mauritius, Morocco, Oman, Pakistan, Qatar, Saudi Arabia, Somalia, Sudan, Tunisia, United Arab Emirates, Yemeni Republic.

ROMAN CATHOLICISM (11) Argentina*, Colombia*, Costa Rica, Dominican Republic, Haiti, Malta, Panama*, Paraguay†, Peru†, Seychelles*, Venezuela*.

EVANGELICAL LUTHERAN CHURCH (4) Denmark, Iceland, Norway, Sweden.

BUDDHISM (3) Bhutan, Cambodia (Kampuchea), Thailand.

GREEK ORTHODOX CHURCH (1) Greece.

JUDAISM (1) Israel.

HINDUISM (1) Nepal.

CHURCH OF ENGLAND (1) United Kingdom (England).

PRESBYTERIANISM (1) United Kingdom (Scotland).

PANCASILA (1) ‡ Indonesia.

---

* Quasi-state religion.
† Roman Catholicism is the official religion, although the constitution guarantees religious freedom.
‡ A national secular-state ideology, stressing unity and social justice, which is a compulsory belief for all social organisations.

2.11 Unusual Constitutional Features

Some constitutions contain unusual or unique provisions, most of them being products of the country's history, geography or social structure.

The Mexican constitution, reflecting the country's history of exploitation by the wealthy and powerful, places restrictions on the activities of the Church, large landowners and foreign organisations. Following a record of unequal educational opportunities, the constitution also stresses the importance attached to state education. In similar vein, the constitution of Paraguay provides for agrarian reform in its Chapter 6.

The Soviet Union's constitution specifically enshrines (Articles 40–45) certain socio-economic rights. These include 'the right to work, the right to rest and leisure, the right to health protection, the right to maintenance in old age and sickness, the right to housing, the right to education and the right to enjoy cultural benefits'.

Because of the small size of the country, the constitution of Nauru permits the President, who combines the roles of head of state and head of government, to take on additional personal portfolios in a cabinet of only five or six.

To ensure a balance between the religious communities, the Lebanese constitution prescribes that if the President is a Christian the Prime Minister must be a Muslim, and vice versa.

The constitution of Liberia includes a provision for monitoring and ensuring the maintenance of a one-party state.

Different geographical bases are required of the President and Vice-President by the Tanzanian constitution; if one is from the mainland, the other must be from the island of Zanzibar.

Finally, the recently adopted Brazilian constitution, whose 245 articles and 70 clauses took 19 months to be scrutinised and approved by the federal Congress, contains the most detailed statement of specific social and economic rights currently in force in a non-communist regime. These include a prescribed 44 hours for the working week and stipulated rights to five days of paternity leave and extended maternity leave. In addition, the new constitution, in its economic chapter, restricts the future levying of real interest rates to a maximum level 12.5 per cent above inflation.

2.12 How Important are Constitutions?

Are constitutions merely statements of a grand design and, as such, removed from the realities of the political process? In the final analysis surely naked military power must prevail? The answers to these questions, based on recent experience, must be yes and no.

In liberal democratic countries with long-established codified constitutions, such as the United States, there can be no doubt about their supreme significance. The content and importance of the American constitution are made clear to every school child and the newest immigrants will cherish the freedoms it proclaims. Specific provisions are frequently quoted in contemporary life. Both Rear-Admiral John Poindexter and Lieutenant-Colonel Oliver North pleaded the fifth amendment, the right to remain silent in a criminal case, when required to testify at the 1986 'Irangate' hearings. Since the Watergate affair all Americans must be aware of the impeachment powers contained in Articles I–II of the constitution. It is sufficiently alive to have accumulated no less than 26 amendments, the last being as recently as 1971.

Even in a country such as the United Kingdom, with an uncodified constitution, constitutional controversies arise over such matters as the powers of the House of Lords, devolution, parliamentary sovereignty *vis-à-vis* the European Community, electoral reform and the possibility of introducing a Bill of Rights.

Admittedly, given the necessary political will and military might, any constitution can be suspended or annulled and at the present time there are about ten which fall into this category. Nevertheless, the aura of legitimacy which, accurately or not, a constitution brings is almost universally sought, even by clearly despotic regimes.

Recommended Reading

Bahl, R., *Financing State and Local Government in the 1980s,* Oxford University Press, 1984.

Banting, K. and Simeon, R. (eds), *The Politics of Constitutional Change in Industrial Nations: Redesigning the State,* Macmillan, 1985.

Burgess, M. (ed), *Federalism and Federation in Western Europe,* Croom Helm, 1986.

Charlton, R., *Comparative Government,* Longman, 1986, Ch 4.

Duchacek, I., *Federalism: The Territorial Dimension of Politics,* Holt Rinehart Winston, 1970.

Duchacek, I., *Power Maps: The Comparative Politics of Constitutions,* ABC Clio, Santa Barbara, California, 1973.

Finer, S., *Five Constitutions,* Harvester Press, 1979.

Griffith, J. A. G., *The Politics of the Judiciary,* 3rd edn., Fontana, 1985.

Hague, R. and Harrop, M., *Comparative Government and Politics: An Introduction,* 2nd edn., Macmillan, 1987, Ch 9.

Hicks, U. K., *Federalism: Failure and Success, A Comparative Study,* Macmillan, 1978.

Hodder-Williams, R., *The Politics of the US Supreme Court,* Allen and Unwin, 1980.

House, P. W. and Steger, W. A., *Modern Federalism: An Analytic Approach,* Lexington Books, 1982.

Reagan, M. and Sanzone, J. G., *The New Federalism,* 2nd edn., Oxford University Press, 1981.

Roberts, G. K., *An Introduction to Comparative Politics,* Edward Arnold, 1986, Chs 3 and 10.

Sawyer, G., *Modern Federalism,* Pitman, 1976.

Simons, W. B. and White, S. (eds), *The Party Statutes of the Communist World,* Lancaster Nijhoff, 1984.

Smith, G., *Politics in Western Europe: A Comparative Analysis,* 4th edn., Gower Publishing, 1986, Chs 5 and 9.

Unger, A. L., *Constitutional Development in the USSR: A Guide to the Soviet Constitutions,* Methuen, 1981.

Chapter 3

THE IDEOLOGICAL BASES

3.1 The Nature of Ideology

We are now entering the treacherous world of ideologies where we are as likely to be misled as informed. Nevertheless, it is an area which must be explored if we are to make distinctions between political systems which get beneath the layers of institutions to the cultures and attitudes which have shaped them.

It is not particularly important to the ordinary citizen that there is a two-chamber assembly or that the head of state is a King or a President. Whether the economy is planned from the centre or left to market forces, or whether there is a choice of political parties to support or only one: these things are important.

Identifying the ideology on which a political system is based or influenced will help us penetrate the façade of institutions and slogans, but we must first clarify what we mean by ideology.

It is generally recognised that the political system of the Soviet Union had its theoretical beginning in the writings of Karl Marx (1818–83) and Friedrich Engels (1820–95), subsequently developed and adapted by Vladimir Ilyich Lenin (1870–1924), and that the current regime in Iran is motivated by the religion of Islam, through its Shia branch, but what about the system in the United Kingdom? Is it not too evolutionary and pragmatic to have any substantial theoretical or philosophical basis?

It depends on how we construe ideology. It is a much abused, and over-used, word. In recent years it has, more often than not, been associated with zealots and fanatics. The spread of international terrorism has built up a picture of ruthless groups imbued with a single-mindedness which rejects customary morality so as to advance the aims of some particular ideology. Too often ideology has come to mean blind faith and irrationality. This is too narrow an interpretation, and indeed a distortion, of the word.

The definition which will be used for our purposes is one which might be found in any good general dictionary. An ideology is a body of ideas which reflects the beliefs and values of a nation and its political system. Such a definition is wide enough to encompass a variety of political cultures, from the mature, rational attitudes to be found in many states of Western Europe to the more inspirational, and often emotive, ideas found in countries with less experienced political systems.

Ideologies can be individually or socially inspired. More often than not they are both. Politicians are essentially doers rather than thinkers, even though some of them would have the public believe they are both. They adopt and use philosophies as a platform for political action.

But why and how does a philosophy eventually become so much a part of the beliefs and values of a country that it can be said to be the ideology on which its political system is based? Initially, it usually results from a revolution of one kind or another and then proceeds through a process of what might be called evolutionary absorption.

For example, the *'ancien régime'* of seventeenth- and eighteenth-century France was ended abruptly by the revolution of 1789. Opposition to the profligacy and inequity of the absolute monarchy, allied to the democratic message of the 'Enlightenment' philosophers and writers such as Jean-Jacques Rousseau (1712–78), brought about the dramatic change. Then, over a much longer period, the forces which had initially impelled the revolution were modified and absorbed into the French psyche so as to become the ideology which now underlies its political system.

Other writers, such as John Stuart Mill (1806–73) in England, expanded and amended Rousseau's concept of liberal democracy into a more practical idea of representative democracy, while in other countries French and British experience was adapted to suit differing social and political needs. Thus, liberal democracy became the ideology of a wide family of nations.

The inequities of the Tsarist regime in Russia also ended abruptly in the revolution of 1917, with practical discontent again, allying itself with theoretical justification through the writings of Marx and Engels and the 'praxis' of Lenin. The communist theology of the Soviet Union was, over the years, adopted and modified by another, mixed family of nations.

We have identified two major and contrasting ideologies, liberal democracy and communism, but it would be a distortion of reality if we tried to fit all the 165 states we have under review into one or other of these two categories. Indeed, a purist might argue that each nation has its own unique ideology and any classification would be misleading. If this view were accepted then the very notion of comparative politics would be questionable and a study such as this would have to be abandoned. The idea of the whole world being divided into one of two ideological camps is clearly unacceptable, so a wider, but still manageable, classification must be found.

Accepting again the arbitrary nature of the choice, a sevenfold grouping is offered, in the belief that any classification is preferable to none at all. At the same time, some of the deficiencies in the process should be noted.

The first is that the ideology associated with particular countries is, inevitably, a 'broad brush' description of something more subtle and complicated than the simple 'label' would suggest. The second defect is that a static situation has been assumed. This may be acceptable as far as long-established states, with stable political systems, are concerned, but less so for newer states whose systems are still in a state of flux. Where such conditions are believed to exist an appropriate caveat will be added.

With the foregoing reservations, the following ideologies will be identified and used:

1 Liberal democracy
2 Emergent democracy
3 Communism
4 Nationalistic socialism
5 Authoritarian nationalism
6 Military authoritarianism
7 Absolutism

South Africa is one state whose political system cannot be fitted into any one of these seven categories with confidence. It contains elements of several of them but, since any interpretation would be based on racial origins, and particularly on skin pigmentation, it must fall into a unique category of racism, because this ideology overwhelms and supplants any other beliefs or attitudes which may exist.

3.2 Liberal Democracy

Liberal democracy is a product of two concepts: the right to representative government and the right to enjoy individual freedom. The term 'liberal' is derived from the first concept and 'democracy' from the second. The tests for a political system claiming to be based on this philosophy would therefore seem to be the extent to which the government truly represents the mass of the people and the extent to which rights which individuals claim to have are protected.

In practice the essential features of a liberal democratic system can be identified as:

1 Representative institutions based on majority rule, through free elections and a choice of political parties.
2 Limitations on the power of government, implying a pluralistic society in which the state is not all-embracing and exists alongside other, sometimes competing, interests.
3 Accountablity of the government to the electorate.
4 Freedom of expression, assembly and the person, guaranteed by an independent judiciary.
5 A skilled and impartial permanent public service responsible to the government of the day and, through it, to the electorate.

Of the 165 states under examination 50 have been identified as having political systems founded on liberal democracy and they are listed in Table 4. They embrace more than 1.6 billion people, a figure which corresponds to a third of the world's total population. The oldest are to be found in Western Europe but by no means all or even a majority because, although its roots are European, it is an ideology which has been successfully exported to all parts of the world. There is however a tendency, which is apparent from the national income data provided in Table 4, for this type of political system to flourish best in high-income, 'First World', states. Thus, liberal democracies are found in 21 of the world's 'Top 30' countries in terms of per capita incomes, but in only six of the 'Bottom 50'.

In compiling this list of liberal democratic states, the following seven markers have been looked for:

1 Evidence of constitutional government.
2 Evidence of free elections for assemblies and executives.
3 The active presence of more than one political party.
4 Evidence of checks and balances among the three elements of government: executive, legislative and judicial.
5 Evidence of an independent judiciary.
6 Evidence of the protection of personal liberties through constitutional or other legal guarantees.
7 Evidence of stability in liberal democratic government.

Only those political systems displaying all these features have been included in Table 4. Others showing many of the identified attributes but failing the test of stability have, therefore, been placed in the second category of emergent democracies.

It should be noted, however, that included in Table 4 are two borderline cases: Mexico and Singapore. In both these states, effective opposition movements are particularly weak, being hampered by alleged pro-government ballot-rigging in the first and by increasing direct harassment in the second. Despite this, however, in comparative terms the degree of liberal freedom which is tolerated in these two countries remains tolerably high. Moreover, the longevity and stability of the PRI and PAP party regimes in place render alternative classification in the emergent democracy category inappropriate. A more accurate descriptive term for these two countries would, however, be 'restricted' or 'partial' liberal democracies.

	TABLE 4 LIBERAL DEMOCRATIC SYSTEMS (50)		
Region & Country	Index of Democratisation* (1970–79)	Human Rights Rating (%)† (1986)	Per Capita National Income‡ ($ 1985)‡
WESTERN EUROPE (16)			
Austria	30.8 (WR 9)	96	7,631 (WR 19)
Belgium	38.0 (WR 4)	96	7,408 (WR 21)
Denmark	40.3 (WR 1)	98	9,709 (WR 10)
Finland	19.4 (WR 19)	98	9,211 (WR 13)
France	33.4 (WR 6)	94	8,126 (WR 17)
Germany			
West Germany	32.8 (WR 8)	97	8,950 (WR 16)
East Germany	0.1 (WR 76)	33	5,400 (WR 31)
Iceland	N/A	N/A	9,118 (WR 15)
Ireland	24.2 (WR 16)	86	4,090 (WR 37)
Italy	38.4 (WR 3)	87	5,592 (WR 30)
Luxembourg	N/A	N/A	11,960 (WR 6)
Malta	N/A	N/A	2,800 (WR 45)
The Netherlands	39.8 (WR 2)	98	7,710 (WR 18)
Norway	32.9 (WR 7)	97	11,784 (WR 7)
Sweden	35.9 (WR 5)	98	10,315 (WR 9)
Switzerland	22.3 (WR 17)	95	13,720 (WR 5)
United Kingdom	30.0 (WR 11)	94	7,156 (WR 22)
NORTH AMERICA (2)			
Canada	24.4 (WR 15)	96	11,778 (WR 8)
United States	17.6 (WR 22)	90	14,565 (WR 2)

Table 4—*Liberal Democratic Systems* (contd)

Region & Country	Index of Democratisation* (1970–79)	Human Rights Rating (%)† (1986)	Per Capita National Income‡ ($ 1985)‡
CENTRAL AMERICA AND THE CARIBBEAN (13)			
Antigua & Barbuda	N/A	N/A	1,850 (WR 56)
Bahamas	N/A	N/A	5,000 (WR 32)
Barbados	N/A	N/A	4,400 (WR 34)
Belize	N/A	N/A	990 (WR 82)
Costa Rica	18.6 (WR 20)	91	1,304 (WR 69)
Dominica	N/A	N/A	1,040 (WR 79)
Dominican Republic	8.2 (WR 31)	84	684 (WR 99)
Jamaica	13.0 (WR 27)	77	810 (WR 92)
Mexico	3.4 (WR 41)	62	1,990 (WR 54)
St Kitts & Nevis	N/A	N/A	1,300 (WR 70)
St Lucia	N/A	N/A	1,100 (WR 74)
St Vincent & the Grenadines	N/A	N/A	900 (WR 87)
Trinidad & Tobago	6.6 (WR 35)	79	5,556 (WR 31)
SOUTH AMERICA (1)			
Venezuela	22.2 (WR 18)	88	2,519 (WR 48)
MIDDLE EAST AND NORTH AFRICA (1)			
Israel	29.4 (WR 12)	74	4,346 (WR 35)
CENTRAL AND SOUTHERN AFRICA (3)			
Botswana	3.1 (WR 43)	78	850 (WR 91)
The Gambia	N/A	N/A	260 (WR 137)
Mauritius	N/A	N/A	970 (WR 83)
ASIA (5)			
India	16.1 (WR 24)	60	226 (WR 144)
Japan	26.5 (WR 14)	88	9,452 (WR 12)
Malaysia	10.1 (WR 30)	53	1,770 (WR 61)
Singapore	N/A	59	6,100 (WR 26)
Sri Lanka	16.6 (WR 23)	52	330 (WR 125)
OCEANIA (9)			
Australia	30.1 (WR 10)	94	9,196 (WR 14)
Kiribati	N/A	N/A	350 (WR 122)
Nauru	N/A	N/A	7,000 (WR 22)
New Zealand	27.7 (WR 13)	98	6,100 (WR 26)
Papua New Guinea	N/A	91	598 (WR 108)
Solomon Islands	N/A	N/A	500 (WR 114)
Tuvalu	N/A	N/A	350 (WR 123)
Vanuatu	N/A	N/A	600 (WR 107)
Western Samoa	N/A	N/A	620 (WR 105)

ABBREVIATION:

WR=World Ranking

*This index has been compiled by G.T. Kurian from data collected by Tatu

Vanhanen on the basis of two empirical political variables: *(a)* a competition variable based on 'the share of the smaller parties and independents of the votes cast in parliamentary and/or presidential elections'; and *(b)* a participation variable based on the degree of voter participation in elections. 119 states were covered. (Source: G.T. Kurian, *New Book of World Rankings,* Macmillan, 1984, Table 43, pp. 65–6).

†Source: C. Humana, *World Human Rights Guide,* Pan Books, 1987.

‡Source: *The World in Figures,* Economist Publications, 1987, p. 13.

3.3 Emergent Democracy

The states identified as emergent democracies bear many of the characteristics of liberal democracies except evidence of stability in their political systems, the majority having experienced at least one non-democratic coup or change of government at some time or other during the past two decades. Some have enjoyed stable liberal democratic government for extensive periods only to revert to militaristic or other autocratic rule. Others have emerged from a prolonged spell of autocracy in relatively recent years and it is still too early to judge how permanent the new regime will be.

The three most prominent examples of emergent democracies in Western Europe are Spain, Portugal and Greece. Here liberal democratic regimes have been in operation for more than a decade, with registered civil rights ratings now matching those of their fellow European Community member-states.

By contrast, the roots of democratic and civil freedoms have barely been planted in more recently emergent regimes such as Afghanistan, Bangladesh, Liberia, Nicaragua, Pakistan and Uganda. In these states, the armed forces remain influential background watchdog arbiters who might be tempted to reassert direct control in the near future if the democratisation process moves ahead in a direction which sharply conflicts with their own interests. At present, however, the existence of multi-party politics in these states, despite its fragile, nascent form, merits their tentative inclusion in this political category.

In the 'newly re-democratised' states of Eastern Europe, such as Bulgaria, Czechoslovakia, Hungary, Poland, Romania and Yugoslavia, pluralist politics are still at an early, undeveloped stage. Chile and Panama have only recently moved from military to civilian rule and Mongolia has very lately discarded Marxist-Leninism as its guiding principle. Equally, the African states of

37

Algeria, the Comoros, Gabon, the Côte d'Ivoire, Mozambique and Sao Tome and Principe are new converts to the idea of multi-party politics, while Namibia has only enjoyed full independence since late 1989.

Despite these clear variations in degrees of 'democratisation', all the states categorised as emergent democracies might usefully be described as liberal democracies on trial and the 51 so identified are listed in Table 5. The dates of origin of the current regimes are also shown.

Similar movements in other countries in Central and Southern Africa are predictable but change there seems likely to be slower.

TABLE 5   EMERGENT DEMOCRATIC SYSTEMS (51)*

Region & Country	Date of Origin of Current Liberal Democratic Regime	Index of Democratisation (1970–79)	Human Rights Rating (%) (1986)	Per Capita National Income ($ 1985)
WESTERN EUROPE (5)				
Cyprus	1975	N/A	N/A	3,186 (WR 41)
Greece	1974	10.3 (WR 28)	92	2,971 (WR 42)
Portugal	1976	4.6 (WR 37)	91	1,820 (WR 59)
Spain	1978	3.0 (WR 44)	84	3,880 (WR 38)
Turkey	1983	18.1 (WR 21)	41	960 (WR 84)
EASTERN EUROPE (6)				
Bulgaria	1990	0.1 (WR 74)	23	3,200 (WR 39)
Czechoslovakia	1990	0.1 (WR 75)	36	6,000 (WR 27)
Hungary	1990	0.5 (WR 65)	55	1,722 (WR 62)
Poland	1989	0.3 (WR 69)	41	1,900 (WR 55)
Romania	1990	0.5 (WR 66)	20	2,687 (WR 47)
Yugoslavia	1990	0.6 (WR 64)	50	1,850 (WR 56)
CENTRAL AMERICA AND THE CARIBBEAN (7)				
El Salvador	1983	8.1 (WR 32)	Poor	1,113 (WR 74)
Grenada	1983	N/A	N/A	780 (WR 93)
Guatemala	1985	6.7 (WR 34)	Poor	1,300 (WR 70)
Haiti‡	1990	0.0 (WR 93)	Poor	360 (WR 120)
Honduras	1985	0.4 (WR 67)	Poor	696 (WR 98)
Nicaragua	1987	2.6 (WR 45)	Poor	1,000 (WR 80)
Panama‡	1989	0.0 (WR 109)	79	2,038 (WR 52)
SOUTH AMERICA (10)				
Argentina	1983	1.7 (WR 50)	88	2,000 (WR 53)
Bolivia	1982	0.0 (WR 82)	70	700 (WR 95)
Brazil	1985	0.0 (WR 83)	71	1,300 (WR 70)
Chile‡	1990	1.9 (WR 49)	35	1,050 (WR 78)

Table 5—Emergent Democratic Systems (contd)

Region & Country	Date of Origin of Current Liberal Democratic Regime	Index of Democratisation (1970–79)	Human Rights Rating (%) (1986)	Per Capita National Income ($ 1985)
SOUTH AMERICA—contd				
Colombia	1978	10.1 (WR 29)	57	1,100 (WR 74)
Ecuador	1978	0.8 (WR 58)	83	1,472 (WR 67)
Guyana†	1966	15.3 (WR 25)	N/A	515 (WR 112)
Peru	1980	0.0 (WR 110)	62	669 (WR 102)
Suriname‡	1987	N/A	N/A	2,700 (WR 46)
Uruguay	1985	2.6 (WR 46)	91	1,520 (WR 65)
MIDDLE EAST AND NORTH AFRICA (6)				
Algeria	1989	0.0 (WR 80)	54	2,400 (WR 50)
Egypt§	1970	1.4 (WR 52)	59	960 (WR 84)
Lebanon	1980	5.0 (WR 36)	N/A	850 (WR 90)
Morocco**	1972	0.8 (WR 59)	52	530 (WR 110)
Tunisia	1967	0.0 (WR 116)	60	1,040 (WR 79)
Yemeni Republic	1990	N/A	Bad	555 (WR 109)
CENTRAL AND SOUTHERN AFRICA (8)				
The Comoros	1990	N/A	N/A	270 (WR 132)
Côte d'Ivoire	1990	0.0 (WR 95)	Poor	510 (WR 113)
Gabon	1990	N/A	N/A	2,500 (WR 48)
Liberia‡	1984	0.0 (WR 100)	39	350 (WR 121)
Mozambique	1990	N/A	25	120 (WR 158)
Namibia	1989	N/A	N/A	1,084 (WR 75)
Sao Tome and Principe	1990	N/A	N/A	270 (WR 132)
Uganda‡	1986	0.0 (WR 117)	Poor	150 (WR 151)
ASIA (7)				
Afghanistan‡	1987	0.0 (WR 78)	Bad	180 (WR 148)
Bangladesh‡	1986	1.9 (WR 48)	44	150 (WR 151)
South Korea	1987	0.8 (WR 61)	59	1,830 (WR 58)
Mongolia	1990	0.0 (WR 105)	N/A	950 (WR 86)
Nepal	1991	0.0 (WR 106)	Poor	137 (WR 156)
Pakistan‡	1986	4.1 (WR 38)	40	330 (WR 125)
Taiwan§	1986	N/A	50	2,871 (WR 44)
Thailand	1983	0.9 (WR 57)	57	661 (WR 103)
OCEANIA (2)				
Fiji	1987	13.3 (WR 26)	N/A	1,500 (WR 66)
Philippines	1987	0.8 (WR 60)	86	524 (WR 111)

*For sources see Table 4.

†Ballot rigging in Guyana has, since 1980, begun to establish the elements of a quasi one-party regime, representing a retrogression from liberal-democracy, although opposition parties do continue to operate.

‡The military remain an important political force.

§A quasi-one-party system still effectively operates.

**The monarch remains the dominant political force.

3.4 Communism

As an ideology communism stems from the writings of Marx and Engels which were subsequently taken up by Vladimir Ilyich Lenin and his associates and adapted to meet the needs of early twentieth-century Russia. According to Marx, communism is an ideal which is eventually reached when all private property and class distinctions have been abolished and the state has become redundant and 'withered away'. In these terms, the nations which are commonly referred to as communist can hardly be said to be 'without states'. Indeed, they possess some of the most elaborate structures of state institutions in the world.

Nor were the origins of the Soviet Union, established now as the 'model' for all communist systems, congruent with the classic texts of Marx and Engels. According to these, anti-capitalist revolutions should have first taken place in Western Europe, the most developed region of the world, where the industrial proletariat (working class) were expected to rise up in revolt against mounting exploitation by the bourgeoisie (industrial/ business middle class). This would then have led on to an intermediate 'socialist' phase in which the state remained in place, serving as the instrument of the working classes in a 'revolutionary dictatorship', and in which inequalities continued to be tolerated, with each producer being remunerated in accordance with work done. Later, as affluence increased, a final, 'higher' phase of full communism would be achieved, no longer requiring the apparatus of government for its sustenance, in which all labour divisions would be ended and each worker would be able to receive 'according to his needs'.

In reality, however, revolution occurred first in under-developed Russia, in October 1917. This revolution was, moreover, far from a spontaneous uprising of industrial workers. Instead, it was a wartime 'coup', stimulated and led by Lenin, a member of the white-collar intelligentsia, with most of its 'revolutionary troops' drawn from peasant stock. Theoretical justification for this was provided by Lenin's theory of 'Imperialism: The Highest Stage of Capitalism', with the 'vanguard' position it ascribed to disciplined communist parties, fomenting revolution at the periphery so as to sever the links which bound together the global capitalist system and thus precipitating a final revolutionary cataclysm in the advanced West. This subsequent revolution failed to take place, however, leaving the Soviet Union to protect and 'build socialism' alone during the inter-war period. Only since the end of the Second World War have significant new communist regimes become established. As in the Soviet case, however, they are to be found in the backward 'Second and Third Worlds' of Eastern Europe and Asia, having been imposed either by military force or following guerrilla-based, anti-colonial liberation struggles.

Today, the followers of Marx and Lenin reluctantly agree that the ideal of communism has not yet been reached and that the intermediate condition of socialism remains a truer description of the contemporary Soviet system and those of its imitators. In none of these countries has the state 'withered away'. Instead, the Communist Party is firmly in charge, dominating state institutions, having assumed its prescribed role as the 'vanguard of the proletariat', so as to protect socialist society before the advent of true communism. Events in the Soviet Union and its former satellite states since the accession of Mikhail Gorbachev to leadership of the Communist Party in 1985 mean that the achievement of this theoretical ideal has been abandoned.

Nevertheless, although not 'communist' as such, it can be said, without too much distortion, that there are states which still subscribe to the ideology of communism, in Marxist terms. They are shown in Table 6 and currently number eight, but the likelihood of their all remaining adherents to the principles of Marx and Lenin is very remote.

There have been significant departures from the Soviet model in several countries in this category, notably China and Cuba, which under the dominant leadership of Mao Zedong (and since 1978 Deng Xiaoping) and Fidel Castro, have pursued varying 'paths to socialism'.

Four distinguishing features characterise communist states:

1 Marxism-Leninism (in the case of China, Maoism-Dengism) has been adopted as the official ideology, source of legitimacy and vocabulary of political affairs.
2 The bulk of economic activity is under state ownership and subject to administrative (central) planning.
3 One party, the Communist Party, dominates the political scene and is tightly controlled from above in accordance with the Leninist precept of 'democratic centralism'.
4 The influence of the Communist Party, constitutionally ascribed a 'leading role' in the nation's affairs, is all-

pervasive, controlling state-organs, trade unions, the media, the judiciary and industrial and agricultural enterprises through both supervision and direct membership.

TABLE 6   COMMUNIST SYSTEMS (8)*

Region & Country	Date Regime Established	Index of Democratisation (1970–79)	Human Rights Rating (%) (1986)	Per Capita National Income ($ 1985)
EASTERN EUROPE (2)				
Albania	1944	0.0 (WR 79)	Bad	860 (WR 89)
Soviet Union †‡	1917	0.1 (WR 77)	20	4,200 (WR 35)
CENTRAL AMERICA AND THE CARIBBEAN (1)				
Cuba†	1959	0.0 (WR 90)	26	1,600 (WR 64)
ASIA (5)				
China	1949	0.0 (WR 89)	23	270 (WR 132)
Cambodia	1975	0.7 (WR 62)	Bad	50 (WR 166)
North Korea	1948	0.0 (WR 108)	17	900 (WR 87)
Laos	1975	N/A	Bad	100 (WR 163)
Vietnam†	1945 (North) 1976 (South)	0.0 (WR 118)	25	130 (WR 156)

*For sources of data in columns 3–5 see Table 4.   †Current (1988) full members of Comecon.

‡Current (1988) members of the Warsaw Treaty Organisation (Warsaw Pact).

Other states which claim to apply Marxist-Leninist principles, but which in practice have substantially adapted and modified both the Soviet model and Marxist-Leninist theories to accommodate their own individual needs, have been placed in the next ideological category of nationalistic socialism. This embraces nine nations: Angola, Benin, Cape Verde, The Congo, Ethiopia, Guinea-Bissau, Madagascar, Somalia and Zimbabwe, two of which, Angola and Ethiopia, currently enjoy membership of several Comecon institutions. One state, Ghana, which is also sometimes described as 'Marxist', has been assigned to the military authoritarian category, and four 'liberalising' quasi-Marxist regimes, Afghanistan, Guyana, Nicaragua and Suriname, to the category of emergent democracy.*

*This list of contemporary regimes which have been popularly ascribed as Marxist has been derived from B. Szajkowski (ed), *Marxist Governments: A World Survey*, 3 vols, Macmillan, 1981, and the recent 33-country title *Marxist Regimes Series* produced by Pinter Publishers.

3.5 Nationalistic Socialism

Countries which have been placed in this category display many of the attributes of a communist state but in a less developed and structured form. A key feature is the existence of one political party of avowed socialist orientation, but whose role, in practice, has been more that of a promoter of nationalism and an opponent of imperialism than of a 'guardian of the proletariat' and radical transformer of the country's economic structure. Private farming and petty manufacturing have, for example, remained predominant in these states.

In many countries subscribing to nationalistic socialism the presence of a 'charismatic leader' has been a distinctive characteristic. Muammar al-Kadhafi of Libya, Julius Nyerere of Tanzania, Kenneth Kaunda of Zambia and Robert Mugabe of Zimbabwe are obvious examples, each of the latter three having established his reputation as a guerrilla or political leader during his nation's independence struggle. In addition, a significant number of the states included in this category, Angola, Ethiopia, Iraq, Libya, Somalia and Syria being the most prominent examples, have been involved in recent years in military border disputes with their neighbours. This has served to enhance the nationalist standing and inclination of their leaderships.

The 16 states which have been identified as having nationalistic socialist regimes are set out in Table 7 below. They embrace 0.15 billion people, or just over 3 per cent of the world's total population. Almost three-quarters (13) of the total are to be found in Central and Southern Africa, a region where one-party regimes of a strongly left-of-centre slant constitute the predominant political type. In addition, it is notable that nationalistic socialist regimes are to be found in some of the world's 50 poorest states.

In terms of civil rights restrictions, the overall ratings recorded by most of the 16 nationalistic socialist regimes are disappointingly low. Five regimes, Benin, Senegal, Tanzania, Zambia and Zimbabwe, despite the monism of their political structures, stand out, however, as significantly more 'liberal', exceeding the rating registered by several emergent democratic nations.

The most liberal of these regimes is Senegal, which continues to allow opposition parties, currently numbering 17, to register freely and contest elections. Such, however, is the long-standing *de facto* dominance of the ruling Senegalese Socialist Party, regularly being returned in disputed circumstances with in excess of 70 per cent of the national vote and 80 per cent of the country's legislative assembly seats, that it has been sensible to include this regime in the nationalistic socialist category in preference to that of an emergent democracy.

TABLE 7 NATIONALISTIC SOCIALIST SYSTEMS (16)*

Region & Country	Date Regime Established	Index of Democratisation (1970–79)	Human Rights Rating (%) (1986)	Per Capita National Income ($ 1985)
MIDDLE EAST AND NORTH AFRICA (3)				
Iraq	1968	0.0 (WR 94)	19	2,900 (WR 43)
Libya	1969	0.0 (WR 101)	23	6,000 (WR 28)
Syria	1971	0.2 (WR 72)	29	1,800 (WR 60)
CENTRAL AND SOUTHERN AFRICA (13)				
Angola	1975	N/A	Poor	500 (WR 114)
Benin	1972	0.0 (WR 81)	59	260 (WR 137)
Cape Verde	1981	N/A	N/A	280 (WR 129)
The Congo	1964	0.9 (WR 56)	N/A	1,100 (WR 75)
Ethiopia	1984	0.0 (WR 91)	13	110 (WR 162)
Guinea-Bissau	1981	N/A	N/A	160 (WR 151)
Madagascar	1977	1.1 (WR 53)	Poor	210 (WR 147)
Senegal	1966	1.0 (WR 55)	77	400 (WR 118)
Seychelles	1979	N/A	N/A	2,300 (WR 51)
Somalia	1979	0.0 (WR 113)	Poor	250 (WR 139)
Tanzania	1977	1.7 (WR 51)	47	220 (WR 145)
Zambia	1972	3.7 (WR 39)	51	272 (WR 130)
Zimbabwe	1988†	N/A	45	620 (WR 105)

*For sources see Table 4.   †Year in which one-party state was officially declared.

3.6 Authoritarian Nationalism

In its starkest form nationalism is a belief that people of the same racial stock are so distinctive that only they have the right to be regarded as members of a nation. This extreme kind of nationalism is so intolerant of other races and creeds that, at the best, they are disenfranchised and, at the worst, eliminated. Nazi Germany exhibited this attitude in its most brutal form and the present white-dominated regime in South Africa pursues its own version of the 'final solution' through the operation of the system of apartheid.

Fortunately, extreme examples of this kind are rare and most present-day exponents of nationalism use it as a device to claim the loyalty and obedience of members of the public. Even liberal democratic states have nationalistic tendencies, even though they may disguise the fact under the banner of patriotism. The national flag and the national anthem are manifestations of nationalism under the guise of patriotism and even sport has succumbed to its temptations.

A state which subscribes to the ideology of authoritarian nationalism displays the following three features:

1 Restrictions on the activities of all political parties, or a limitation to one which gives undivided and uncritical support to the state.
2 An authoritarian personal or collective executive.
3 Either the absence of an assembly to balance the power of the executive or the presence of an assembly which is essentially the servant of the executive.

For many states adherence to authoritarian nationalism will be a stage in the progression of independence from the rule of a colonial power to emergent democracy and, eventually, to a full, pluralistic democracy. Given a much longer time span, it is conceivable that all states will eventually abandon nationalistic tendencies and move towards regional, and even global, groupings. These developments are examined in Chapter 9.

The 12 countries identified as proponents of authoritarian nationalism are listed in Table 8. Within this grouping, it must be stressed, however, that there exist considerable differences between both the policy outlooks and the degree of illiberalism of the regimes in power.

At one extreme, for example, stands the fundamentalist Islamic nationalist regime of the IRP in Iran, bent on a revolutionary transformation of both the polity and society and which has become infamous for its human rights violations, most notably its summary executions of dissident Kurdish and left-wing opponents.

Towards the other end of the scale is the KANU regime of Kenya, headed by Daniel Arap Moi, which has pursued a pro-Western foreign policy and a free-enterprise orientated domestic policy programme and has a relatively 'liberal' human rights record. It remains intolerant, however, of direct political opposition and retains tight control over such institutions as the media, judiciary and trade union movement, in a classic one-party manner.

In the middle ground between these two regimes are ranged the majority of the residual authoritarian nationalist states, pursuing policy programmes which range from right-of-centre to left-of-centre in a non-transformatory manner. Cameroon, Malawi and Sierra Leone are, for example, three examples of broadly centrist regimes.

Despite these clear variations, two elements remain common to all 12 states:

1 The existence of one-party dominance.
2 Policy orientations which fall short of being fully socialist.

The second characteristic serves to distinguish these states from those included in the nationalistic socialist category above, thus making their inclusion in this group defensible.

The 12 states identified embrace 0.31 billion people, or just over 6 per cent of the global population. Two-thirds, that is eight, of the total are located in Central and Southern Africa, while a similar proportion are to be found in states which rank among the poorest 50 in the world. The single most important authoritarian nationalist regime in demographic terms, accounting for half the combined population total, is Indonesia. Here the Golkar Party, the most dominant of the three political parties which are permitted to operate, controls affairs in a relatively sophisticated manner, ruling conjointly with the military in accordance with its own unique Pancasila philosophy.

TABLE 8   AUTHORITARIAN NATIONALIST SYSTEMS (12)*

Region & Country	Date Regime Established	Index of Democratisation (1970–79)	Human Rights Rating (%) (1986)	Per Capita National Income ($ 1985)
MIDDLE EAST AND NORTH AFRICA (2)				
Djibouti	1981	N/A	N/A	730 (WR 94)
Iran	1979	0.3 (WR 68)	Bad	3,600 (WR 39)
CENTRAL AND SOUTHERN AFRICA (8)				
Cameroon	1966	0.0 (WR 86)	53	710 (WR 95)
Chad	1982	0.0 (WR 88)	N/A	90 (WR 165)
Kenya	1969	0.0 (WR 97)	48	270 (WR 132)
Malawi	1966	0.0 (WR 102)	Poor	140 (WR 153)
Mali	1974	0.0 (WR 103)	Poor	120 (WR 158)
Sierra Leone	1978	3.2 (WR 42)	64	250 (WR 138)
Togo	1973	0.0 (WR 115)	Poor	190 (WR 148)
Zaire	1972	0.2 (WR 72)	30	100 (WR 163)
ASIA (2)				
Indonesia‡	1966	3.5 (WR 40)	30	483 (WR 116)
Maldives†	1968	N/A	N/A	400 (WR 118)

*For sources of data see Table 4.   †There are no political parties.

‡Three political parties are permitted to operate, but the government party, Golkar, is predominant.

3.7 Military Authoritarianism

Military authoritarianism is a form of authoritarian nationalism whereby military leaders take it upon themselves to impose a government on the people, claiming invariably that it is for the public good. History is littered with examples of regimes when 'men of action' have felt it necessary to use their military strength to overthrow and replace civilian administrations. In some cases the transition is short-lived; in others military rule has become a permanent feature.

The characteristics of a state accepting authoritarian nationalism will be found also in this category with, of course, a military regime always in control. Sometimes a state based on military authoritarianism will try to disguise itself by using a civilian administration as a façade, fronting the military power behind. Panama in recent years has provided an example of this.

The 14 states subscribing to military authoritarianism are listed in Table 9. They embrace 0.22 billion people, or 4.4 per cent of the global total, more than 85 per cent being located in Central and Southern Africa.

TABLE 9 MILITARY AUTHORITARIAN SYSTEMS (14)*				
Region & Country	Date Regime Established	Index of Democratisation (1970–79)	Human Rights Rating (%) (1986)	Per Capita National Income ($ 1985)
SOUTH AMERICA (1)				
Paraguay	1954	7.2 (WR 33)	48	1,405 (WR 68)
CENTRAL AND SOUTHERN AFRICA (12)				
Burkina Faso	1980	1.1 (WR 54)	Poor	120 (WR 158)
Burundi	1987	0.0 (WR 85)	Poor	215 (WR 146)
Central African Republic†	1981	0.0 (WR 87)	Bad	240 (WR 142)
Equatorial Guinea†	1979	N/A	N/A	140 (WR 154)
Ghana	1981	0.6 (WR 63)	46	370 (WR 120)
Guinea	1984	0.0 (WR 92)	Poor	280 (WR 129)
Lesotho	1986	0.0 (WR 99)	Poor	270 (WR 132)
Mauritania	1978	0.0 (WR 104)	N/A	350 (WR 122)
Niger†	1974	0.0 (WR 107)	Poor	240 (WR 142)
Nigeria	1983	0.2 (WR 70)	53	660 (WR 103)
Rwanda†	1973	0.0 (WR 111)	Poor	250 (WR 139)
Sudan	1989	0.2 (WR 71)	Poor	310 (WR 128)
ASIA (1)				
Myanma (Burma)	1989	0.0 (WR 84)	Poor	162 (WR 149)

*For sources of data see Table 4.   †In a state of transition towards a pluralist system.

3.8 Absolutism

Absolutism is an ideology which can be traced back to *The Leviathan* written by Thomas Hobbes (1588–1679) soon after the mid-seventeenth-century English Civil War (1642–52), in support of the English monarchy as the guarantor of stability and order. The ideology had even earlier roots in the medieval European doctrine of 'The Divine Right of Kings'. It argues that no limits whatsoever should be placed on the activities of a legitimate government, which will usually be in the form of an absolute monarch. Legitimacy is often claimed through the accident of birth, although it is convenient to forget that at some stage in history that legitimacy must have been acquired by force.

For a nation in an early stage of economic and social development, or one threatened by external forces, absolutism is an attractive ideology to accept, offering a guarantee of stability and order. For some countries it may represent only a stage in their development, to be superseded by a republican form of government or by a constitutional monarchy. For others it has become a permanent condition.

The characteristics of a state based on absolutism are:

1 The absence of any constitutional form of government, or a popular assembly or judiciary to counter executive power.
2 The denial of the right to form political parties or other forms of organised interests.

The twelve states adhering to absolutism are listed in Table 10. In Bhutan there are signs of emergent democracy and the monarchies in Jordan and Tonga, although absolute in the final analysis, do have vestiges of constitutional checks and balances. One other state, Morocco, is also characterised by monarchical rule, but within a more fully developed and party-based constitutional structure. For this reason it has been assigned instead to the emergent democracy category.

The eleven absolutist regimes embrace a population of 40 million, corresponding to less than 1 per cent of the world total. Seven are located in the Middle East, in which region it constitutes the predominant political type. It should also be noted that seven of these absolutist states, including six in the Middle East, are, as a consequence of their mineral oil wealth, among the world's 'Top 25' nations in terms of per capita national income. On the other hand, Bhutan is to be found among the world's 'Bottom 10'.

	Index of Democratisation (1970–79)	Human Rights Rating (%) (1986)	Per Capita National Income ($ 1985)
TABLE 10 ABSOLUTIST SYSTEMS (11)*			
Region & Country			
MIDDLE EAST AND NORTH AFRICA (7)			
Bahrain	N/A	N/A	7,500 (WR 20)
Jordan	0.0 (WR 96)	Poor	1,658 (WR 63)
Kuwait	0.0 (WR 98)	49	13,980 (WR 3)
Oman	N/A	N/A	6,700 (WR 24)
Qatar	N/A	N/A	9,600 (WR 11)
Saudi Arabia	0.0 (WR 112)	28	6,900 (WR 24)
United Arab Emirates	N/A	N/A	16,100 (WR 1)
CENTRAL AND SOUTHERN AFRICA (1)			
Swaziland	N/A	N/A	680 (WR 100)
ASIA (2)			
Bhutan	N/A	N/A	105 (WR 162)
Brunei	N/A	N/A	13,600 (WR 5)
OCEANIA (1)			
Tonga	N/A	N/A	700 (WR 95)

*For sources of data see Table 4.

3.9 The Future State of Ideologies

We have already defined an ideology as a body of ideas which reflects the beliefs and values of a nation and its political system. We should not, however, see the practical implementation of an ideology as something immutable and 'set in stone'. A political system is both the product of and guardian of an economic system and, as a nation seeks to change the structure and working of its economy, so, inevitably, its political system will change with it.

Therefore, the pluralism which a market-orientated economy demands will, sooner or later, be reflected in a country's politics and, eventually, but over a longer time scale, the ideology will undergo change.

The dramatic changes in the political systems of the states of Eastern Europe in recent years highlight this link between economic and political factors. The centralised 'command' economy of the Soviet Union simply failed to deliver the output, particularly in consumer goods, which its citizens demanded. The economic system had to change to one more determined by market forces, and, with this shift, the political system inevitably began to follow suit. It was no longer possible for the state, and its single-party apparatus, to provide the necessary incentives, a pluralist approach became inevitable.

The advent of Mikhail Gorbachev was the fuse which produced the eventual explosion. It is reasonable to suppose that the changes would ultimately have taken place, under a different leader or leaders. Under Gorbachev they were greatly accelerated. The example of the monolithic empire of the Soviet Union was enough to trigger similar, and even speedier, movements among its satellite neighbours.

Whereas, as short a time ago as 1979, it was possible to identify 16 well-entrenched communist systems throughout the world, their number has now been halved and the contraction is likely to continue as economic forces, influenced by the market, inexorably drive political systems into a pluralist pattern.

It can be argued that what we have called liberal democracy is so inextricably allied to market economics that the ultimate situation will be a world of liberal democracies. That view is probably a little too simplistic, for we should also remember that the capitalistic system, if uncontrolled, contains as many pitfalls and dangers as its alternative.

The mixed economy, where public and private enterprise co-exist, is most likely to be the model for future generations and political ideologies and systems which are best able to accommodate such an economy are the ones which will survive.

The classification of ideologies used in this book was devised shortly before the cataclysmic changes in Eastern Europe and the rest of the world and there was, consequently, a great temptation to completely rethink that classification. It was resisted, however, because the global political map is still in such a fluid state that speculation, rather than certainty, remains the order of the day.

Recommended Reading

Brown, A. (ed), *Political Culture and Communist States*, Macmillan, 1984.

Cammack, P., Pool, D. and Tordoff, W., *Third World Politics: A Comparative Introduction*, Macmillan, 1988, Ch. 2.

Charlton, R., *Comparative Government*, Longman, 1986, Chs. 1 and 8.

Clapham, C., *Third World Politics: An Introduction*, Croom Helm, 1985, Ch. 3.

Decalo, S., *Coups and Army Rule in Africa: Studies in Military Rule*, Yale University Press, 1976.

Deutsch, K.W., Dominguez, J.I. and Heclo, H., *Comparative Government: Politics of Industrialized and Developing Nations*, Houghton Mifflin, 1981.

Finer, S.E., *Comparative Government: An Introduction to the Study of Politics*, Penguin, 1970.

Finer, S.E., *The Man on Horseback: The Role of the Military in Politics*, 2nd enl. edn. rev., Pinter, 1988.

Furtak, R., *The Political Systems of the Socialist States: An Introduction to Marxist-Leninist Regimes*, Wheatsheaf, 1986.

Ghayasuddin, G. (ed), *The Impact of Nationalism on the Muslim World*, Open Press, 1986.

Hague, R. and Harrop, M., *Comparative Government and Politics*, 2nd edn., Macmillan, 1987, Ch 4.

Hiro, D., *Islamic Fundamentalism*, Paladin, 1988.

Lijphart, A., *Democracies: Patterns of Majoritarian and Consensual Government in Twenty-One Countries*, Yale University Press, 1984.

Nordlinger, E.A., *Soldiers in Politics: Military Coups and Governments*, Prentice-Hall, 1977.

Bingham Powell Jr, G., *Contemporary Democracies: Participation, Stability and Violence*, Harvard University Press, 1982.

Smith, G., *Politics in Western Europe: A Comparative Analysis*, 4th edn., Gower Publishing, 1986, Chs 1–3.

White, S., Garner, J. and Schopflin, G., *Communist Political Systems: An Introduction*, 2nd edn., Macmillan, 1987, Chs. 1 & 2.

Wiles, P. (ed), *The New Communist Third World: An Essay in Political Economy*, Croom Helm, 1982.

Chapter 4

EXECUTIVES

4.1 Political Executives

It is usual to make a distinction between the political executive and the non-political, or permanent, executive. The latter is the salaried civil service which normally remains in office to work for whichever politicians happen to be in power. They in turn constitute the political executive and, as such, provide the leadership for both the political system and the state.

The modern political executive can be personal or collective and is found in a variety of forms including President, Prime Minister and party chairman or Secretary-General. Whatever the contemporary form and title, each is a direct descendant of the personal autocrat or absolute monarch, at one time universal.

States with more than one political party operating have been identified as liberal democracies or emergent democracies. With only a few exceptions, their executives are either Presidents or Prime Ministers. We shall refer to them respectively as presidential or parliamentary executives. In the exceptions a dual executive, usually of a President and a Prime Minister, operates.

One-party states have been subdivided into communist, nationalistic socialist, authoritarian nationalist and military authoritarian. In these cases the most common form of executive is, again, presidential, although in those we have identified as communist the executive assumes a distinctive form, partly collective and partly personal, as at the apex of power the state and party machines merge.

Finally, there are the few surviving absolutist states, where political parties have no role to play, and the executives are individuals exercising virtually unbridled power in very much the same way as the original precursors of what we now call democratic governments.

4.2 The Parliamentary Executive

This is the second most common form of political executive in the world today, 43 states having adopted it, embracing over 28 per cent of the global population. Twenty-seven of them are constitutional monarchies and 16 republics. It is sometimes referred to as the 'Westminster model' because it originated, and is found in its clearest form, in the United Kingdom. It is not coincidental that of the 43 nations with parliamentary political executives 26, including Britain, were formerly part of the British Empire and are now independent members of the Commonwealth. It is useful therefore to examine the United Kingdom system, even though the executives of other countries have been adapted from the original example to suit their particular needs. All parliamentary executives are found in multi-party liberal (37) or emergent democracies (6), with 16 of the total being in Western Europe, eleven in the Caribbean region and eight in Oceania. More than half, 56 per cent, are located in island states. The full list, showing geographical distributions, is given in Tables 11 and 12.

The parliamentary executive displays three essential features.

1 The role of head of state is separate from that of head of government and is distant from party politics, serving mainly as the patriotic and ceremonial focus of the nation. The head of state can be a President, as in West Germany or India, or a monarch, as in the Netherlands or the United Kingdom. In the majority of Commonwealth countries with parliamentary executives, the head of state is still the British monarch, represented by a resident Governor-General.
2 The executive is drawn from the assembly and directly responsible to it, and its security of tenure is dependent on the support of the assembly, or parliament. In other words, a 'no confidence' vote in parliament can bring down the government, resulting in a change of executive or a general election. It is in such circumstances that the non-political head of state may become temporarily involved in politics by either inviting the leader of a party in opposition to form a new government, or by dissolving parliament and initiating elections.

A particular characteristic of the 'Westminster model' is that it is historically based on the concept of a two-party system. The House of Commons, for example, is physically constructed to accommodate two opposing parties, the government party sitting on benches to the right of the chairman of the House, or Speaker, and the opposition party to his left. Also, the Leader of the Opposition is acknowledged formally in legislation, provided with suitable office accommodation, and paid a salary out of public funds. This practice is followed in several Commonwealth states, most notably Australia and New Zealand, but is not an essential feature of a parliamentary executive. Indeed, the majority of European states, including West Germany, Austria, Belgium, Denmark, Ireland, Italy, the Netherlands and Norway, have a wide range of parties, and governments are frequently, and in some cases invariably, formed by coalitions of these parties. Conversely, in a number of Asian states with parliamentary executive systems, for example, Japan, Malaysia and Singapore, effective one-party electoral dominance has been the norm, although opposition parties do operate.

3 The leader of the party, or coalition of parties, commanding the support of parliament is called upon by the head of state, monarch or President, to become Prime Minister and form a government. The Prime Minister then chooses a cabinet, drawn from parliament, and they, with other non-cabinet ministers, form the government.

The fact that the parliamentary executive is drawn from and responsible to the assembly makes it, in theory at least, particularly accountable. In reality much depends upon the state of the parties in parliament. A British Prime Minister for example, enjoying a clear parliamentary majority, usually has greater executive power and discretion than a United States President, subject to the checks and balances of a constitution which gives significant power and authority to an independent Congress. In countries where coalition governments are the norm prime ministerial authority is invariably weaker, with power being diffused among ministers drawn from a variety of parties. Special arrangements have been devised in a number of such cases, however, to buttress the chief executive's authority. The most notable example is West Germany in which, under the terms of the Basic Law (constitution) of 1949, members of the assembly can only force the replacement of the Chancellor (Prime Minister) through a 'constructive vote of no confidence' by which a majority of members vote positively in favour of a proposed successor.

TABLE 11   STATES WITH PARLIAMENTARY EXECUTIVES (43)

State	Date Parliamentary Executive Established*	Area ('000 km²)	Pop (m) (c 1985)
Antigua & Barbuda (CM, C)	1981	0.44	0.085
Australia (CM, C)	1901	7,686.85	15.763
Austria (R)	1920/45	83.85	7.546
Bahamas (CM, C)	1973	13.94	0.235
Barbados (CM, C)	1966	0.43	0.255
Belgium (CM)	1831/1971	30.51	9.868
Belize (CM, C)	1981	22.97	0.168
Canada (CM, C)	1867/1982	9,975.22	25.625
Denmark (CM)	1849/1953	43.08	5.087
Dominica (R, C)	1978	0.75	0.074
Fiji (R, C)	1970	18.33	0.715
Germany (R)	1949/1990	375.00	78.400
Greece (R)	1975	131.99	9.954
Grenada (CM, C)	1974	0.34	0.100
Iceland (R)	1944	102.85	0.244
India (R, C)	1949	3,287.59	785.000
Ireland (R)	1937	68.39	3.624
Israel (R)	1948†	20.70	4.208
Italy (R)	1948	301.28	57.226
Jamaica (CM, C)	1962	11.42	2.366
Japan (CM)	1946	371.86	121.402
Luxembourg (CM)	1868/1956	2.59	0.367
Malaysia (CM, C)	1957	332.37	15.820
Malta (R, C)	1974	0.32	0.355
Mauritius (CM, C)	1968/69	2.04	1.029
Netherlands (CM)	1814/1983	34.00	14.481
New Zealand (CM, C)	1853†	269.06	3.305
Norway (CM)	1814	323.90	4.165
Papua New Guinea (CM, C)	1975	462.84	3.395
Pakistan (R, C)	1988	803.90	101.900
St Kitts-Nevis (CM, C)	1983	0.27	0.040
St Lucia (CM, C)	1979	0.62	0.123
St Vincent & the Grenadines (CM, C)	1979	0.39	0.103
Singapore (R, C)	1965	0.62	2.584
Solomon Islands (CM, C)	1978	29.79	0.283
Spain (CM)	1978	504.88	39.074
Sweden (CM)	1809	449.70	8.357
Thailand (CM)	1978	514.00	52.438
Trinidad & Tobago (R, C)	1976	5.13	1.204
Tuvalu (CM, C)	1978	0.03	0.009
United Kingdom (CM, C)	1689†	244.10	56.458
Vanuatu (R, C)	1980	14.76	0.136
Western Samoa (R, C)	1962	2.84	0.180
Total (27 CM, 16 R, 26 C)	—	26,527.94	1,433.811

CM=Constitutional Monarch; R=Republic; C=Commonwealth member.
*Date of constitution/amended constitution.   †No formal written constitution.

TABLE 12   DISTRIBUTION OF PARLIAMENTARY EXECUTIVES

(a) By Region

(Commonwealth Members in Brackets)

Region	Number		Region	Number	
Asia	6	(4)	Middle East &	1	(—)
Central America	11	(11)	North Africa		
& the Caribbean			North America	1	(1)
Central & Southern	1	(1)	Oceania	8	(8)
Africa			South America	0	(—)
Eastern Europe	0	(—)	Western Europe	15	(2)
			Total	43	(27)

(b) By State Population Size

Population (m) (c 1985)	Number	Population (m) (c 1985)	Number
Below 0.1	4	50–100	4
0.1–1	13	100–200	2
1–10	14	200–500	0
10–20	3	500–1,000	1
20–50	2		
		Total	43

(c) By State Areal Sizes

State Areal Size ('000 km²)	Number	State Areal Size ('000 km²)	Number
Below 1	10	500–1,000	3
1–10	4	1,000–5,000	1
10–100	11	5,000–10,000	2
100–500	12		
		Total	43

4.3 The Limited Presidential Executive

The limited presidency is now the most common form of political executive in the world today, 52 states having adopted it, embracing 25 per cent of the global population. It should be noted, however, that 16 of the countries listed in Table 13 have only very recently adopted this type of executive, having moved from unlimited presidential or military executive systems. Their ability to sustain this form of democratic government must, therefore, be viewed with caution. The United States provides the clearest example and, although there are practical differences between individual systems, the essentials as found in the United States are virtually the same. Like parliamentary executives, all limited presidential executives occur in multi-party liberal (9) or emergent democracies (43). The full list with geographical distributions is given in Tables 13 and 14.

It should be remembered, however, that democracy is a rather delicate plant and in most of the states classified as emergent democracies, which adopted pluralist politics within the past decade, the plant is still at a tender age.

The evidence of a multi-party system has been taken as the main criterion for describing political systems as democratic and in five states, Afghanistan, Bangladesh, Liberia, Nicaragua and Taiwan, democracy in a genuine sense is, as yet, more in the realms of anticipation than realisation. In each of these states considerable obstacles have been placed in the way of the unfettered operation of opposition parties, while the military also remain influential arbiters in the political process. In one other state, Uganda, political conditions are at present in a state of flux, with constitutional arrangements remaining unsettled.

In the five former satellites of the Soviet Union, Bulgaria, Czechoslovakia, Hungary, Poland and Romania, economic and political re-education are proceeding side-by-side; it is proving to be a difficult, and sometimes unpredictable, process, while Yugoslavian democracy is threatened by ethnic and cultural divisions. The civilian presidencies in Chile, Haiti and Panama still operate within the context of a strong military presence, while the pluralist systems of Gabon, the Côte d'Ivoire, Mongolia, Mozambique, Sao Tome and Principe and the Yemeni Republic are virtually untested and could disappear overnight in a sudden coup. The politics of Algeria and Turkey are in a more settled state and the prospects for the new state of Namibia seem auspicious.

A general point which does however emerge from these tables is the predilection for this system of executive in the mainland countries of the Americas. Of the 21 states in this broad region, only five, Belize, Canada, Chile, Paraguay and Suriname, have differing executive systems. The two former British colonies, Belize and Canada, have parliamentary executives; the former Dutch colony of Suriname a dual executive; and the remaining two states of Chile and Paraguay military executives. For the remaining states of the region, which secured independence from the early nineteenth century onwards, the influence of United States political and constitutional conventions and republican ideals is clear. In addition, the limited presidential executive form of government has been a popular model which has been adopted in recent years by newly emergent or re-established democracies, the most prominent recently being Argentina, Brazil, the Philippines and South Korea.

There are are four key features present in a limited presidential executive.

1 The President is elected for a fixed term to perform the dual role of head of state and head of government. As head of state he occupies a mainly ceremonial position and is the focus of popular patriotism. As head of government, he leads the executive branch of government, and is usually head of the armed forces and the state civil service. Also as head of government he is in charge of foreign affairs and is the main initiator of legislation.

2 The President's tenure is secure unless he commits a grave unconstitutional act. The United States President, for example, cannot be removed by Congress except by impeachment.

3 He governs with an advisory cabinet of non-elected departmental secretaries, whom he chooses and appoints and who are fully responsible to him.

4 Presidential powers are limited by the need for the approval of the assembly for certain executive actions. Under the United States constitution, for example, Congress has sole legislative powers and the President's veto of an Act of Congress can be overridden by a two-thirds vote. Although the President is expected to provide national leadership, his ability to do so is constrained by his ability to carry Congress with him. The United States Senate, in particular, has strong counterbalancing powers whereby the President can only make key federal appointments, judicial and cabinet, with Senate approval. Foreign treaties require a two-thirds majority of the chamber before coming into effect.

It is this balanced relationship between the President of the United States and Congress, as well as the clear statement of their respective roles written into the constitution, which make the presidency, although powerful, a limited form of executive and these are features which are found in the other 34 states whose political executives fall into this category. The degrees of emphasis differ, however, as do the arrangements for the election of Presidents and the restrictions on their length and terms of office. This information is set out in detail in the individual country entries in Part II.

In general, it would be true to say that few states with limited presidential executives approach the high degree of dispersal of power that exists in the United States. As a consequence, the effective authority of most of the Presidents included in Table 13 significantly exceeds that of the US chief executive.

Even in some countries which might have been valid democracies for a number of years, such as Egypt, Guyana and Mexico, true competition from opposition parties remains circumscribed, further enhancing presidential authority. There are also some states, notably Afghanistan, Bangladesh, Chile, Haiti, South Korea, Liberia, Nicaragua, Pakistan, Panama and Taiwan, where the military remain an influential force. In such cases, the presidential system can only be viewed as partially limited.

TABLE 13   STATES WITH LIMITED PRESIDENTIAL EXECUTIVES (53)

State	Date Executive Established	Area ('000 km²)	Pop (m) (c 1985)
Afghanistan*	1987	647.50	18.136
Algeria	1989	2,381.75	22.972
Argentina	1853/1983	2,780.00	31.200
Bangladesh*	1986	144.00	104.100
Bolivia	1826/1947	1,098.60	6.430
Botswana	1966	600.40	1.100
Brazil	1969/1985	8,512.00	143.300
Bulgaria INT	1990	110.84	9.000
Chile*	1990	756.95	12.300
Colombia	1886/1974	1,139.00	30.000
The Comoros	1990	1.86	0.469
Costa Rica	1949	50.70	2.700
Côte d'Ivoire	1990	322.46	10.500

Table 13—States with Limited Presidential Executives (contd)

State	Date Executive Established	Area ('000 km²)	Pop (m) (c 1985)
Cyprus	1960	9.25	0.666
Czechoslovakia	1990	127.90	15.502
Dominican Republic	1966	48.73	6.614
Ecuador	1945/1979	283.56	9.600
Egypt	1971	1,001.50	50.500
El Salvador	1983/1985	21.39	5.100
Gabon INT	1990	266.70	1.200
The Gambia	1970	11.30	0.800
Guatemala	1985	108.89	8.600
Guyana‡	1980	215.00	0.800
Haiti*	1990	27.75	5.900
Honduras	1982/1985	112.09	4.600
Hungary INT	1990	93.03	10.644
Kiribati	1979	0.68	0.062
South Korea	1987	98.50	43.300
Liberia*	1984	111.40	2.300
Mexico	1917	1,972.55	81.700
Mongolia INT	1990	1,565.00	1.900
Mozambique INT	1990	799.38	14.000
Namibia	1990	823.16	1.151
Nauru§	1968	0.02	0.008
Nicaragua*	1987	130.00	3.300
Panama*	1989	77.08	2.227
Peru	1980	1,285.22	20.200
Philippines	1987	300.00	58.100
Poland INT	1990	312.68	37.500
Romania INT	1990	237.50	22.800
Sao Tome and Principe INT	1990	1.00	0.105
South Africa**	1961/1984	1,222.16	33.200
Suriname	1987	163.82	0.400
Switzerland††	1874	41.29	6.470
Taiwan*	1947	36.00	19.600
Tunisia	1959	164.15	7.260
Turkey	1989	779.45	51.819
Uganda INT	1969	236.88	15.200
United States of America	1787	9,372.57	241.000
Uruguay	1966	186.93	3.000
Venezuela	1961	912.05	17.800
Yemeni Republic INT	1990	531.57	8.600
Yugoslavia INT	1990	255.80	23.200
Total	—	42,489.99	1,228.935

*The military remain influential. ‡Although presidential, operates like a parliamentary executive.

§No formal parties. **White-only democracy.

††The Swiss presidency is, in reality, collective or collegial, comprising all seven members of the Federal Council (Bundesrat), one of whom is selected annually to assume the formal title of president of the Swiss Confederation (Bundespräsident).

INT: in an interim state and in the process of establishing fully democratic institutions.

**TABLE 14   DISTRIBUTION OF LIMITED PRESIDENTIAL
EXECUTIVES**

(a) By Region

Region	Number	Region	Number
Asia	5	Middle East &	4
Central America	9	North Africa	
& the Caribbean		North America	1
Central & Southern	11	Oceania	3
Africa		South America	11
Eastern Europe	6	Western Europe	3
		Total	53

(b) By State Populations

Population (m) (c 1985)	Number	Population (m) (c 1985)	Number
Below 0.1	2	50–100	4
0.1–1	6	100–200	2
1–10	20	200–500	1
10–20	9	500–1,000	0
20–50	9		
		Total	53

(c) By State Areal Sizes

Areal Size ('000 km²)	Number	Areal Size ('000 km²)	Number
Below 1	2	500–1,000	8
1–10	3	1,000–5,000	9
10–100	10	5,000–10,000	2
100–500	19		
		Total	53

4.4 The Dual Executive

The dual executive is found in a minority of liberal and emergent democracies, the most notable example being France. Altogether there are six identifiable dual executives: in Finland, France,

Lebanon, Morocco, Portugal and Sri Lanka. There are significant differences between them, however, and, although the French system is usually cited as the model, it should not be assumed that the others contain all, or even most, of its features. In Finland, France, Lebanon, Portugal and Sri Lanka the executive consists of a working partnership between the President and the Prime Minister while in Morocco the partnership is between the monarch and the Prime Minister. The full list, with geographical distributions, is given in Tables 15 and 16.

Although not really a 'model' of the other systems, a description of how the dual executive operates in France will be helpful to an understanding of the variations which are found in other countries.

The constitution for the French Fifth Republic was framed in the short time span of three months, during the summer of 1958, while the new administration of Charles de Gaulle was settling into office. Conscious of the recent history of instability in French governments, its authors tried to combine elements of the United States and British constitutions, while at the same time they sought to strengthen the executive and encourage greater party discipline and stability. To these ends, provision was made for a two-headed executive of a President, to be elected by an electoral college for a seven-year term, and a Prime Minister, chosen by the President but responsible to the National Assembly.

Under the terms of the constitution the President has considerable powers, including, as well as the appointment of the Prime Minister, control of the armed forces, the right to preside over cabinet and Defence Council meetings, the right to dissolve the Assembly once a year, and powers to negotiate treaties, countersign legislation approved by the Assembly, and appoint ambassadors.

Nevertheless, the constitution made provision (Articles 20 and 21) for the Prime Minister and Council of Ministers to wield ultimate power while the President was expected to remain aloof from day-to-day government and act as a mediator and conciliator who ensured that the different factions in whatever coalition was formed on the basis of Assembly support worked successfully together.

The respective roles of President and Prime Minister were altered when, in October 1962, President de Gaulle forced through, by referendum, a change in the constitution making the President directly elected by the people. This gave him a justifiable claim of popular support and he and his immediate successors used this to dominate policy-making so that the Prime Minister became, in effect, the political servant of the President, who governed in the style of the United States presidency, but without the congressional checks and balances which limit it.

As long as the French President was able to appoint a Prime Minister amenable to his directions and acceptable to the National Assembly the unbalanced twin executive worked. In 1986, however, following Assembly elections which swept to power the opposition conservative coalition, President Mitterrand was forced to appoint a Prime Minister, Jacques Chirac, whose political stance was well to the right of his. An experiment of 'cohabitation' thus began, in which the Prime Minister assumed the upper hand. This lasted, at times uneasily, until the presidential and Assembly elections of April-June 1988, which were won by President Mitterrand and his Socialist Party, restored the *status quo*. The period of 'cohabitation' did at least prove that the constitution was sufficiently flexible to allow a President and Prime Minister from different parts of the political spectrum to work together, if need be, for an interim period with reasonable success.

The dual executive in Lebanon closely resembles that of France but the relationship between the President and Prime Minister is as much conditioned by religious as political factors. With the object of maintaining religious harmony, the President has always been, by tradition, a Christian and the Prime Minister a Muslim. The President is elected for a six-year, non-renewable, term by the National Assembly. In 1988 the inability to agree on a new Christian President resulted in the creation of two rival governments, which threatened the unity of the country.

In Finland, the dual executive is also very similar to that of France, with the President, who is popularly elected for a renewable six-year term, having responsibility for foreign affairs, the dissolution of the Eduskunta (parliament), the formation and dismissal of governments and the appointment of senior civil servants. The President also has substantial veto powers over legislation passed by the Eduskunta and, more limited, decree powers. The multi-party, coalition nature of Finnish politics has served to enhance the effective role of the President, as has the sensitivity and importance of foreign relations with Finland's neighbour, the Soviet Union. This was particularly the case between 1956 and 1981 when Urho Kekkonen, of the Centre Party of Finland (KP), was President and used the office to ensure the continuance in power of centre-left parliamentary coalitions, and to promote a foreign policy of 'active neutrality', despite dwindling electoral support. In recent years, however, there have been proposals to reduce significantly presidential powers in the legislative and executive spheres.

The Portuguese variant of the dual executive has been evolving since the adoption of a new constitution in 1976. To effect a smooth transition to civilian government after a long period of dictatorship and military rule, the role of the President was cast as a 'watchdog' for the army, to ensure that its interests were not neglected by a civilian Prime Minister. The relationship between the two parts of the executive depended as much on personalities as constitutional rules. The revised constitution of 1982 reduced the powers of the presidency and four years later the first civilian for 60 years was elected to that office. Political power is now weighted towards the Prime Minister but he does not yet head a genuine parliamentary executive.

The Sri Lankan constitution of 1978 is based loosely on the French model and provides for a directly elected President and a Prime Minister, drawn from the assembly, who is appointed by the President and acts as his 'parliamentary manager'. The President has considerably more powers than the Prime Minister and can hold several portfolios himself. Sri Lanka thus represents a weak form of dual executive, compared with the French version, yet falls short of being a full presidential executive, as in the United States.

In Morocco the executive partnership is between the monarch and the Prime Minister but it is a very one-sided affair, with the King holding a near-monopoly of power. Although in legalistic terms Morocco is a constitutional monarchy the near-absolutism of the King has been given a formal legitimacy and the Prime Minister and cabinet function more as royal advisers than independent politicians.

The dual executives of these six states demonstrate the variety of ways in which a constitution can be adapted to suit the circumstances of a particular political environment at a particular time.

TABLE 15   STATES WITH DUAL EXECUTIVES (6)

	Date Executive Established*	Area ('000 km²)	Pop (m) (c 1985)
Finland	1919	337.05	4.931
France	1958	547.03	55.400
Lebanon	1927/1947	10.40	2.700
Morocco†	1972	458.73	23.700
Portugal	1976/1982	92.08	16.600
Sri Lanka	1978	65.61	16.344
Total	–	1,510.90	119.675

*Date of constitution/amended constitution.   †Not termed president.

TABLE 16   DISTRIBUTION OF DUAL EXECUTIVES

(a) By Region

Region	Number	Region	Number
Asia	1	Middle East & North Africa	2
Central America & the Caribbean	0	North America	0
Central & Southern Africa	0	Oceania	0
Eastern Europe	0	Western Europe	3
		Total	6

(b) By State Population Size

Population (m) (c 1985)	Number	Population (m) (c 1985)	Number
Below 0.1	0	50–100	1
0.1–1	0	100–200	0
1–10	2	200–500	0
10–20	2	500–1,000	0
20–50	1		
		Total	6

(c) By State Areal Sizes

State Areal Size ('000 km²)	Number	State Areal Size ('000 km²)	Number
Below 1	0	500–1,000	1
1–10	0	1,000–5,000	0
10–100	3	5,000–10,000	0
100–500	2		
		Total	6

4.5 The Communist Executive

Until recently the Soviet Union provided the 'classic' example of a communist political executive, with its interlocking web of party and state personnel and interests, culminating in a concentration of power at the apex of the political system. Now, however, the constitution is undergoing dramatic change and moving nearer to the US model of a limited presidency.

In the communist system as it used to operate in the Soviet Union, it was the party which determined policy objectives and it is the state apparatus which implements them. Whereas in a liberal democratic country, such as the United States, the constitution determines the distribution and exercise of power, in a communist country, the constitution is subservient to the needs of the state, as interpreted by the party. In fact, constitutions are fairly frequently changed to meet party requirements.

Although currently undergoing rapid change, it is useful to describe the 'classic' Soviet system in order to understand how a communist system works.

The word 'soviet' means elected council and the Supreme Soviet, the national assembly, is constitutionally, but not in reality, the supreme body of state power. It consists of some 542 members, elected by the broader Congress of the USSR People's Deputies and, in turn, elects a Council of Ministers (COMs) from its membership, as the equivalent of a formal government. The Council has about 70 members, embracing the heads of around 50 specialist ministries, state committees and defence and security institutions, as well as the chairmen of the 15 Union Republic COMs, and meets in full session four times a year. Day-to-day decision-making responsibilities are devolved to its Presidium, or permanent committee, which, with 13 or so members, can, in some respects, be viewed as a partial equivalent to a state cabinet in a liberal democratic system.

The chairman of this Presidium is usually referred to as Prime Minister or Premier; however, the office is by no means fully the equivalent of a head of government in a Western parliamentary system. The nearest to a head of state in the Soviet system is the chairman of the Presidium of the Supreme Soviet, a 39-member body, which represents the assembly when it is not sitting.

The state machinery of the Presidium of the Council of Ministers and the Presidium of the Supreme Soviet are the external constitutional manifestations of political power but the real power lies within the Communist Party, which ensures its hold on policy-making through its membership of the state institutions and the policy of *nomenklatura*. This means that key posts throughout Soviet society and government are reserved for persons of 'sound' judgement who have been vetted and approved by the party's apparatus. Presently around 3 million positions fall into this category.

It is in the 251-member Central Committee of the Communist Party where true authority can first be perceived and it is in the Politburo, a 12–20-member cabinet body which is 'elected' by the Central Committee and meets weekly, and the twelve-member Secretariat, its administrative and policy-formulating wing, where ultimate power lies. Leading members of these bodies, at the apex of the party, also hold key positions, including the chairs, in the Presidiums of the Supreme Soviet and the Council of Ministers. It is also usual for the General Secretary of the party, who is the country's effective political leader, to take a major state position, such as chairman of the Presidium of the Supreme Soviet, as formal insignia of office. His real power derives, however, from his position as head of the party.

The other Eastern European states formerly within the Soviet bloc had political systems broadly similar to that of the Soviet Union. The two principal exceptions were Yugoslavia and Romania. After the death of Marshal Tito, Yugoslavia had a unique, rotating, collective leadership and a significant degree of regional decentralisation. In Romania, there was a quasi-presidential system, tailored to the needs of the pre-eminent figure of Nicolae Ceausescu.

The Asian communist states, including China, and Castro's Cuba, where a personalised, plebiscitarian form of leadership prevails, also display a number of significant variations from the Soviet model. In all cases, however, control of the state, including its full range of economic institutions, through the party is the dominant, and clearly recognisable, characteristic. It is this, more than anything else, that distinguishes communist from other one-party states.

The distribution of states with communist, or, as they should more correctly be termed, socialist, executives and their date of establishent are set out in Tables 17 and 18. As only the Soviet Union's dates back to pre-1945, it is evident that this political type is a relatively recent development. It is, in addition, with the notable exception of Cuba in the Caribbean, to be found concentrated geographically in only two regions, Asia and Eastern Europe. The relatively small number (8) of states falling into this category embrace, in total, nearly a third of the world's population.

TABLE 17   STATES WITH COMMUNIST EXECUTIVES (8)

State	Date Established*	Area ('000 km²)	Pop (m) (c 1985)
Albania	1946/1950	28.75	3.046
Cambodia	1975/1981	181.00	7.284
China	1949/1982	9,561.00	1,050.000
Cuba	1959/1976	114.52	10.200
North Korea	1948/1972	121.25	20.500
Laos	1975†	236.80	4.117
Soviet Union	1917/1977	22,402.20	280.000
Vietnam	1945/76(80)	329.60	62.000
Total	—	32,975.12	1,437.147

*Date of establishment of communist regime/most recent state constitution.

†Lacks a formal constitution.

TABLE 18   DISTRIBUTION OF COMMUNIST EXECUTIVES

(a) By Region

Region	Number	Region	Number
Asia	5	Middle East & North Africa	0
Central America & the Caribbean	1	North America	0
Central & Southern Africa	0	Oceania	0
		South America	0
Eastern Europe	2	Western Europe	0
		Total	8

Table 18—Distribution of Communist Executives (contd)

(b) By State Population Size

Population (m) (c 1985)	Number	Population (m) (c 1985)	Number
Below 0.1	0	50–100	1
0.1–1	0	100–200	0
1–10	3	200–500	1
10–20	1	500–1,000	0
20–50	1	1,000–1,500	1
		Total	8

(c) By State Areal Sizes

State Areal Size ('000 km²)	Number	State Areal Size ('000 km²)	Number
Below 1	0	500–1,000	0
1–10	0	1,000–5,000	0
10–100	1	5,000–10,000	1
100–500	5	10,000–30,000	1
		Total	8

4.6 The Unlimited Presidential Executive

The term unlimited is used to describe the executive presidency in one-party, non-communist states, but in politics nothing is really unlimited. Even the seemingly all-powerful military dictator can be, and is at times, overthrown. Nevertheless, the states which have been classified as nationalistic socialist and authoritarian nationalist have considerably fewer limitations on their political executives than those in their liberal and emergent democratic counterparts.

As in communist systems, the party is the ultimate source of power but, unlike communist states, a strong, and sometimes charismatic, leader often predominates and the objectives of the party, even in socialist states, are subordinated to national interests. Most of the countries with this type of executive have comparatively short histories of release from rule by a colonial power and have felt the need to assert their independence. Many also have tribal, ethnic or regional differences which require strong leadership if all social groups are to cohere into a single state. More than 90 per cent of countries with unlimited presidential executives are to be found in Africa and the adjoining Middle East.

Despite this regional concentration, these states display considerable variations in their political systems and it is something of a distortion to group them together in this way. Some have, for example, histories of instability and their current leaders have reached the top through a bloody or bloodless military coup. This has been the experience of the Congo, the Seychelles, Syria and Togo, for example. Some, such as Angola, Chad and Ethiopia, have been racked by recent wars and border insurgency. In contrast, other states, such as Djibouti and Senegal, have long records of political stability.

Nevertheless, their political executives have certain features in common, including a much greater authoritarianism than is found in liberal and emergent democratic states. This results mainly from the absence of competition and choice which a multi-party political system clearly provides. They have no opposition party 'waiting in the wings' to take over should the electorate express a wish for a change. Some unlimited executive states, the most prominent example being Senegal, do formally tolerate opposition groupings but elections are so heavily stacked in the governing party's favour, through its control of the media and state sector resources, and through resort to electoral chicanery, that there is little or no possibility of its being defeated.

The importance of the political leader in such states cannot be overstressed. Some have been in office for much longer periods than their counterparts in liberal democratic states could ever hope for. Some became or are becoming virtual legends. Ahmadou Ahidjo led Cameroon for 22 years, between 1960 and 1982. Hastings Banda of Malawi, Mobutu Seseseko of Zaire, and Kenneth Kaunda of Zambia, have similar records. President Suharto of Indonesia has been at the helm for more than 20 years, as have Moussa Traore of Mali, Gnassingbe Eyadema of Togo, and General Ne Win of Burma, until his 'retirement' in July 1988. They are closely followed by figures such as Muammar al-Kadhafi of Libya, and Mohammed Siad Barre, the former leader of Somalia.

In Iran, on the other hand, the focus of leadership in recent years has tended to shift from one individual to another, as different factions have wrestled for power. Sometimes the religious leader, Ayatollah Khomeini, a revered, charismatic figure, seemed to have the strongest voice and at other times the pragmatic Speaker of the Assembly, Hojatoleslam Ali Akbar Rafsanjani, seemed more influential. Eventually, on the Ayatollah's death in 1989, Rafsanjani succeeded him.

To people accustomed to life in liberal democratic political systems the concept of one-party government and strong personal leadership may seem repressive and undemocratic. It would be unwise, however, to make such a sweeping judgement. A country's political system is inevitably the product of its history, culture and resource-base and the majority of the states with unlimited presidential executives are still on a 'learning curve' in their political development. Indeed some systems are so volatile that there are fundamental changes currently taking place or likely to become evident in the foreseeable future. In other cases, particularly across black Africa, the system of one-party monopoly appears to be firmly embedded, drawing its sustenance from older tribal political traditions, with their inclusive decision-making processes, and from the argument that open democracy, with its costly campaigns and inter-party quarrels, is an indulgence that cannot yet be afforded.

Table 19 shows that the Maldives, although categorised as having an unlimited presidential executive, does not follow the usual pattern of being a one-party system. Indeed, political parties, as such, do not exist at all. However, since it operates within a constitutional framework, it was thought more sensible to place it in this category rather than regard it as having an absolute executive.

TABLE 19 STATES WITH UNLIMITED PRESIDENTIAL EXECUTIVES (28)

State	Date of Start of One-Party System	Date Current President First Took Office	Area ('000 km²)	Pop (m) (c 1985)
Angola (S)	1975	1979	1,246.70	8.200
Benin (S)	1975	1972	112.60	4.100
Cameroon	1966	1982	474.00	10.000
Cape Verde (S)	1981	1975	4.03	0.312
Chad*	1983	1982	1,284.00	5.200
Congo (S)	1964	1979	342.00	1.800
Djibouti	1981	1977	23.39	0.300
Ethiopia (S)	1984	1977	1,221.90	43.900
Guinea-Bissau (S)	1981	1980	36.13	0.900

Table 19—States with Unlimited Presidential Executives (contd)

State	Date of Start of One-Party System	Date Current President First Took Office	Area ('000 km²)	Pop (m) (c 1985)
Indonesia*	1967	1967	1,925.00	173.103
Iran*	1978	1989	1,648.00	46.600
Iraq* (S)	1979	1979	444.00	16.278
Kenya	1982	1978	583.00	21.000
Libya† (S)	1969	1969	1,759.54	3.900
Madagascar (S)	1977	1975	595.79	10.300
Malawi	1966	1964	118.48	7.300
Maldives‡	—	1978	0.30	0.180
Mali	1974	1968	1,240.00	7.908
Senegal* (S)	1966	1980	197.00	6.900
Seychelles (S)	1979	1977	0.45	0.066
Sierra Leone	1978	1985	73.33	3.883
Somalia (S)	1979	1969	637.66	7.800
Syria* (S)	1973	1971	185.18	10.535
Tanzania (S)	1977	1985	945.09	22.400
Togo	1979	1967	56.79	3.023
Zaire	1978	1965	2,345.00	31.300
Zambia (S)	1972	1964	752.62	7.100
Zimbabwe* (S)	1987	1980	390.60	9.000
Total (S=17)	—		18,642.58	463.288

S=Avowedly socialist.   *Legally pluralist but effectively one-party.

†Leader is not termed president.   ‡No political parties operate.

TABLE 20   DISTRIBUTION OF UNLIMITED PRESIDENTIAL EXECUTIVES

(a) By Region

Region	Number	Region	Number
Asia	2	Middle East & North Africa	5
Central America & the Caribbean	0	North America	0
Central & Southern Africa	21	Oceania	0
		South America	0
Eastern Europe	0	Western Europe	0
		Total	28

Table 20—*Distribution of Unlimited Presidential Executives* (contd)

(b) By State Populations

Population (m) (c 1985)	Number	Population (m) (c 1985)	Number
Below 0.1	1	50–100	0
0.1–1	4	100–100	1
1–10	13	200–500	0
10–20	4	500–1,000	0
20–50	5		
		Total	28

(c) By State Areal Sizes

State Areal Sizes ('000 km^2)	Number	State Areal Sizes ('000 km^2)	Number
Below 1	2	500–1,000	5
1–10	1	1,000–5,000	8
10–100	4	5,000–10,000	0
100–500	8		
		Total	28

4.7 The Military Executive

Of the 14 states listed in Table 21 as having military executives one is in South America, twelve in Central and Southern Africa and one in Asia. The American state of Paraguay is long-established whereas the African are all post-Second World War creations. The majority, however, share a common feature, a long record of military conflicts and coups. For good or ill, in each case the army has established order, though often at the expense of the loss of civil liberties.

Some countries have seen the pendulum swing from civilian to military rule with bewildering frequency. Burkina Faso, for example, has experienced no fewer than six coups in 20 years. In Latin America and Central and Southern Africa as a whole, nearly three-quarters of the 65 states have endured at least one military coup since 1960.

Some have suffered long periods of genuinely despotic rule. Jean-Bedel Bokassa, of the Central African Republic, who was in power between 1965 and 1979, brought his nation almost to economic ruin through his personal excesses, which included an elaborate ceremony to crown him emperor. The Duvalier family ruled Haiti for many years like gang bosses with their own private armies. In Burundi, in Central Africa, military rule has been ruthlessly used to sustain tribal despotism, in particular the economic and political pre-eminence of the minority Tutsis.

In contrast, some military rulers have brought great political stability. General Alfredo Stroessner of Paraguay enjoyed absolute power, without any real challenge, for 35 years, from 1954 to 1989, by dealing swiftly and harshly with dissidents and astutely allowing potential rivals to share in the spoils of office.

The policies pursued by some military regimes, most especially those in South America, have been strongly reactionary and conservative, designed to protect the interests of narrow business élites and stifle popular social movements. Others, often drawing their leaders and in-service support from the middle officer ranks, have pursued radical economic and social policies. These reformist regimes, usually having been prompted to seize power because of the corrupt excesses of preceding civilian administrations, have also tended to follow puritanical governing styles. The most notable contemporary examples are the populist, if not necessarily popular, regimes of Flight-Lieutenant Jerry Rawlings in Ghana and Captains Thomas Sankara (1983–87) and Blaise Compaore (1987–) in Burkina Faso.

The identification of the 14 military states has been comparatively straightforward but inevitably a little arbitrary. In at least a further 26 states classified under other categories the military remain an influential background political force. These include twelve countries identified as limited presidential executives: Afghanistan, Bangladesh, Chile, Egypt, Guatemala, Haiti, South Korea, Liberia, Nicaragua, Pakistan, Taiwan and Uganda. Thailand, which has been classified as a parliamentary executive, is another example of a state with a military presence in the background, as well as Suriname, categorised as a limited presidential executive. Laos, Cambodia, North Korea and Vietnam, which have been listed as communist executives, also fall into this category, as do the unlimited presidential executives of Benin, Burma, Ethiopia, Indonesia, Iraq, Libya, Syria and the Yemeni Republic.

Of the countries listed in Table 21, five, Burkina Faso, Burundi, Equatorial Guinea, Lesotho and Rwanda, are one-party states, and in Myanma (Burma) opposition to the military executive has been suppressed. Paraguay has more than one party and the remaining seven, Central African Republic, Ghana, Guinea, Mauritania, Niger, Nigeria and Sudan, have banned all political activity. In all 13, however, the chief identifying feature is that the military are, overtly or more discreetly, in effective control. In Paraguay, for example, the military hide behind a civilian façade.

Nevertheless, just as no political leader has the gift of eternal life, so no political system can be expected to last for ever in whatever form it has reached, and there is evidence that at least some of the military executive systems are becoming a little more democratic. In the Central African Republic, Guinea, Niger, Nigeria and Rwanda promises of a return to more liberal and constitutional regimes have been made. Time will reveal whether or not such promises are honoured.

TABLE 21 STATES WITH MILITARY EXECUTIVES (14)

State	Date Established	Date of Recent Coup*	Area ('000 km²)	Pop (m) (c 1985)
Burkina Faso	1960	1987	274.20	7.100
Burundi	1962	1987	27.83	4.900
Central African Republic†	1960	1981	625.00	2.744
Equatorial Guinea	1968	1979	28.10	0.360
Ghana	1957	1981	238.54	13.552
Guinea†	1958	1984	245.86	5.750
Lesotho	1966	1986	30.35	1.555
Mauritania	1960	1984	1,030.70	1.750
Myanma (Burma)	1962	1989	678.00	37.700
Niger†	1960	1974	1,267.00	6.715
Nigeria†	1960	1985	923.80	105.448
Paraguay	1811	1954	406.75	4.119
Rwanda†	1962	1973	26.34	6.500
Sudan	1956	1989	2,505.80	22.070
Total			8,308.27	220.263

*Most recent successful coup. (There have been unsuccessful coups subsequent to the date shown in Equatorial Guinea—in 1981 and 1983—and Guinea—in 1985.)

†Movement towards more democratic government.

TABLE 22   DISTRIBUTION OF MILITARY EXECUTIVES

(a) By Region

Region	Number	Region	Number
Asia	1	Middle East &	0
Central America	0	North Africa	
& the Caribbean		North America	0
Central & Southern	12	Oceania	0
Africa		South America	1
Eastern Europe	0	Western Europe	0
		Total	14

(b) By State Population Size

Population (m) (c 1985)	Number	Population (m) (c 1985)	Number
Below 0.1	0	50–100	0
0.1–1	1	100–200	1
1–10	9	200–500	0
10–20	1	500–1,000	0
20–50	2		
		Total	14

(c) By State Areal Sizes

State Areal Sizes ('000 km²)	Number	State Areal Sizes ('000 km²)	Number
Below 1	0	500–1,000	3
1–10	0	1,000–5,000	3
10–100	4	5,000–10,000	0
100–500	4		
		Total	14

4.8 The Absolute Executive

All the states listed in Table 23 as having absolute executives are monarchies of one kind or another. Bahrain, Brunei, Jordan, Kuwait, Oman, Qatar and Saudi Arabia are all Arab monarchies, sultanates or emirates and the United Arab Emirates are a federation of no fewer than seven emirates. Bhutan, Nepal, Swaziland and Tonga are hereditary monarchies.

Another factor they all have in common is a history of association with Britain, through either a treaty of protection or trade, or both. In ten of them political parties do not operate at all. In Brunei there is a quasi-party of businessmen loyal to the Sultan, and in Swaziland one party subservient to the ruling regime.

Unlike the military states, the absolute executives have not been imposed following a coup. They have usually been part of the social and political lives of the respective communities for many years, surviving during the colonial period as largely autonomous entities, and the rule, though autocratic, has usually been paternalistic.

The Kingdom of Jordan shows clear evidence of constitutionality, with a written constitutional code and two-chamber assembly but true democracy has had a fluctuating existence, with political activity banned in 1963, restored in 1971 and then banned again in 1976. Today only informal 'associations' are allowed to function. Despite a constitutional appearance, ultimate power remains with the King.

The one universal, and most certain, characteristic is that of government by personal, or, in the case of Saudi Arabia, family decree, rather than by collective discussion and agreement, and it is this which attracts the description of absolute executive.

TABLE 23   STATES WITH ABSOLUTE EXECUTIVES (12)

State	Date Established	Date of Accession of Present Monarch	Area ('000 km^2)	Population (m) (c 1985)
Bahrain (C)	1971†	1961	0.62	0.442
Bhutan	1947†	1972	46.60	1.446
Brunei (C)	1984	1968	5.80	0.240
Jordan (C)	1946	1952	98.00	3.515
Kuwait (C)	1961 †	1977	19.00	1.771
Nepal (C)*	1923/47†	1972	141.40	17.422
Oman	1951†	1970	212.00	1.271
Qatar (C)	1971†	1972	11.44	0.305

Table 23—States with Absolute Executives (contd)

State	Date Established	Date of Accession of Present Monarch	Area ('000 km²)	Population (m) (c 1985)
Saudi Arabia	1926–32‡	1982	2,150.00	11.519
Swaziland (C)	1968	1986	17.40	0.692
Tonga (C)	1970	1965	0.75	0.105
United Arab Emirates (C)	1971†	1971	83.60	1.326
Total	—	—	2,786.61	40.054

C=written constitution; Jordan also has some constitutionality.

*Likely to become a full constitutional monarchy.

†Never formally under colonial control.

‡Date of unification (Saudi Arabia was never subject to European colonial rule).

TABLE 24   DISTRIBUTION OF ABSOLUTE EXECUTIVES

(a) By Region

Region	Number	Region	Number
Asia	3	Middle East & North Africa	7
Central America & the Caribbean	0	North America	0
Central & Southern Africa	1	Oceania	1
Eastern Europe	0	South America	0
		Western Europe	0
		Total	12

(b) By State Population Size

Population (m) (c 1985)	Number	Population (m) (c 1985)	Number
Below 0.1	0	50–100	0
0.1–1	5	100–100	0
1–10	5	200–500	0
10–20	2	500–1,000	0
20–50	0		
		Total	12

Table 24—Distribution of Absolute Executives (contd)

(c) By State Areal Sizes

State Areal Sizes ('000 km²)	Number	State Areal Sizes ('000 km²)	Number
Below 1	2	500–1,000	0
1–10	1	1,000–5,000	1
10–100	6	5,000–10,000	0
100–500	2		
		Total	12

TABLE 25 WORLD DISTRIBUTION OF EXECUTIVE SYSTEMS

(a) By Region

Region	Parliamentary Executives	Limited Presidential Executives	Dual Executives	Unlimited Presidential Executives	Communist Executives	Military Executives	Absolute Executives	Total
Asia	6	5	1	2	5	1	3	23
Central America and the Caribbean	11	9	—	—	1	—	—	21
Central and Southern Africa	1	11	—	21	—	12	1	46
Eastern Europe	—	6	—	—	2	—	—	8
Middle East and North Africa	1	4	2	5	—	—	7	19
North America	1	1	—	—	—	—	—	2
Oceania	8	3	—	—	—	—	1	12
South America	—	11	—	—	—	1	—	12
Western Europe	15	3	3	—	—	—	—	21
Total	43	53	6	28	8	14	12	164

Table 24—World Distribution of Executive Systems (contd.)

(b) By Population and Land Area

Executive Type	Number of States	Area ('000 km²)	% of World Area	Pop (m) (c 1985)	% of World Pop	Population Density (per km²)
Parliamentary executives	43	26,528	19.4	1,434	28.9	54.1
Limited presidential executives	53	42,490	31.1	1,229	24.8	28.9
Dual executives	6	1,511	1.1	120	2.4	79.4
Unlimited presidential executives	28	18,643	13.7	463	9.4	24.9
Absolute executives	12	2,787	2.0	40	0.8	14.3
Military executives	14	8,308	6.1	220	4.4	26.5
Communist executives	8	32,975	24.2	1,437	29.0	43.7
Semi-sovereign states	5	0.7	—	0.1	—	162.0
Colonies and dependent territories*	43	3,212	2.4	13	0.3	4.0
World Total	212	136,455	100.0	4,956	100.0	36.5

*The figures here exclude Corsica and Western Sahara (whose areas and populations are included, with France and Morocco respectively, under the dual executive heading); the South African Bantustans (whose totals are included under the limited presidential executive heading); Xizang (Tibet) (whose totals are included with China under the communist executive heading); and the uninhabited Antarctic Territories.

Table 25—World Distribution of Executive Systems (contd.)

(c) By State Population Size

State Population Size (m) (c 1965)	Parliamentary Executives	Limited Presidential Executives	Dual Executives	Unlimited Presidential Executives	Communist Executives	Military Executives	Absolute Executives	Total
Below 0.1	4	2	—	1	—	—	—	7
0.1–1	13	6	—	4	—	1	5	29
1–10	14	20	2	13	3	9	5	66
10–20	3	9	2	4	1	1	2	22
20–50	2	9	1	5	1	2	—	20
50–100	4	4	—	—	1	1	—	10
100–200	2	2	1	1	—	—	—	6
200–500	—	1	—	—	1	—	—	2
500–1,000	1	—	—	—	—	—	—	1
1,000–1,500	—	—	—	—	1	—	—	1
Total	43	53	6	28	8	14	12	164

(d) By State Areal Sizes

State Areal Size ('000 km²)	Parliamentary Executives	Limited Presidential Executives	Dual Executives	Unlimited Presidential Executives	Communist Executives	Military Executives	Absolute Executives	Total
Below 1	10	2	—	2	—	—	2	16
1–10	4	3	—	1	—	—	1	9
10–100	11	10	3	4	1	4	6	39
100–500	12	19	2	8	5	4	2	52
500–1,000	3	8	1	5	—	3	—	20
1,000–5,000	1	9	—	8	—	3	1	22
5,000–10,000	2	2	—	—	1	—	—	5
10,000–25,000	—	—	—	—	1	—	—	1
Total	43	53	6	28	8	14	12	164

Recommended Reading

Baynham, R. (ed), *Military Power in Black Politics*, Croom Helm, 1986.

Blondel, J., *World Leaders: Heads of Government in the Postwar Period*, Sage Publications, 1980.

Blondel, J., *The Organization of Governments: A Comparative Analysis of Government Structures*, Sage Publications, 1982.

Blondel, J., *Government Ministers in the Contemporary World*, Sage Publications, 1985.

Carter, S. and McCauley, M. (eds), *Leadership and Succession in the Soviet Union, Eastern Europe and China*, Macmillan, 1986.

Cartwright, J., *Political Leadership in Africa*, St Martin's Press, 1983.

Charlton, R., *Comparative Government*, Longman, 1986, Ch. 2.

Clapham, C. and Philip, G. (eds), *The Political Dilemmas of Military Rule*, Croom Helm, 1985.

Hague, R. and Harrop, M., *Comparative Government and Politics: An Introduction*, 2nd edn, Macmillan, 1987, Ch. 11.

Hodgson, G., *All Things to All Men, the False Promise of the Modern American Presidency*, Penguin Books, 1984.

Jackson, R. H. and Rosberg, C. G., *Personal Rule in Black Africa: Prince, Autocrat, Prophet, Tyrant*, University of California Press, 1982.

Johnson, N., *State and Government in the Federal Republic of Germany: The Executive at Work*, 2nd edn., Pergamon Press, 1983.

Kellerman, B., *The Political Presidency: Practice of Leadership*, Oxford University Press, 1984.

King, A. (ed), *Both Ends of the Avenue: The Presidency, the Executive Branch and Congress in the 1980s*, American Enterprise Institute, 1983.

King, A. (ed), *The British Prime Minister*, 2nd edn., Macmillan, 1985.

Lowenhardt, J., *The Soviet Politburo*, Canongate, 1982.

McKay, D., *Politics and Power in the USA*, Penguin, 1987, Ch. 5.

O'Brien and Cammack, P. (eds), *Generals in Retreat: The Crisis of Military Rule in Latin America*, Manchester University Press, 1985.

Ridley, F. F. (ed), *Government and Administration in Western Europe*, Martin Robertson, 1979.

Rose, R. and Sulieman, E. (eds), *Presidents and Prime Ministers*, American Enterprise Institute, 1980.

Saich, T., *China: Politics and Government*, Macmillan, 1981.

Smith, G. B., *Soviet Politics: Continuity and Contradiction*, Macmillan, 1988, Ch. 5.

Weller, P., *First Among Equals: Prime Ministers in Westminster Systems*, Allen and Unwin, 1985.

Wright, V., *The Government and Politics of France*, 2nd edn., Hutchinson, 1983, Chs. 1–4 and 6.

Chapter 5

ASSEMBLIES

5.1 The Nature of Assemblies

Although in formal constitutional terms the three arms of government are described as the executive, the judiciary and the legislature, the term assembly has been deliberately preferred for the third arm because the role of the vast majority of legislatures in the world today is deliberative and policy-influencing, rather than law-making. Indeed the old term parliament, which is still used in some political systems, best identifies the chamber as a place for debate.

Assemblies do, of course, play a major role in the law-making process but they now mostly legitimise policies presented to them by the executive, rather than initiate them themselves. In doing so, they usually also have a modifying, revising function, based on the concept that assembly members are more likely to have an understanding of what is practicable and acceptable to the electorate than politicians in government who, inevitably, become insulated in their positions of power from the real world outside.

Popularly elected assemblies have always epitomised democracy and it is not surprising, therefore, that even the most autocratic rulers have sought to make their regimes 'respectable' by establishing a façade of democratisation through puppet assemblies. In South Africa three separate assemblies have been created to give a semblance of democracy but only one, restricted to the white population, has any real political meaning, and the majority of South Africans are completely unrepresented within the system.

The nineteenth century was the 'golden age' of assemblies, characterised by the parliament in London where individual members had a genuine role to play before they were to become overwhelmed by the tyranny of the party system and the burgeoning, and increasingly specialist, scope of legislative affairs. Since that time the balance of power has shifted inexorably towards the executive until we are left with but a few shining examples of assemblies which can, and do, wield real political power. The most notable one today is undoubtedly the United States Congress. It is closely followed by the Riksdag of

Sweden, with the Camera dei Deputati and Senato in Italy and the Legislative Assembly in Costa Rica also being influential bodies. Legislative chambers elsewhere are mostly pale shadows of these.

Despite the relative decline in assembly importance, they still operate in the vast majority of states and are found within a wide range of ideologies and working alongside all types of political executive. Table 26 gives the basic facts about them, showing that at the present time only 13 of the 164 states under consideration do not have active assemblies and, of these 13, only five, Brunei, Oman, Qatar, Saudi Arabia and the United Arab Emirates, have never had an institution which could be described as a popular assembly and show no disposition to establish one. In each of the other 8 cases either an established assembly is in abeyance, invariably as a result of the establishment of a military regime, or the constitution is in a transitional state with the likelihood of elections being held in the foreseeable future.

The contemporary scene, therefore, reveals little diminution in the number of assemblies but a marked deterioration in their power and influence, particularly *vis-à-vis* the political executive. Undoubtedly, the major reason for this decline is the increase in party strength. The political systems with parliamentary executives, drawn from and responsible to their assemblies, have in many cases seen the virtual disappearance of the independent politician and the rise of strong, highly disciplined parties, demanding unfailing allegiance from their members and consistent support in the voting lobbies. The United Kingdom parliament, and particularly the House of Commons, provides clear evidence of this trend, which in Britain has been reinforced by the simple plurality electoral system. This method of voting, almost presupposing the existence of a two-party regime, meant that the arrival of a significant third party in 1981 guaranteed parliamentary domination by whichever party gained 40 per cent or more of the popular vote. In the UK elections of 1979, 1983 and 1987, for example, the Conservatives' share of the national vote was, respectively, 43.9 per cent, 42.4 per cent and 42.3 per cent. Similar trends have been noted in the case of the Australian House of Representatives. Here the alternative vote majoritarian system is in force.

In one-party states, assemblies have traditionally always been more subservient, providing a comforting democratic gloss of legitimacy to policy decisions taken behind the closed doors of party caucuses. In communist states, the sheer size of 'parliamentary' bodies such as the pre-1989 Supreme Soviet (1,500 members) in the Soviet Union, and the National People's Congress (c 3,000 members) in China, and the fact that they meet in plenary session for, at most, only 10–14 days a year has been one factor behind such impotence. The new Supreme Soviet of the Soviet Union is, however, a 'full-time' assembly. The most important reason for their relative powerlessness, however, has been the rigid control over agenda and placements exerted by the party leadership above, buttressed by the principle of 'democratic centralism'. Similar tight leadership control is exerted in non-communist, one-party states.

The political systems where assemblies still retain a degree of virility are those with limited presidential executives and those parliamentary executive states with voting systems which encourage a multiplicity of parties.

In a limited presidential executive state, the constitution places clear restraints on the powers of the executive and protects the assembly in its counterbalancing role. This is evident in its purest and most extreme form in the United States, where it is enhanced by the notorious weakness of party structures. It is also the case, though to lesser degrees, in Brazil, Colombia, Costa Rica, the Dominican Republic, the Philippines and Venezuela. These are all countries where efforts have been made to copy the 'US model'.

In parliamentary states with electoral systems which stimulate party multiplicity, coalition executives are the norm and accountabilty to the assembly becomes a reality. Several West European countries fall into this category, most notably Italy, which has had more than 50 governments since the Second World War. Others include Belgium, Denmark and the Netherlands.

In the region we have called Oceania, the political system of Papua New Guinea, where more than six minor political parties effectively function, is an even more notable example of assembly atomisation, with votes of no-confidence being frequently registered against incumbent administrations, as members shift fluidly in and out of coalition groups.

TABLE 26   ASSEMBLIES OF THE WORLD

State	Name	First Chamber		Second Chamber		
		No	Term	Name	No	Term
Afghanistan	Council of Reps (E)	234	5	Senate (E/A)	128	3-5
Albania	People's Assembly (E)	250	4	—		
Algeria	Nat People's Assembly (E)	281	5	—		

Table 26—Assemblies of the World (contd)

State	First Chamber Name	No	Term	Second Chamber Name	No	Term
Angola	People's Assembly (E/A)	223	3	—		
Antigua	House of Reps (E)	17	5	Senate (A)	17	5
Argentina	Camara de Diputados (E)	254	4	Senado (E)	46	9
Australia	House of Reps (E)	148	3	Senate (E)	76	4
Austria	Nationalrat (E)	183	4	Bundesrat (E)	63	—
The Bahamas	House of Assembly (E)	49	5	Senate (A)	16	5
Bahrain	—					
Bangladesh	Jatiya Sangsad (E/A)	330	5	—		
Barbados	House of Assembly (E)	27	5	Senate (A)	21	5
Belgium	Chamber of Reps (E)	212	4	Senate (E/A)	182	4
Belize	House of Reps (E)	28	5	Senate (A)	8	5
Benin	Nat Revolutionary Ass (E)	196	5	—		
Bhutan	Tshongdu (E/A)	151	3	—		
Bolivia	Chamber of Deputies (E)	130	4	Senate (E)	27	4
Botswana	National Assembly (E/A)	40	5	—		
Brazil	Chamber of Deputies (E)	479	4	Senate (E)	69	8
Brunei	—					
Bulgaria	Grand National Assembly (E)	400	5	—		
Burkina Faso	—				—	
Burma	People's Assembly (E)	489	4	—		
Burundi	National Assembly (E/A)	65	5	—		
Cambodia	National Assembly (E)	117	5	—		
Cameroon	National Assembly (E)	180	5	—		
Canada	House of Commons (E)	295	5	Senate (A)	104	—
Cape Verde	Nat People's Ass (E)	79	5	—		
Central African Republic TRAN	National Assembly (E)			Econ & Reg Council	—	
Chad TRAN	National Assembly (E)	123	5	—		
Chile	Chamber of Deputies (E)	120	4	Senate (E/A)	47	8
China	Nat People's Congress (E)	2,970	5	—		
Colombia	House of Reps (E)	199	4	Senate (E)	114	4
The Comoros	Federal Assembly (E)	42	5	—		
The Congo	People's Nat Assembly (E)	135	5	—		
Costa Rica	Legislative Assembly (E)	57	4	—		
Cuba	National Assembly of People's Power (E)	510	4	—		
Cyprus	House of Reps (E)	80	5	—		
Czechoslovakia	Chamber of the People (E)	200	5	Chamber of Nations (E)	150	5
Denmark	Folketing (E)	179	4	—		
Djibouti	Chamber of Deputies (E)	65	5	—		
Dominica	House of Assembly (E/A)	30	5	—		
Dominican Republic	Chamber of Deputies (E)	120	4	Senate (E)	30	4
Ecuador	Nat Chamber of Reps (E)	72	4	—		
Egypt	People's Assembly (E/A)	458	5	—		
El Salvador	National Assembly (E)	60	3	—		
Equatorial Guinea	House of Reps of the People (E)	41	5	—		
Ethiopia	National Assembly (E)	835	5	—		
Fiji	House of Reps (E)	70	5	Senate (A)	34	6
Finland	Eduskunta (E)	200	4	—		
France	National Assembly (E)	577	5	Senate (E)	321	9
Gabon	National Assembly (E/A)	120	5	—		
Gambia	House of Reps (E/A)	36	5	—		
Germany	Bundestag (E)	662	4	Bundesrat	69	—
Ghana	—				—	
Greece	Parliament (E)	300	4	—		
Grenada	House of Reps (E)	15	4	Senate (A)	13	4

Table 26—Assemblies of the World (contd)

State	First Chamber Name	No	Term	Second Chamber Name	No	Term
Guatemala	National Assembly (E)	100	5	—		
Guinea	—				—	
Guinea-Bissau	National People's Ass (E)	150	5	—		
Guyana	National Assembly (E)	65	5	—		
Haiti TRAN	Chamber of Deputies			Senate	—	
Honduras	National Assembly (E)	134	4	—		
Hungary	National Assembly (E)	394	5	—		
Iceland	Althing (E)	65	4	*		
India	House of the People (Lok Sabha) (E)	544	5	Council of States (Rajya Sabha) (E)	245	6
Indonesia	House of Rep (E/A)	500	5	—		
Iran	Majlis (Islamic Consultative Assembly) (E)	270	4			
Iraq	National Assembly (E)	250	4	—		
Ireland	Dail (E)	166	5	Seanad (E/A)	60	5
Israel	Knesset (E)	120	4	—		
Italy	Camera del Deputati (E)	630	5	Senato (E/A)	322	5
Ivory Coast	National Assembly (E)	175	5	—		
Jamaica	House of Reps (E)	60	5	Senate (A)	21	5
Japan	House of Reps (E)	512	4	House of Councillors (E)	252	6
Jordan	House of Deputies (E)	80	4	House of Notables (A)	30	8*
Kenya	National Assembly (E/A)	202	5	—		
Kiribati	Maneaba (E/A)	39	4	—		
North Korea	Supreme People's Ass (E)	615	4	—		
South Korea	National Assembly (E)	299	4	—		
Kuwait	—				—	
Laos	Supreme People's Ass (E)	79	5	—		
Lebanon	National Assembly (E)	99	4	—		
Lesotho	—				—	
Liberia	House of Reps (E)	64	6	Senate (E)	26	6
Libya	General People's Congress (E)	1,112	1	—		
Luxembourg	Chamber of Deputies (E)	64	5	—		
Madagascar	National People's Ass (E)	137	5	—		
Malawi	National Assembly (E/A)	112	5	—		
Malaysia	House of Reps (E)	177	5	Senate (E/A)	58	6
Maldives	Majlis (E/A)	48	5	—		
Mali	National Assembly (E)	82	3	—		
Malta	House of Reps (E)	65	5	—		
Mauritania	—				—	
Mauritius	Legislative Assembly (E/A)	70	5	—		
Mexico	Chamber of Deputies (E)	400	3	Senate (E)	64	6
Mongolia	Ardyn Ih Hural (E)	370	5	—		
Morocco	Chamber of Reps (E)	306	6	—		
Mozambique	People's Assembly (E)	250	9	—		
Namibia**	National Assembly (E)	72	5	—		
Nauru	Parliament (E)	18	3	—		
Nepal	Rashtriya Panchayat (E/A)	140	5	—		
Netherlands	2nd Chamber (E)	150	4	1st Chamber (E)	75	6
New Zealand	House of Reps (E)	97	3	—		
Nicaragua	National Constituent Assembly (E)	c.90	6	—		
Niger	—				—	
Nigeria	—				—	
Norway	Storting (E)	165	4	*		
Oman	—				—	
Pakistan	National Assembly (E/A)	237	5	Senate (E)	87	6
Panama	Legislative Assembly (E)	67	5	—		

Table 26—Assemblies of the World (contd)

State	First Chamber Name	No	Term	Second Chamber Name	No	Term
Papua New Guinea	National Parliament (E)	109	5	—		
Paraguay	Chamber of Deputies (E)	c.60	5	Senate (E)	c.30	5
Peru	Chamber of Deputies (E)	180	5	Senate (E)	60	5
Philippines	House of Reps (E/A)	250	3	Senate (E)	24	6
Poland	Sejm (E)	460	4	Senate (E)	100	4
Portugal	Assembly (E)	250	4	—		
Qatar	—				—	
Romania	Marea Adunare Nationala (E)	396	5	Senate (E)	119	5
Rwanda	National Development (E) Council	70	5	—		
St Kitts Nevis	National Assembly (E/A)	14	5	—		
St Lucia	House of Assembly (E)	17	5	Senate (A)	11	5
St Vincent and the Grenadines	House of Assembly (E/A)	19	5	—		
Sao Tome & Principe	National People's Assembly (E)	40	5	—		
Saudi Arabia	—				—	
Senegal	National Assembly (E)	120	5	—		
Seychelles	National Assembly (E/A)	25	5	—		
Sierra Leone	House of Reps (E/A)	127	5	—		
Singapore	Parliament (E)	81	5	—		
Solomon Islands	National Parliament (E)	38	4	—		
Somalia	People's Assembly (E/A)	177	5	—		
South Africa	House of Assembly (E/A)	178	5	—		
Soviet Union	People's Council of the Union (E)	271‡	5	Soviet of the Nationalities (E)	271‡	5
Spain	Congress of Deputies (E)	350	4	Senate (E)	280	4
Sri Lanka	National State Assembly (E)	168	6	—		
Sudan	Legislative Assembly (E)	301	4	—		
Suriname	National Assembly (E)	51	5	—		
Swaziland	House of Assembly (E/A)	50	4	Senate (E/A)	20	4
Sweden	Riksdag (E)	349	3	—		
Switzerland	National Council (E)	200	4	Council of States (E)	46	4
Syria	Majlis al-Sha'ab (E)	250	4	—		
Taiwan	Legislative Yuan (E/A)	313	3	—		
Tanzania	National Assembly (E)	243	5	—		
Thailand	House of Reps (E)	347	4	Senate (A)	261	6
Togo	National Assembly (E)	77	5	—		
Tonga	Legislative Assembly (E/A)	29	3	—		
Trinidad and Tobago	House of Reps (E)	36	5	Senate (A)	31	5
Tunisia	National Assembly (E)	136	5	—		
Turkey	Grand National Assembly (E)	450	5	—		
Tuvalu	Parliament (E)	12	4	—		
Uganda	National Resistance Council (E/A)	278	5	—		
United Arab Emirates	—				—	
United Kingdom	House of Commons (E)	650	5	House of Lords (A)	1,150	+ —
United States	House of Reps (E)	435	2	Senate (E)	100	6
Uruguay	Federal Chamber of Deputies (E)	99	5	Senate (E)	30	5
Vanuatu	Parliament (E)	46	4	—		
Venezuela	Chamber of Deputies (E)	196	5	Senate (E/A)	44+	5
Vietnam	National Assembly (E)	496	5	—		

Table 26—Assemblies of the World (contd)

State	First Chamber Name	No	Term	Second Chamber Name	No	Term
Western Samoa	Assembly (E)	47	3	—		
Yemeni Republic TRAN	National Assembly (E)	301	5	—		
Yugoslavia	Federal Chamber (Skupstina) (E)	220	4	Chamber of Republics & Provinces (E)	88	4
Zaire	National Legislative Council (E)	210	5	—		
Zambia	National Assembly (E/A)	135	5	—		
Zimbabwe	House of Assembly (E)	100	5	Senate (E/A)	40	5

KEY:

E/A—Elected/Appointed.
No—Number of members.
Term—Normal length of term in years.
*Formed from first chamber after election.
**Second chamber to be formed in 1992.
†Assembly not currently functioning.
‡Elected by and from the 2,250-member Congress of People's Deputies (CUPD).
TRAN—In a transitional state.

5.2 Assembly Functions

Whatever degree of virility or supineness they display, what are the functions of contemporary assemblies?

First, they have the obvious task of legitimising policies, in other words turning political decisions into law. Although, at its worst, this may mean little more than 'rubber stamping' the actions of the executive, it is a basic function of an assembly and the foundation of what states which claim to be democratic call the 'rule of law'.

Second, they are required to act as the people's representatives and, as such, carry their views to the executive. This is what representative democracy is supposed to be about, but if it is to be effective then the assembly must be able to influence the executive. This brings us back to the question of an assembly's virility.

Third, they are expected to be a 'talking shop': the national debating chamber. This is the role for which assemblies in liberal and emergent democracies are best equipped and which they generally best perform. In one-party states it is the party, through whatever closed institutions it devises, which predominantly fulfils this function. However, in one-party states which may be going through a transitional period, as is the case in several contemporary communist regimes, or are riven with internal factions, as for example in contemporary Iran, assembly debates can be surprisingly lively and relatively open.

Fourth, in liberal and emergent democracies, assemblies perform the vital 'reactive' role of supervising and scrutinising the actions of the political executive and bureaucracy, calling attention to abuses of authority and inefficiencies, and suggesting improvements to legislative packages presented to them.

5.3 Comparing Assemblies

Table 26 provides a variety of data with which to compare assemblies in different states but if it is to be used effectively some criteria need to be established.

For example, is it important that some assembles are unicameral, with one chamber, and others, bicameral, with two? Why, in two-chamber assemblies, are the 'upper' chambers usually less powerful than the 'lower'? Is it important that membership of some chambers is on the basis of election and in others by appointment? Does the duration of the term of office of assembly members have any real significance?

Before these questions can be answered sensibly they must be qualified in some way.

The relationship between assemblies and political executives is arguably the most important basis of comparison because if democratic, rather than autocratic, government is to be achieved then there must be some limits on executive power and in most political systems the only representative body likely to be able to impose such limits is a popular assembly.

As the basis for objective comparisons, we shall, therefore, look at single- and two-chamber assemblies, and, where there are two, the relationships between them; the membership of assemblies and the criteria for membership; and the relationships between assemblies and executives.

5.4 One Chamber or Two?

First, the question of one or two chambers. There is a clear link between federalism and two-chamber assemblies. Of the 20 federal states listed in Table 2, 16, or 80 per cent, have two-chamber assemblies, compared with only 35 of the 144 unitary states, or just over 24 per cent. In the majority of cases the reason for the link will be obvious and this is illustrated in Table 27. In this Table the generic term second chamber or upper house has been used for convenience, but this can be slightly misleading. As we will see later, the so-called 'upper house' is often the weaker of the two and in the Netherlands what is listed in Table 27 as the 'second chamber' is in fact the 'first chamber' of the bicameral States-General.

It is interesting to observe that two states, Iceland and Norway, ostensibly have single-chamber assemblies but, after election, these divide into two. In Iceland the 63-member Althing becomes a lower house of 42 and an upper house of 21. Members may speak in either house but only vote in the one for which they have been chosen. Legislation must be passed by both houses and on some occasions, for example, when considering the budget and dealing with parliamentary questions, they both sit together as the Combined Althing. In Norway a quarter of the 165-member Storting becomes an upper house, the Lagting, and the remaining three-quarters the lower house, the Odelsting. Legislation must start in the Odelsting and then be passed by the Lagting. If there is a conflict of view between the two houses they can consider legislation jointly, as a combined Storting, and approve it by a two-thirds majority.

In making this first comparison between states with one- or two-chamber assemblies, Table 27 is relevant, indicating whether the state is unitary or federal, whether members are elected or appointed on a national or regional basis, and whether or not a representative or appointee is required to reside in the constituency he or she represents.

Of the 16 federal states with bicameral assemblies, 14, or 88 per cent, have second chambers which are regionally representative, whereas only five out of 35, or 15 per cent, unitary states have similar regionally representative bases. There are eight states where the representation is part-national and part-regional, and one federal and seven unitary states fall into this category.

This pattern illustrates one of the chief reasons for having a second chamber: to help resolve regional differences in countries which are geographically large and/or socially and culturally diverse. Regional interests which might object to a centralised government are to some extent pacified by the knowledge that they are formally represented at the centre by a 'local' politician.

Incidentally, it is interesting to note that, whereas the majority of states recognise regional aspirations through second chamber representation, two, Peru and Uruguay, seek to achieve this in a reverse way, by having national representation in the second chamber and regional representation in the first.

A minority of constitutions carry this regional representation a stage further by requiring politicians to reside in the region they represent. Argentina, Canada and the United States have adopted this rule.

The relationship between first and second chambers in terms of political power and authority is another interesting basis of comparison. It is not easy to make clear distinctions and, inevitably, a certain amount of subjectivity will creep in. Table 27 attempts this comparison, using criteria such as the ability to veto legislation, the respective controls of financial legislation and the extent to which a chamber has powers to interrogate the executive and curb its powers. On the basis of such criteria, it will be seen, in Table 27, that the majority of second chambers are weaker than, or enjoy parity with, first chambers and only one, the United States Senate, can, with certainty, be said to be stronger.

TABLE 27   SECOND CHAMBERS OR UPPER HOUSES

State	Federal or Unitary	Relative Term (yrs)	Relative Powers	Basis of Representation
Afghanistan	U	Varies	*	Mixed
Antigua	U	5/5	<	National
Argentina	F	9/4	<	Regional
Australia	F	4/3	<	Regional
Austria*	F	Varies	<	Regional
Bahamas	U	5/5	<	National
Barbados	U	5/5	<	National
Belgium	U	4/4	=	Mixed
Belize	U	5/5	<	National
Bolivia	U	4/4	=	Regional
Brazil	F	8/4	=	Regional
Canada	F	*	<	Regional
Central African Republic*	U		<	Regional
Chile	U	4/4	*	Regional
Colombia	U	4/4	=	National
Czechoslovakia*	F	5/5	=	Regional
Dominican Republic	U	4/4	=	Regional
Fiji	U	6/5	<	Mixed
France	U	9/5	<	Mixed
Germany*	F	*	<	Regional
Haiti	U		<	
Grenada	U	4/4	<	National

93

Table 27—Second Chambers or Upper Houses (contd)

State	Federal or Unitary	Relative Term (yrs)	Relative Powers	Basis of Representation
India*	F	6/5	<	Regional
Ireland	U	5/5	<	National
Italy	U	5/5	=	Regional
Jamaica	U	5/5	<	National
Japan*	U	6/4	<	National & Local
Jordan*	U	8/4	>	National
Liberia	U	6/6	=	National
Malaysia	F	6/5	<	Mixed
Mexico	F	6/3	=	Regional
Netherlands*	U	6/4	<	Regional
Pakistan	F	6/5	<	Regional
Paraguay	U	5/5	<	National
Peru	U	5/5	=	National
Philippines	U	6/3	*	National
Poland	U	4/4	<	National
Romania*	U	2/2	<	National
St Lucia	U	5/5	<	National
Soviet Union*	F	5/5	=	Regional
Spain	U	4/4	<	Mixed
Swaziland	U	4/4	=	Mixed
Switzerland	F	4/4	=	National
Thailand	U	6/4	=	National
Trinidad & Tobago	U	5/5	<	National
United Kingdom*	U	*	<	National
United States	F	6/2	>	Regional
Uruguay	U	5/5	=	National
Venezuela	F	5/5	=	Regional
Yugoslavia*	F	4/4	=	Regional
Zimbabwe	U	5/5	<	Mixed

KEY:

Relative Term: compared with First Chamber or Lower House
Relative Powers: compared with First Chamber or Lower House;
=is equal;<is weaker;>is stronger; *see notes below
Basis of Representation: National/Regional/Mixed
Most second chambers are termed 'senates'; where another name applies this is noted below.

*NOTES

Afghanistan	In transitional state
Austria	Bundesrat
Canada	Senators appointed for life
Central African Republic	In transitonal state
Chile	In transitional state
Czechoslovakia	Chamber of Nations

Table 27—Second Chambers or Upper Houses (contd)

*NOTES (contd)

Germany	The Bundesrat's composition varies as state governments change, rather than being dependent on elections
Haiti	In transitional state
India	Council of States
Japan	House of Councillors
Jordan	House of Notables
Netherlands	First chamber
Philippines	In transitional state
Romania	In transitional state
Soviet Union	Council of Nationalities
United Kingdom	House of Lords composed of hereditary and life members
Yugoslavia	Chamber of Republics

5.5 Membership of Assemblies

Table 26 shows that in the vast majority of states membership of an assembly is on the basis of election. It would be surprising if it were otherwise since the main purpose of having an assembly is to ensure, or at least suggest, that the ordinary person has an opportunity to be represented by a politician who has been freely chosen. How this is done and whether or not it is done successfully will be examined in the next chapter.

There are a few first chambers or single chambers where a combination of election and appointment is used. In the vast majority of such cases the non-elected members are executive appointees, giving a President or monarch the opportunity of placing his own people. Occasionally appointments are made to try to ensure a particular distribution of membership. In Tanzania, for example, a complicated mixture of election and appointment makes provision for regional, female and party representation as well as presidential nominees. Similarly, in Bangladesh and Pakistan a set quota of National Assembly seats, 30 and 20 respectively, are reserved for women appointees. In India, two Lok Sabha seats are reserved for the Anglo-Indian community.

In the majority of one-party states assembly representatives, whether elected or appointed, are initially selected by the party. In communist systems there is an interweaving of party and state membership, with the party nominees, because of their greater experience and 'professionalism', dominating proceedings. The non-party deputies are selected as exemplary representatives of the full cross-section of society by sex, age, ethnic and occupational groups. They serve their constituents as mandated delegates on a part-time basis, being given only minor 'out of pocket' expenses for the five to ten days spent each year at the national assembly.

Of the 51 states with second chambers, members are wholly elected in 25, wholly appointed in 13 and part-elected and part-appointed in ten. In some of the small states, with a parliamentary executive fashioned on the 'Westminster model', the mixture of election and appointment is constructed so as to reflect the political balance in the first chamber. In Antigua, the Bahamas, Barbados, Belize, Grenada, St Lucia, and Trinidad & Tobago, for example, the Prime Minister and the official Leader of the Opposition are entitled to nominate members.

In states with political systems modelled on the United States, most notably those in Latin America, direct popular election of the second chamber predominates.

In Europe and South Asia, by contrast, members of the second chambers are predominantly elected indirectly, in the majority of cases by regional assemblies. Austria, Belgium, France, India, Ireland, Germany, the Netherlands, Pakistan and Yugoslavia all provide examples of indirectly elected second chambers.

The most popular term of membership is five years. The complete analysis is given in Table 28.

TABLE 28   ASSEMBLY TERMS OF MEMBERSHIP

Term	First or single chamber		Second chamber	
(years)	Number	%	Number	%
1	1	0.7	—	—
2	2	1	—	—
3	13	9	—	—
4	43	29	11	25
5	84	57	17	39
6	4	3	11	25
8	—	—	3	7
9	1	0.7	2	4
Total	148	100	44	100

The popularity of a five-year term is understandable. A newly

elected government, with a policy package it wished to implement, would probably spend at least the first two years framing
the necessary legislation and ensuring its passage through the
legislative machine. If a proposal was thought to be beneficial in
the long term but unpopular in a short time span then a
reasonable period would be needed for the public to appreciate its
benefits. That would be the government's view. On the other
hand, immediately popular proposals might be innately flawed
and these defects might only reveal themselves over time. A
five-year term of office would give the electorate time to assess a
government's performance before it submitted itself again for
election. That would be the opposition's view.

Politicians in states with first chambers with limited lives of
three years, such as Australia, have expressed reservations from
time to time about the shortness of the term and some of the
practical consequences. Short-term assemblies tend to make
governments cautious in their policy proposals, fearing a loss of
public support with insufficient time to prove that short-term
unpopularity can be replaced by long-term satisfaction.

It should be remembered, however, that assemblies in states
with parliamentary executives rarely run their full terms. They
may end because the government loses assembly support or, as
frequently happens, it or a coalition partner seeks a dissolution at
what it considers to be the most propitious time to ensure
electoral success.

In states with limited presidential executives assembly terms
are invariably of a fixed duration. This is of potential value to
opposition parties, removing the incumbent administration's
control over the election timetable and thus subjecting all
members equally to the whims of random external forces. It also
serves, however, to institutionalise electioneering, sometimes to
an unhealthy degree. This is most clearly seen in the case of the
United States House of Representatives whose members, facing
biennial elections, find themselves condemned to a non-stop
cycle of campaigning and fund-raising. Fixed-term assemblies are
also the norm in two Scandinavian countries with parliamentary
executives, Norway and Sweden, and also in Switzerland.

Second chambers with terms of six years or more often stagger
those of individual members, with half or a third submitting
themselves for election at a time. This serves to 'keep fresh' the
accountability of the assembly, but can create problems for a new
administration assuming office following a sudden election swing

in the lower chamber. The states falling into this staggered category are:

Nine-year term with a third retiring
    every three years: Argentina and
                                       France

Eight-year term with a third and
two-thirds retiring alternately every
    four years: Brazil

Eight-year term with a half retiring
    every four years: Jordan

Six-year term with a half retiring
    every three years: Japan and
                                       Netherlands

Six-year term with a third retiring
    every two years: United States,
                                       India and Pakistan

Finally, constitutions invariably specify qualifications for candidates in assembly elections, including a mimimum age. Most states with two-chamber assemblies stipulate a more mature entry age for members of the second chamber. In Venezuela, for example, the minimum ages are 21 years for the Chamber of Deputies and 30 years for the Senate. In Argentina and the United States they are 25 years for the Chamber of Deputies/House of Representatives and 30 years for the Senate. In Thailand and the Philippines the figures are 25 years for the House of Representatives and 35 years for the Senate. In Italy, the ages are 25 years for the Camera dei Deputati and 40 years for the Senato.

This requirement of greater maturity, frequently combined with a longer term of office than in the first chamber, tends to add to the authority of second chamber members, who have often already had sufficiently long political careers to qualify them for the description of 'elder statesmen'.

5.6 Assembly Size

In Table 29 The size distribution of contemporary world assemblies, lower and upper chambers, is set out and in Table 30 general population per lower house member has been calculated for each state with an assembly.

TABLE 29   SIZE DISTRIBUTION OF CONTEMPORARY
WORLD ASSEMBLIES

Membership Size	Lower Chambers	Upper Chambers	Lower Chambers (%)	Upper Chambers (%)
10 or Below	—	1	—	2
11–50	26	22	18	45
51–100	29	12	20	24
101–200	40	6	27	13
201–300	22	5	15	10
301–400	10	2	7	4
401–500	7	—	5	—
501–750	9	—	6	—
751–1,000	1	—	1	—
1,001–3,000	2	1	1	2
Total	146	49	100	100

TABLE 30   POPULATION PER LOWER HOUSE MEMBER*

State	Thousands of People per Lower House Member	State	Thousands of People per Lower House Member
Nauru	0.44	Luxembourg	5.73
Tuvalu	0.75	Belize	6.00
Kiribati	1.51	Guinea-Bissau	6.00
Dominica	2.47	Grenada	6.67
Sao Tome & Principe	2.63	St Lucia	7.24
Seychelles	2.64	Solomon Islands	7.45
St Kitts-Nevis	2.86	Suriname	7.84
Vanuatu	2.96	Equatorial Guinea	8.78
Libya	3.51	Barbados	9.44
Tonga	3.62	Bhutan	9.58
Maldives	3.75	Gabon	10.00
Iceland	3.81	Comoros	11.17
Western Samoa	3.83	Congo	11.76
Djibouti	4.62	Cyprus	11.89
Bahamas	4.80	Albania	12.18
Antigua	5.00	Guyana	12.31
Mongolia	5.14	Fiji	13.75
St Vincent & Grenadines	5.42	Swaziland	13.84
Malta	5.46	Mauritius	14.49
Cape Verde	5.57	Namibia	15.99
		The Gambia	16.00

Table 30—Population per Lower House member* (contd)

State	Thousands of People per Lower House Member	State	Thousands of People per Lower House Member
Cuba	20.40	Romania	61.79
Benin	20.92	Taiwan	62.62
Ireland	21.83	Iraq	65.11
Bulgaria	22.50	Portugal	66.40
Sweden	23.94	Paraguay	68.65
Finland	24.65	Malawi	72.28
Norway	26.53	Sri Lanka	72.64
Lebanon	27.27	Madagascar	75.18
Botswana	27.50	Burundi	75.38
Hungary	27.50	Burma	77.10
Denmark	28.42	Morocco	77.45
Uruguay	30.30	Czechoslovakia	77.50
Papua New Guinea	31.15	Poland	81.52
North Korea	31.30	El Salvador	85.00
Singapore	31.90	Guatemala	86.00
Switzerland	32.35	United Kingdom	86.86
Greece	33.18	Sudan	87.01
Panama	33.23	Algeria	87.36
Trinidad & Tobago	33.44	Malaysia	89.38
New Zealand	34.07	Zimbabwe	90.00
Honduras	34.33	Venezuela	90.82
Nicaragua	34.38	Italy	90.83
Israel	35.07	Canada	90.87
Liberia	35.94	France	96.01
Angola	36.77	Mali	96.44
Sierra Leone	37.34	Netherlands	96.54
Togo	39.26	Tanzania	96.97
Jamaica	39.43	Chile	102.50
Austria	41.23	Yugoslavia	105.45
Somalia	44.07	Australia	106.51
Belgium	46.55	Egypt	110.26
Costa Rica	47.37	Spain	111.64
Bolivia	49.46	Peru	112.22
Laos	52.11	Turkey	115.15
Ethiopia	52.57	Germany	118.43
Zambia	52.59	Uganda	120.63
Tunisia	53.38	Kenya	122.09
Syria	54.03	Argentina	122.83
Dominican Rep	55.12	Nepal	124.44
Cameroon	55.56	Vietnam	125.00
Mozambique	56.00	Ecuador	135.21
Senegal	57.50	South Korea	144.82
Jordan	58.58	Thailand	146.89
Cambodia	59.21	Zaire	149.05
Côte d'Ivoire	60.00	Colombia	150.75

Table 30—Population per Lower House Member* (contd)

State	Thousands of People per Lower House Member	State	Thousands of People per Lower House Member
Mexico	163.40	Indonesia	346.21
Iran	172.59	China	353.54
South Africa	186.52†	Soviet Union	373.33
Philippines	232.40	Pakistan	429.96
Japan	237.11	United States	554.02
Brazil	299.16	India	1,443.01
Bangladesh	315.45		

*Population:member ratios have not been calculated for Afghanistan or the Yemeni Republic, whose political systems remain in a transitional condition.

†This has been calculated by dividing the total population by a figure corresponding to the 178-members of the House of Assembly. In reality, however, South Africa's unique, racially discriminatory, political system has resulted in the establishment of three separate chambers for the white, coloured and Asian communities, while, at the same time, excluding blacks from the national political process entirely. To be truly accurate, separate deputy-population ratios have been calculated for each community. The resulting figures are: for the white community–33.57 (thousands of persons per member); for the coloured community–39.05; for the Asian community–22.13; for the black community—not applicable.

From Table 29, it emerges that almost two-thirds of the world's lower chambers have memberships of 200 or fewer, with the median size being around 150. In addition, it is apparent that upper houses of bicameral assemblies are almost uniformly smaller than their lower house counterparts, being on average half the size. As a consequence, 73 per cent of upper chambers have memberships of 100 or fewer, the median figure being 58.

From Table 30, it emerges, not surprisingly, that a state's population size is the principal determinant both of the membership size of its assembly and of the resultant population-:member ratio. Thus, the larger in demographic terms the state, the larger on average the size of its assembly and, notwithstanding this, the higher its population:member ratio. For this reason, India, the second most populous country in the world, appears at the bottom of the Table 30 ratio listings, followed by the United States, the world's fourth most populous state. Conversely, tiny island states such as Nauru, Tuvalu and Kiribati are to be found clustering at the head of the listings, having small assemblies, with memberships substantially fewer than 50, yet despite this still registering unusually low population:member ratios.

There are two notable exceptions to this general, regular pattern.

First, communist or nationalistic socialist states usually have assemblies far larger than equivalent-sized liberal or emergent democracies, or one-party non-socialist states. As a natural corollary, their resulting population:member ratios are lower than might be expected. China, with its 2,970-member National People's Congress; Libya, with its 1,112-member General People's Congress; the Soviet Union, with its 2,250-member Congress of the USSR People's Deputies (CUPD); Ethiopia, with its 835-member National Assembly; and North Korea, with its 655-member Supreme People's Assembly are the most prominent examples. The rationale behind the election of these 'jumbo-assemblies' would, in theory, appear to be a desire to broaden the participation base. In practice however, as has been noted earlier, these assemblies meet in plenary session for less than two weeks a year. They delegate their authority to smaller 'inner assemblies', standing committees and general secretariats, which generally comprise between 40 and 140 members, a figure substantially below the membership average for the permanent assemblies in liberal or emergent democracies.

In three other countries, Afghanistan, Indonesia and Taiwan, large quasi-assemblies are found, with memberships in excess of 900, which have powers to amend their constitutions and, in the first three, to appoint the state Presidents. These are, however, only *ad hoc* bodies, meeting variously at two-, five-, six- or seven-year intervals, unless specially summoned. In the interim periods, they delegate effective authority to smaller, regular national assemblies below them. For this reason, they have not been treated as full assemblies in this chapter, being excluded from the listings in Table 26 and from the calculations made for Table 30 above.

The second, and more specific, anomaly which emerges when Tables 29 and 30 are studied, in conjunction with Table 26, is found in the United Kingdom. The United Kingdom has by far the largest lower house, 650 members, of all the world's liberal democracies and, for this reason, has a comparatively low population:member ratio for its total population size. Furthermore, it is the only country in the world having an upper chamber with a larger membership than its lower. This results from the anachronistic combination of hereditary succession and government appointment that is still used to fill the House of Lords, as well as the fact that in earlier years it was the pre-eminent chamber. Today the House of Lords comprises roughly 800 hereditary peers and 400 life peers, including the law lords and the 'lords spiritual', but in practice its active membership is less than 400. Indeed, 300 hereditary peers have never even visited the chamber to take the oath of membership.

5.7 Assembly-Executive Relationships

There are three possible bases on which to examine the assembly-executive relationship. First, the extent to which an assembly can initiate legislation. Second, the extent to which an assembly can influence policy-making. Third, the extent of an assembly's ability to criticise the executive, block its policies and even dismiss it.

The vast majority of contemporary assemblies are not significant initiators of legislation. They are, as has already been said, mainly amenders and approvers. For this reason they have frequently been categorised as 'reactive' chambers. There are, however, some notable exceptions which stand out as examples of 'active' legislatures. Non-adversarial Sweden, where assembly members are mainly grouped in constituency rather than party blocks, is one. So, to an even greater extent, is the United States.

In Sweden private members' proposals (*motioner*) are ten times as numerous in the Riksdag as government bills (*propositioner*), although the bulk of the former are amendments or party alternatives to government bills, designed to spark off new discussion and inquiries.

In the United States Congress thousands of bills and resolutions are introduced each year by Senators and Representatives, several hundred of which ultimately become law. Even here, however, the key legislative measures are those proposed in January by the President in his annual 'State of the Union' address to both chambers and which are subsequently adopted by party supporters within Congress under the promptings of the White House's liaison staff.

The ability of assemblies to influence policy-making is also slight, Sweden again being somewhat unusual in this respect. An assembly in a state with a parliamentary executive is, in theory, in a strong position to make policy since the executive is drawn from it and responsible to it. In practice, however, an assembly member who has joined the executive to a great extent loses his or her allegiance to the assembly and becomes, psychologically but not physically, separate from it. The obvious example is the distinction between a front-bench, government, member of the United Kingdom House of Commons and a back-bencher.

So we are left with the third basis on which to examine the assembly-executive relationship: the ability to criticise, block policies and, *in extremis*, to dismiss an executive.

Most assemblies in parliamentary executive systems have built-in mechanisms for regular questioning of ministers. The United Kingdom House of Commons has an hour set aside for this for four days per week, and on two of these days fifteen minutes for questions specifically addressed to the Prime Minister. Although probably the most popular event of the parliamentary week in Britain, as far as the media and public are concerned, there is little evidence that Question Time in the House of Commons is anything more than an opportunity for rival parties to score points against each other. In West Germany and Finland 'interpellation' seems more successful, the oral questioning of a minister often being accompanied by a snap vote.

Most assemblies in limited presidential and parliamentary executive systems have strong committee structures, partly to expedite the legislative process and partly to oversee the actions of the executive. The United States Congress undoubtedly has the strongest committees of any contemporary assembly in the world. The power and authority of these committees, well provisioned with research staff and armed with extensive rights to subpoena staff from the executive, have been dramatically highlighted in recent years through the wide publicity given to the Watergate and 'Irangate' hearings. The fact that sessions of the congressional committees can receive nationwide television coverage has increased public awareness and enhanced their influence.

By comparison, assembly committees in other states seem weak. In the United Kingdom, as the result of the composition of the House of Commons and the disciplined party system, standing committees which consider government legislation are government-dominated, introducing only minor amendments to bills presented. Even weaker are the investigative select committees which were introduced into the chamber in 1979 to 'shadow' the work of government departments. Although producing informative reports, their impact as parliamentary watchdogs has not been great. Their counterparts in Canada and France have been only marginally more successful.

Stronger committee systems operate in Germany, Italy and Japan, all three having constitutions partly modelled on that of the United States. These committees are primarily concerned with legislation but, from time to time, *ad hoc* investigative committees have been influential. In Japan in 1976 an assembly committee vigorously investigated the Lockheed bribes scandal, its work eventually resulting in the arrest and trial of former Prime Minister Tanaka. More recently in what was West Germany, a committee successfully probed the 'Flick scandal' which was concerned with illegal party financing.

In one-party states, assemblies are inevitably subservient to the party, and hence the executive. However, in the Soviet Union, working with, rather than against, the party, the 34 or so specialised permanent standing commissions of the Supreme Soviet have, in recent years, grown in stature and become part of the policy-making machine. Similar bodies are also influential in the Polish Sejm and Hungary's National Assembly.

On balance, however, it must be said that, with some rare exceptions, contemporary assemblies have shown little sign of keeping up with, let alone overtaking, the increasing power and authority of executives of all types.

5.8 The Representation of Interests

The representation of interests is one activity that assemblies usually do well, especially in liberal democratic and emergent democratic states. This representation falls into three broad categories: constituency representation, party representation and specific group representation.

Constituency representation is a traditional function of all assemblies. In the United States Congress it has been developed to a high degree and is reinforced by the residential factor in both the House of Representatives and the Senate. Some Congressmen have devoted virtually their entire political careers to the economic advancement of the constituencies they represent, knowing that this is the surest route to re-election.

Similar, but less well-developed, examples can be found in assemblies in other parts of the world, including Kenya, the Philippines, South Korea, Yugoslavia, France and the United

Kingdom. In the British House of Commons, for example, it is not unknown for a member to ignore a major policy line of his party in order to support his constituency. Some United Kingdom Labour Party MPs have in recent years been confronted with 'dilemmas of conscience' in trying to follow a non-nuclear power policy when their constituents have been dependent on nuclear generation for their livelihoods.

Party representation has been the fastest-growing activity in most assemblies in recent years. The last independent MP in the British House of Commons disappeared in the 1960s and there is now only a minority of assemblies that accommodate them. Kiribati, the Maldives, Nauru and Tuvalu seem to be the few contemporary states where assembly elections are contested by politicians standing as independents.

The representation of group interests is another growing activity of assembly members, particularly in liberal democratic countries. In the British House of Commons many Labour members are sponsored by trade unions and some Conservatives are paid by a variety of interests to present their points of view. In an effort to bring this activity into the open, the House of Commons has produced a Register of MPs' Interests and members are requested, but not compelled, to register their interests as well as declare them during the course of debates. In the United States, with the growing influence of Political Action Committees, which provide a quarter of the funds used in contesting congressional elections, the influence of single-issue ideological interest groups is substantially stronger.

Recommended Reading

Arter, D., *The Nordic Parliaments: A Comparative Analysis*, Hurst, 1984.

Blondel, J. *et al* in: M. Curtis (ed), *Introduction to Comparative Government*, Harper & Row, 1985.

Blondel, J., *Comparative Legislatures*, Prentice-Hall, 1973.

Charlton, R., *Comparative Government*, Longman, 1985, Ch 3.

Goodwin, Jr, G., 'The New Congress', in: P. J. Davies and F. A. Waldstein (eds), *Political Issues in America Today*, Manchester University Press, 1987.

Hague, R. and Harrop, M., *Comparative Government and Politics: An Introduction*, 2nd edn., Macmillan, 1987, Ch 10.

Inter-Parliamentary Union, *Parliaments of the World: A Reference Companion*, Macmillan, 1976.

Judge, D., *The Politics of Parliamentary Reform*, Heinemann, 1983.

Kim, C. *et al*, *The Legislative Connection: The Politics of Representation in Kenya, Korea and Turkey*, Duke University Press, 1984.

Lees, J. and Shaw, M. (eds), *Committees in Legislatures: A Comparative Analysis*, Duke University Press, 1979.

Loewenberg, G. and Patterson, S. C., *Comparing Legislatures*, Little Brown, 1979.

Lovenduski, J. and Woodall, J., *Politics and Society in Eastern Europe*, Macmillan, 1987, Ch 9.

Mann, T. E. and Ornstein, N. J. (eds), *The New Congress*, American Enterprise Institute, 1981.

Mezey, M., *Comparative Legislatures*, Duke University Press, 1979.

Nelson, D. and White S. (eds), *Communist Legislatures in Comparative Perspective*, Macmillan, 1982.

Norton, P. (ed), *Parliament in the 1980s*, Basil Blackwell, 1985.

Paxton, P., *World Legislatures*, Macmillan, 1974.

Roberts, G. K., *An Introduction to Comparative Politics*, Edward Arnold,   1985, Ch 7.

Smith, G., *Politics in Western Europe: A Comparative Analysis*, 4th edn., Gower Publishing, 1986, Ch 7.

Sundquist, J. L., *The Decline and Resurgence of Congress*, The Brookings Institution, 1981.

Vanneman, P., *The Supreme Soviet: Politics and the Legislative Process in the Soviet Political System*, Duke University Press, 1977.

Waller, D. J., *The Government and Politics of the People's Republic of China*, 3rd edn., Hutchinson, 1981, Ch 3.

White, S., Gardner, J. and Schopflin, G., *Communist Political Systems: An Introduction*, 2nd edn., Macmillan, 1987, Ch. 3.

Chapter 6

ELECTIONS AND VOTERS

6.1 The Importance of Elections

The majority of contemporary states claim to be democratic and seek to prove their democratic credentials under the banner of representation. The right to vote is almost the only universal right in the world today. Of the 164 states we are examining only five, Brunei, Oman, Qatar, Saudi Arabia and the United Arab Emirates, do not have, and never have had, any institutions which can, even in the loosest sense, be described as popularly representative. A further eight states have 'suspended' legislatures and thus no currently functioning electoral systems. Among the other 151 there are wide differences in kinds and degrees of representation.

The first, and obvious, difference is between multi-party and one-party political systems. It is reasonable to assume that an election in a multi-party state means a choice of policies as well as representatives, whereas in a one-party system a representative may be changed but the basic policy thrust, as derived from the party, remains the same.

Why then do one-party states bother to go through the charade of elections? First, most of them, indeed probably all of them, would claim that the elections were not a charade. They might well argue that the reality of choice is no greater in a multi-party system than in their own. They might, with some justification, select one of the world's oldest democracies, the United Kingdom, and point out that no government in the post-war period has been elected by a clear majority of the people voting. They might also compare turnouts of less than 80 per cent in general elections in the UK with turnouts well in excess of 90 per cent in most communist one-party states.

The politician in a liberal democratic state, while conceding these points, would probably argue that a choice between parties was nonetheless a substantially greater choice even though, through ignorance or apathy, some people failed to exercise it. He would say that the opportunity of voting for a complete change of policy, and even philosophy, was a vital element in a democratic political system and that without it genuine choice was limited.

Leaving aside such arguments, it is clear that in one-party states the voter knows that whatever decision he or she takes in the polling booth the party in power will not change, so the earlier question must be repeated: why are elections held?

The main reason is to demonstrate popular support for the regime. The important work of selecting the candidate has already been done, within the party machine. The election just legitimises the 'behind the scenes' decisions. In some one-party states the question asked is simply 'Yes or No?'. There is only one candidate and therefore choice is given only in a negative form. In other states a choice of candidate may be given. The former communist states of East Germany, Hungary, Poland, Romania and Yugoslavia offered candidate choice for some years and the practice was later adopted in the Soviet Union and China. In non-communist one-party states candidate choice is fairly common.

Although in one-party states the election would appear to make the candidate choice legitimate, the practice is invariably unnecessary on constitutional or practical grounds. The party decision, once taken, is inviolate. The size of the turnout in each constituency will, however, be of interest to party officials because it will indicate the degree of activity, or apathy, in different areas. It will enable them to gauge the work being done by individual candidates and provide public 'feedback' on sensitive issues, allowing them to take steps to improve local morale and efficiency and, if pressed, introduce measures to deal with grass-roots grievances. This is particularly relevant in communist states.

In non-communist one-party states elections may be important on more personal grounds. In some countries, where candidates are fighting each other within the one party, success will often depend on which politician, in the eyes of the voter, offers the best deal. In Kenya, for example, there is usually a large (40–50 per cent) turnover of parliamentary representatives as the record of one politician is judged unsatisfactory in terms of what he has 'delivered' by way of state money for some local development and so is replaced by another who appears to offer more. This is a variant of what is described in congressional elections in the United States as 'pork barrel' politics: the ability to 'bring home the bacon'.

In multi-party political systems elections are much more significant. Not only do they provide the non-politically active public, who invariably comprise more than 95 per cent of the

109

population in most liberal-democratic societies, with an opportunity to participate in the political process. They actually determine who shall wield power. This is why in liberal and emergent democracies so much attention is paid to voting qualifications and voting methods.

6.2 Voting Qualifications

The great majority of constitutions refer to voting on the basis of universal adult suffrage which, in simple terms, means the right of all adults to cast their vote. For some countries this is a comparatively recently acquired right and it is a right which still varies in detail from state to state.

The age of majority varies and, although 18 is the most common, being the rule in 108 states, there are some states, 21 in all, where it is as high as 21 and others, such as Guinea-Bissau and, in presidential elections in Iran, as low as 15. Moreover, in some Latin American states, Colombia being an example, the franchise is extended to married persons at an earlier age, 18, than to those who are single, 21. Under some constitutions literacy is also a necessary qualification, whereas in countries, such as India, Honduras and Madagascar, where the level of literacy is low, there is often provision for people to vote on the basis of symbols rather than names.

Women were the last group in most countries to acquire the right to vote. In New Zealand they were given the franchise as early as 1893, long before it was a fully independent state. In Jordan, by way of contrast, they did not acquire it until 1982.

South Africa remains the one country in the world where a significant proportion of the population are excluded from electoral participation on racial-ethnic grounds. Between 1909 and 1936, a portion of the black and coloured community of Cape Province did enjoy the right to vote. Thereafter, however, the introduction of a series of new laws served effectively to eliminate black suffrage. This was formally acknowledged in 1959, the official date of complete disenfranchisement for blacks. In 1984 voting rights were restored to coloureds, who comprise 11 per cent of the population, and Indians, who constitute another 3 per cent, for elections to their own assemblies. The black community, who comprise more than 68 per cent of the country's total population, still remain excluded from a political process which is effectively controlled by the 18 per cent white minority.

6.3 Voting Systems

Elections are usually held to choose either executives or assemblies, or both. In multi-party states where the executive, usually the President, is separate from, and usually limited by, the assembly, the two elections are quite separate. They may take place at the same time but there are two distinct sets of choices. In parliamentary systems where the executive is drawn from and responsible to the assembly, the assembly determines which party will form the executive and thus only assembly elections are necessary. In one-party states the executive is usually chosen by the party and then 'legitimised' either by the assembly or through a separate election.

The election of executives is generally a fairly straightforward process but considerable ingenuity has been shown in some multi-party states in devising methods of electing assemblies to try to ensure as close a correlation as possible between the number of votes cast for a particular party and the number of seats that party wins.

6.3.1 Simple Plurality (SP)

The most frequently used voting system is the simplest and easiest to understand, the simple plurality, or 'first-past-the-post', method. It is used for assembly elections in the world's two largest liberal democracies, the United States and India, as well as in the United Kingdom and most of the former British colonies which, after independence, retained a 'Westminster model' constitution.

This voting system does not make any pretence of trying to equate the number of seats won with the number of votes cast. Consequently, in countries with two major parties, such as the United Kingdom and New Zealand, third or fourth parties tend to win disproportionately fewer seats than votes, as Table 31 clearly shows. In countries where numerous minor parties, usually regionally or occupationally based, but only one significant national party, operate, the larger grouping is usually consistently able to hold power, despite capturing a relatively low share of the total vote. This has been apparent in India, where the Congress Party has been the predominant force. In countries where there are strong localised ethnic concentrations, such as Northern Ireland and parts of Scotland and Wales, the SP system can be of potential advantage to smaller parties.

**TABLE 31   PARTIES' SHARE OF HOUSE OF COMMONS IN
UK GENERAL ELECTIONS: 1945-87***

(a) By Votes

General Election Year	Conservative Share (%)	Labour Share (%)	Lib/Alliance† Share (%)	Total Votes (m)	Voter Turnout (%)
1945	40	48	9	24.1	73
1950	43	46	9	28.8	84
1951	48	49	2	28.6	82
1955	50	46	3	26.8	77
1959	49	44	6	27.9	79
1964	43	44	11	27.7	77
1966	42	48	8	27.3	76
1970	46	43	7	28.3	72
1974 Feb	38	37	19	31.3	78
1974 Oct	36	39	18	29.2	73
1979	44	37	14	31.2	76
1983	42	28	25	30.7	73
1987	42	31	23	32.6	75

(b) By Seats

General Election Year	Conservative Share (%)	Labour Share (%)	Lib/Alliance† Share (%)	Total Seats (number)	Voter Turnout (%)
1945	33	61	2	640	73
1950	48	50	1	625	84
1951	51	47	1	625	82
1955	55	44	1	630	77
1959	58	41	1	630	79
1964	48	50	1	630	77
1966	40	58	2	630	76
1970	52	46	1	630	72
1974 Feb	47	47	2	635	78
1974 Oct	44	50	2	635	73
1979	53	42	2	635	76
1983	61	32	4	650	73
1987	59	35	3	650	75

*Source: J. D. Derbyshire and I. D. Derbyshire, *Politics in Britain: From Callaghan to Thatcher*, W & R Chambers, 1990, Table 4, p. 6.

†The Alliance fought its first general election in 1983.

Currently, it is employed by 93 states for lower chamber assembly elections, 52 being either liberal or emergent democracies. The remainder are one-party or quasi-one-party states. In some of the latter, Cameroon being an example, 'slate-system' variants of SP operate. Here, the party which gains the majority of votes cast secures all the available assembly seats. In many communist states, the SP system is nominal, no opposition candidates being put up.

The alternatives to the SP system fall into two broad categories, the absolute majority (see 6.3.2–6.3.3) and the proportional systems (6.3.4–6.3.7). Within each of these two groups are variations, sometimes of detail and sometimes of substance.

6.3.2 The Alternative Vote (AV)

The alternative vote (AV) is not theoretically a form of proportional representation in that it cannot guarantee a close relationship between votes and seats and, indeed, can sometimes produce surprising results. It does however go some way towards making the voting system fairer and is relatively simple and easy to understand.

It uses single-member constituencies, the voter choosing a candidate by marking 1 against his name on the ballot paper. If he wants, he can also mark 2 against his second choice and so on, but this is not compulsory. First preference votes are then counted and if any one candidate collects more than 50 per cent of all the votes cast he is automatically elected. If this does not happen the candidate with the least number of first choice votes is eliminated and the second preferences of those who chose him as number 1 are distributed among the other candidates. This process continues until one candidate emerges with more than 50 per cent.

The main objection to AV is that it tends to help compromise candidates and its results can sometimes be quite unpredictable, with the successful candidate being someone whom very few people positively want. At present, only Australia employs this voting system. It was first introduced in 1919 and applies to its lower chamber, the House of Representatives. It has had little perceptible impact on the party system, which remains firmly set in a two- to three-party mould.

6.3.3 The Second Ballot (SB)

The second ballot is similar in some respects to AV. A simple majority election is held and if no one gets more than 50 per cent of the total vote, the candidate with the fewest votes is eliminated and a second election is held, usually within the next week to ten days. The rules concerning who can participate in the 'run-off' contest vary considerably. In France, where the system is used for National Assembly elections, candidates who have received support from at least 12.5 per cent of the registered electorate are entitled to compete in the following week's second ballot. The candidate who achieves a majority in this second contest is the one who is elected. For French presidential elections, only the top two candidates go forward to the 'run-off' ballot.

In terms of achieving better proportionality, the second ballot generally fares worse than AV and even SP. In addition, it is more costly to operate. The reason for its adoption by the framers of France's Fifth Republic constitution was their concern to encourage the emergence of more streamlined and disciplined party groupings, following the '*immobilisme*' of the Fourth Republic, whose assembly had contained representatives from more than a dozen competing parties, elected by the party list system of proportional representation.

Despite these roots, eleven countries currently use the SB system for their lower chamber elections. In addition to France, they are the Côte d'Ivoire, Czechoslovakia, Egypt, Hungary, Iran, Kiribati, Poland, Romania, the Soviet Union and Vanuatu. In the Ivory Coast, the SB system is of a 'slate variety', in which the party which receives the majority of the national vote captures all the available National Assembly seats. SB is also used by several other states, including Cyprus, Ecuador and Peru, for presidential contests, and for governorship contests in some southern states of the United States.

In theory, many communist states can be viewed as SB countries, their constitutions requiring assembly candidates to secure a full majority of the votes. In practice, however, because of a lack of effective competition, national level contests have always been settled by one ballot.

Compared with the SP system, both the SB and AV have had a tendency to promote tactical alliances between minor parties or major and minor parties, to improve their chances of success.

Majority voting systems are concerned principally with returning effective governments, usually of a single party, even though they do not always achieve this. In contrast, proportional electoral systems place their chief priority on the principle of representation, seeking to effect the return of assemblies which, in party, social, gender and ethnic composition, closely mirror the profile and wishes of the electorate. Four principal variants of proportional representation (PR) are currently to be found in operation.

6.3.4 The Party List (PL)

List systems are, potentially, the most truly representative form of PR, being designed to return members reflecting the broadest possible spectrum of public opinion. To achieve this, unlike absolute majority systems, they are, of necessity, based on large multi-member constituencies of either a regional or, in the case of Israel, for example, a national character.

The first stage in the complicated operation of the PL system is the production of lists of candidates by each of the political parties fighting the election. Each list shows names in descending order of preference, as chosen by the party. In many cases, an elector merely votes for the party of his or her choice and seats are then allocated to each party according to the total proportion of votes received. Thus a party winning 30 per cent of the votes would be entitled to 30 per cent of the seats and enough names would be taken from the party's list to fill those seats.

Like AV, the party list system cannot always guarantee full proportional representation. In general, however, it has been calculated that it results in a correspondence between parties' shares of the national vote and assembly seats of 90–98 per cent. In contrast, the 'index of proportionality' for SP systems is, on average, ten points lower, at between 80–92 per cent, while that for Australia's AV stands at 87 per cent and for France's SB 79 per cent.

Some versions of the list system, such as the inflexible 'closed list', used in Israel and Spain, where the voter is given no choice of candidate and simply votes for the party, can make an election very impersonal. Others, however, allow voters to indicate a preference for an individual as well as a party. Varying examples of these are the 'flexible list' system, used in Belgium, and its variant in Italy, the 'open list' system of Finland, and the most liberal of all, the 'free list' system of Luxembourg and Switzerland.

List systems can be 'doctored' by stipulating a 'cut-off' point of percentage votes to be won below which very small parties get no representation at all. If this is not done then virtually any party, whatever it size, will have a chance of winning at least one seat and an assembly could be peppered with 'one off' representatives. The nature and size of the 'cut-off' threshold can vary considerably. In Denmark it is as low as 2 per cent of the vote, in Sweden 4 per cent and in West Germany 5 per cent.

Currently, 32 states employ list systems. Sixteen are in Western Europe. They are Austria, Belgium, Cyprus, Denmark, Finland, Greece, Iceland, Italy, Luxembourg, Netherlands, Norway, Portugal, Spain, Sweden, Switzerland and Turkey. The other 16 are Brazil, Colombia, Costa Rica, the Dominican Republic, Ecuador, Guyana, Honduras, Indonesia, Israel, the Lebanon, Nicaragua, Paraguay, Peru, Sri Lanka, Uruguay and Venezuela. Details of the salient features of these various systems are given in Table 32 below.

On the whole, list systems have tended to favour the development of multi-party coalition politics. In the Netherlands, for example, where the purest possible form of list system is to be found, no 'cut-off' limits being imposed, a dozen or so parties frequently secure representation in the 'Second Chamber', although the three principal parties, the Labour Party (PvdA), the Christian Democratic Appeal (CDA) and the People's Party for Freedom and Democracy (VVD), invariably capture around 80–85 per cent of the total vote and assembly seats. Included in the ranks of the minor parties are Calvinist and Evangelical religious groupings, as well as peace, communist and ecological organisations.

In Italy, Switzerland, Belgium, Finland, Denmark and Iceland, where almost similarly liberal 'cut-off' restrictions are in operation, in the 1987–88 lower chamber elections 14, 13, 11, 9, 8, and 7 parties respectively won seats.

The absence of a suitable cut-off point for elections to the Knesset in Israel has recently resulted in 'hung' assemblies, giving minor parties a disproportionately larger influence over the composition of the government than their voting strengths would normally merit.

In contrast, tighter 'cut-off' variants of the list system are used in some countries so as to favour the larger parties. The most prominent example is Turkey, where parties need 10 per cent of the national vote to secure entry to parliament and 25 or 33 per cent respectively of the vote in three- or four-member constituencies. In addition, bonus seats are given to the party achieving the most votes. This 'up-loaded' system is designed partly to exclude small religious extremist parties from the National Assembly but also as a means of discouraging coalition government. It had the consequence in the November 1987 general election of giving the incumbent Motherland Party (ANAP) 65 per cent of Grand National Assembly (GNA) seats with only a 36 per cent share of the popular vote. Turkey's two other major national parties, the opposition Social Democrats (SHP) and True Path (DYP) parties, captured 25 and 19 per cent of the national vote respectively and 22 and 13 per cent of GNA seats. In contrast, the remaining minor parties, despite receiving 20 per cent of the popular vote, secured no GNA representation at all.

In less democratic countries, even cruder forms of 'up-loading' are to be found. In Paraguay, for example, where congressional elections are fought on single national party lists, the party which receives most votes is automatically awarded two-thirds of the assembly seats. This can be termed a form of 'disproportionate representation'.

An important consequence of the operation of party list systems is the effect on female representation. A clear feature of its working in Western Europe has been to promote the return of substantially higher proportions of female members than has been the case in elections based on absolute majority systems, operating in similar socio-cultural conditions. Thus, at the present time, in the assemblies of the Scandinavian countries where a party list system is used, women comprise more than a quarter of their memberships. In Iceland an all-female political party, the Women's Alliance Movement, has held seats in the Althing since 1983. Elsewhere in continental Europe the proportionate figure for female assembly representation invariably exceeds 10 per cent. In comparison, in the SP legislatures of the United Kingdom, New Zealand and United States the figure stands at less than 5 per cent.

Another useful aspect of list systems is that there is no necessity for by-elections when members retire or depart. Candidates ranking next on the party's previous list are automatically drafted in to fill vacancies as they arise. There are some exceptions to this, however, Greece being one.

By-elections are also avoided in France, where the SB operates, since all candidates must fight with a running-mate (*suppléant*) who will take their place if they resign to assume ministerial office, retire or die in office.

6.3.5 The Additional Member (AM)

The additional member system makes use of party lists but also allows the elector to vote for a candidate, two votes being cast, one for the candidate and one for the party. Half the assembly is then elected on a simple plurality (SP) basis and the other half, using the party lists, is chosen so that the membership of the chamber accurately reflects the national vote. The party lists, therefore, are used to correct any unfairness in the SP system.

The main advantage of the additional member system is that it uses single-member constituencies and so keeps the link between the candidate and the elector. At the same time, however, a high level of 'proportionality', comparable with the 'best' list systems, is achieved.

AM is used principally in elections to West Germany's Bundestag. Here lists operate at the state (*Land*) level, but to qualify for assembly representation on the second list ballot (*Zweitstimme*) parties need to secure at least 5 per cent of the national vote.

Forms of AM also operate in Senegal, where the system was introduced in 1973 with the assistance of West German political consultants; in Guatemala, for a quarter of its Congress; and in South Korea, for a similar proportion of National Assembly seats. Mexico has only a partial AM system used for two-fifths of the 400 seats in the Chamber of Deputies, which are filled predominantly from minority parties' lists. The Upper Chamber of the Japanese Diet has also been elected by a variant of AM since 1982, with 40 per cent of its seats being filled by national level PR.

6.3.6 The Single Transferable Vote (STV)

The single transferable vote (STV) is, in many respects, theoretically the best method of ensuring proportional representation. It uses multi-member constituencies which may be large but which can be small enough to elect three representatives. All the candidates are listed on the ballot form, usually in alphabetical order, and the elector states an order of preference, from 1, 2 downwards. All the votes cast are counted and the 'electoral quota' is calculated, in other words, the minimum number of votes needed to be elected.

The calculation would work as follows:

$$\frac{\text{(total number of votes)}}{\text{(number of seats} + 1)} + 1 = \text{electoral quota (Droop formula)}$$

Thus, in a three-member constituency with a total of 120,000 votes cast, the quota would be:

$$\frac{(120,000)}{(3 + 1)} + 1 = 30,001$$

and any candidate with 30,001 or more first preference votes would automatically be elected.

For example, there might be 12 candidates for the three seats and only one who obtained more than the 30,000 quota, in fact 31,001, or 1,000 more than was needed. All the second preferences of voters who made the top candidate their first choice would be counted and their percentage distribution among the other candidates calculated. The 1,000 'surplus' votes would then be redistributed on this percentage basis. If this redistribution brought another candidate up to to the 30,001 quota he or she would be elected and the process would continue until all three seats were filled. If all the surplus second preference votes were used up and there were still seats to be filled then the bottom candidates would be progressively eliminated, with their second preferences redistributed among the other candidates on a proportionate basis.

STV requires multi-member constituencies but they are often smaller than those used in some varieties of the party list system. STV is also usually more 'personalised' than the list system, theoretically giving electors the power to choose between candidates of the same party. Despite this, high degrees of proportionality, ranging from 90 to 95 per cent, have been achieved.

Described as the 'Anglo-Saxon version of PR', STV is currently used in lower chamber elections by both Ireland and Malta. It is also used for elections to Australia's Senate and to the lower House of the Assembly in the state of Tasmania, as well as for Sri Lankan presidential elections and local government elections in Northern Ireland.

6.3.7 The Limited Vote (LV)

The final PR variant, the limited vote (LV), is currently used in two states, by Japan for lower chamber elections, and by Spain for its upper house contests. Under this system, multi-member constituencies are used, each returning between three to five members, but electors are allowed only one, non-transferable, vote. The three to five candidates winning most votes in each constituency are then subsequently returned on a simple plurality basis.

The use of multi-member constituencies means that minor parties, through restricting themselves to one candidature per constituency, can win seats on relatively low shares, about 15–30 per cent, depending on the size of the constituency, of the total vote. In this respect, the LV system, which is really only 'semi-proportional', differs significantly from the SP, with its single-member constituencies.

6.4 Election Turnouts

The size of the election turnout provides some information about popular participation in the political process but it can also be misleading.

Turnouts in the United Kingdom parliamentary general elections of 1979, 1983 and 1987 were 76.2, 72.7 and 75.4 per cent respectively. These figures compare favourably with those for UK local government elections and for elections to the European Parliament, which were as low as 33 per cent in 1984 and 36 per cent in 1989 for the whole of country, and lower still for England alone. West German Bundestag election turnouts varied between 84 and 91 per cent for the years 1976–87, showing a generally declining tendency. In France, National Assembly election turnouts have invariably ranged between 71 and 83 per cent during the last two decades, while presidential election figures have averaged 86–87 per cent. In the Scandinavian countries of Denmark, Finland, Norway and Sweden, parliamentary election turnouts of between 80 and 90 per cent are the norm.

In general, then, in the liberal democracies of Western Europe turnouts for elections to national assemblies currently cluster within a range band of 70–90 per cent. In all the countries for which turnout figures have been quoted voting is not compulsory. The state, however, shoulders the burden of responsibility for registering electors and compiling the electoral roll in advance of polling day.

In contrast, in the United States the burden of registration falls upon individual citizens, with parties being employed as a private back-up mobilising force. At the present, however, fewer than 70 per cent of the US population of voting age are registered, including only 40 per cent of Hispanics and 50 per cent of those in the lowest socio-economic category. For this reason, US national election turnouts are, by comparative standards, unusually low, standing at barely 50 to 53 per cent of the adult population, though 75 to 80 per cent of those registered, for the presidential elections between 1980 and 1988, and at only 37 per cent for the mid-term congressional and governorship elections of November 1986. Similar low turnout figures can be found in Switzerland, only 49 per cent of the electorate taking the trouble to vote in the October 1987 Nationalrat elections.

Low electoral participation is also, not surprisingly, a feature of many of the world's poorer liberal and emergent democracies. In India and Botswana, for example, turnouts have averaged 50–60 per cent for recent Lok Sabha and National Assembly elections. In Mexico, the figures have been around 50 per cent for presidential and Chamber of Deputies elections, and in Colombia and Thailand, below 40 per cent for elections to their assemblies.

There are, however, some notable exceptions. In Sri Lanka and the Bahamas, for example, parliamentary election turnouts have invariably exceeded 85 per cent; in Gambia, Honduras, Morocco and Vanuatu 80 per cent; in Costa Rica, Dominica and Suriname 75 per cent; in Barbados and Malaysia 70 per cent; and in Papua New Guinea, despite the remoteness of many polling stations, above 66 per cent. In Lebanon, the archaic requirement that electors must cast their ballot in their ancestral villages or towns serves to depress turnouts to a level of 50–55 per cent.

In communist states, turnouts for elections at all levels are invariably high, usually exceeding 95 per cent and sometimes getting as near to a 100 per cent response as is physically feasible. In the Albanian People's Assembly election of 1987, for example, there was, officially, only one spoiled ballot paper among the entire electorate of 1.83 million.

In the USSR's Supreme Soviet elections of 1984 a turnout of 99.99 per cent was registered, implying that fewer than 20,000, out of an electorate of more than 184 million, failed to vote. This does not, however, necessarily denote great popular enthusiam for the party or the electoral process. For such ritualised contests, the local party machine usually puts considerable effort into securing high turnouts, with up to a quarter of the adult population, party members, local state and work council representatives and 'reputable citizens', being brought into action as campaign workers. Special transport is laid on for the house-bound and ballot boxes are posted at every workplace and housing complex, as well as being carried out to those living in remote areas.

Faced with this huge mobilisation and publicity drive, the average citizen who is not a party member may well feel that for the small cost of casting a vote there may be some potential advantage in openly showing support for the official candidate. Only rarely, as was the case in Polish local elections of 1984, do citizens 'rebel' and stay at home. On this occasion, the official turnout slumped to 75 per cent, although government opponents suggested the true figure was closer to 60 per cent.

High electoral turnouts are also invariably the case in one-party nationalistic socialist and authoritarian nationalist regimes. In Indonesia, for example, turnouts are put at over 90 per cent and in Togo at 98 per cent. In Syria and the Côte d'Ivoire, however, they have been as low as 45 and 30 per cent respectively.

Some countries make voting compulsory. This compulsion may be real, in the sense of running the risk of being fined for not voting, but in most cases the offenders are rarely, if ever, prosecuted. Some constitutions, including most in communist states, specify voting as a 'civic' or 'socialist' duty but stop short of compulsion. Whether or not the requirement is enforced, there is evidence that turnouts in countries which formally make voting compulsory are generally perceptibly higher than in those which do not. Turnouts of 95–98 per cent are, for example, the norm in Australia and Belgium. However, lower turnouts of 80 per cent, and sometimes substantially less, have been recorded in the Dominican Republic, Greece and Peru.

TABLE 32 WORLD ELECTION AND VOTING PATTERNS

	Executive Choice	Assembly Choice Lower Chamber	Assembly Choice Upper Chamber	Assembly Choice Assembly Choice	Minimum Voting Age	Voting Compulsory	Date of 1st Female Franchise
Afghanistan	College	UAS SP	UAS SP	Direct	20	Yes	1964
Albania	Party	UAS SP	—	—	18	SD	1946
Algeria	Direct	UAS SP	—	—	18	—	1958
Angola	Party	UAS SP	—	—	18	—	1975
Antigua & Barbuda	Assembly	UAS SP	—	Appointed	18	Yes	1951
Argentina	College	UAS SP	—	College	18	Yes	1947
Australia	Assembly	UAS AV	UAS STV	Direct	18	Yes	1902
Austria	Assembly	UAS PLS	—	College	19	—	1919
Bahamas	Assembly	UAS SP	—	Appointed	18	—	1962
Bahrain	Absolute	—	—	—			—
Bangladesh	Direct	UAS SP	—	—	18	—	1956
Barbados	Assembly	UAS SP	—	Appointed	18	—	1951
Belgium	Assembly	UAS PLS	—	El/Coll	18	Yes	1948
Belize	Assembly	UAS SP	—	Appointed	18	—	1954
Benin	Assembly	UAS SP	—	—	18	—	1956
Bhutan	Absolute	E/A	—	—			—
Bolivia	Direct	UAS SP	UAS SP	Direct	21	Yes	1952
Botswana	Assembly	UAS SP	—	—	21	—	1966
Brazil	Direct	UAS PLS	UAS PLS	Direct	16	Yes	1932
Brunei	Absolute	—	—	—			—
Bulgaria	Party	UAS SP	—	—	18	SD	1947
Burkina Faso	Military	—	—	—			1956
Burma	Party	UAS SP	—	—	18	—	1935
Burundi	Direct	UAS SP	—	—	18	—	1961
Cambodia	Party	UAS SP	—	—	18	SD	1956
Cameroon	Direct	UAS SP	—	—	21	—	1956
Canada	Assembly	UAS SP	—	Appointed	18	—	1920
Cape Verde	Assembly	UAS SP	—	—	18	—	1975

123

Table 32—World Election and Voting Patterns (contd)

	Executive Choice	*Assembly Choice* *Lower Chamber*		*Upper Chamber*		*Minimum Voting Age*	*Voting Compulsory*	*Date of 1st Female Franchise*
Central African Rep	Military	Direct	UAS SP	—	—	—	—	—
Chad	Party	Direct	UAS SP	—	—	—	—	1956
Chile	Military	Direct	UAS SP	E/A	UAS SP	18	—	1949
China	Party	College	UAS SP	—	—	18	SD	1947
Colombia	Direct	Direct	UAS PLS	Direct	UAS PLS	18	—	1957
Comoros	Direct	Direct	UAS SP	—	—	18	—	1978
Congo	Party	Direct	UAS SP	—	—	18	—	1956
Costa Rica	Direct	Direct	UAS PLS	—	—	18	Yes	1949
Cuba	Party	Direct	UAS SP	—	—	16	SD	1934
Cyprus	Direct/SB	Direct	UAS PLS	—	—	21	Yes	1959
Czechoslovakia	Direct	Direct	UAS SB	Direct	UAS SB	18	SD	1919
Denmark	Assembly	Direct	UAS PLS	—	—	18	—	1915
Djibouti	Direct	Direct	UAS SP	—	—	18	—	1957
Dominica	Assembly	E/A	UAS SP	—	—	18	—	1967
Dominican Republic	Direct	Direct	UAS PLS	Direct	UAS SP	18	Yes	1942
Ecuador	Direct/SB	Direct	UAS PLS	—	—	18	Yes	1929
Egypt	Direct	E/A	UAS SB	—	—	18	Yes	1956
El Salvador	Direct	Direct	UAS SP	—	—	18	Yes	1950
Equatorial Guinea	Direct	Direct	UAS SP	—	—	18	—	1982
Ethiopia	Party	Direct	UAS SP	—	—	18	—	1955
Fiji	Assembly	Direct	UAS SP	Appointed	—	18	—	1970
Finland	El/Coll	Direct	UAS PLS	—	—	18	—	1906
France	Direct/SB	Direct	UAS SB	College	—	18	—	1944
Gabon	Direct	E/A	UAS SP	—	—	21	—	1956
Gambia	Direct	E/A	UAS SP	—	—	21	—	1961
Germany	Assembly	Direct	UAS AMS	Appointed	—	18	—	1919
Ghana	Military	—	—	—	—	18	—	1955
Greece	Assembly	Direct	UAS PLS	—	—	18	Yes	1952
Grenada	Assembly	Direct	UAS SP	Appointed	—	18	—	1967
Guatemala	Direct	Direct	UAS AMS	—	—	18	Yes	1965

Table 32—World Election and Voting Patterns (contd)

	Executive Choice	Assembly Choice				Minimum Voting Age	Voting Compulsory	Date of 1st Female Franchise
		Lower Chamber		Upper Chamber				
Guinea	Military	—	UAS SP	—	—	—	—	1956
Guinea-Bissau	Assembly	College	UAS PLS	—	—	15	—	1973
Guyana	Direct	El/Coll	UAS PLS	—	—	18	—	1966
Haiti	Direct	Direct	UAS PLS	—	—	18	—	1950
Honduras	Direct	Direct	UAS SB	—	—	18	Yes	1955
Hungary	Direct	Direct	UAS PLS	—	—	18	—	1945
Iceland	Assembly	Direct	UAS SP	—	—	18	—	1915
India	Assembly	E/A	UAS SP	College	—	18	—	1949
Indonesia	College	E/A	UAS SB	—	—	17	—	1945
Iran	Direct	Direct	UAS SP	—	—	18	—	1963
Iraq	Party	Direct	UAS SP	—	—	18	—	1964
Ireland	Assembly	Direct	UAS STV	Coll/App	—	18	—	1922
Israel	Assembly	Direct	UAS PLS	—	—	18	—	1948
Italy	Assembly	Direct	UAS PLS	E/A	UAS PLS	18	CD	1945
Ivory Coast	Direct/SB	Direct	UAS SB	—	—	21	—	1956
Jamaica	Assembly	Direct	UAS SP	Appointed	UAS AMS	18	—	1944
Japan	Assembly	Direct	UAS LV	Direct	UAS AMS	20	—	1945
Jordan	Heredit	Direct	UAS SP	Appointed	—	20	—	1982
Kenya	Direct	E/A	UAS SP	—	—	18	—	1963
Kiribati	Direct	E/A	UAS SB	—	—	18	—	1979
North Korea	Party	Direct	UAS SP	—	—	17	SD	1946
South Korea	Direct	Direct	UAS AMS	—	—	20	—	1946
Kuwait	Absolute	—	—	—	—	—	—	—
Laos	Party	Direct	UAS SP	—	—	18	—	1956
Lebanon	College	Direct	UAS PLS	—	—	21	—	1957
Lesotho	Heredit	—	—	—	—	—	—	1966
Liberia	Direct	Direct	UAS SP	Direct	UAS SP	18	—	1946
Libya	Party	College	UAS SP	—	—	18	—	1963
Luxembourg	Assembly	Direct	UAS PLS	—	—	18	Yes	1918
Madagascar	Direct	Direct	UAS SP	—	—	18	—	1956

Table 32—World Election and Voting Patterns (contd)

	Executive Choice	Assembly Choice			Minimum Voting Age	Voting Compulsory	Date of 1st Female Franchise
		Lower Chamber	Assembly Choice	Upper Chamber			
Malawi	Direct	UAS SP	—	—	21	—	1964
Malaysia	Assembly	UAS SP	Coll/App	—	21	—	1957
Maldives	Direct	UAS SP	—	—	21	—	1964
Mali	Direct	UAS SP	—	—	18	—	1956
Malta	Direct	UAS STV	—	—	18	—	1947
Mauritania	Military	—	—	—		—	1956
Mauritius	Assembly	UAS SP	—	—	18	—	1956
Mexico	Direct	UAS AMS	Direct	UAS SP	18	—	1953
Mongolia	Direct	UAS SP	—	—	18	SD	1924
Morocco	Heredit	UAS SP	El/Coll	—	21	—	1959
Mozambique	Direct	UAS SP	—	—	18	—	1975
Nauru	Assembly	UAS SP	—	—	20	Yes	1968
Nepal	Heredit	UAS SP	—	—	21	—	1951
Netherlands	Assembly	UAS PLS	College	—	18	—	1919
New Zealand	Assembly	UAS SP	—	—	18	—	1893
Nicaragua	Direct	UAS PLS	—	—	18	—	1955
Niger	Military	UAS SP	—	—		—	1956
Nigeria	Military	—	—	—	18	—	1954
Norway	Assembly	UAS PLS	—	—	18	—	1913
Oman	Absolute	—	—	—		—	—
Pakistan	Direct	UAS SP	College	—	18	—	1956
Panama	Direct	UAS SP	—	—	18	—	1946
Papua New Guinea	Assembly	UAS SP	—	—	18	—	1975
Paraguay	Military	UAS PLS	Direct	UAS PLS	18	Yes	1961
Peru	Direct/SB	UAS PLS	Direct	UAS PLS	18	Yes	1955
Philippines	Direct	UAS SP	Direct	UAS SP	16	Yes	1937
Poland	Direct	UAS SB	Direct	UAS SB	18	—	1918
Portugal	Direct	UAS PLS	—	—	18	—	1975
Qatar	Absolute	—	—	—		—	—
Romania	Direct	UAS SB	—	—	18	—	1948

Table 32—World Election and Voting Patterns (contd)

	Executive Choice		Assembly Choice			Minimum Voting Age	Voting Compulsory	Date of 1st Female Franchise
			Lower Chamber	Upper Chamber				
Rwanda	Military	Direct	UAS SP	—	—	18	—	1962
St Christopher & Nevis	Assembly	E/A	UAS SP	—	—	18	—	1967
St Lucia	Assembly	Direct	UAS SP	Appointed	—	18	—	1967
St Vincent & Grenadines	Assembly	E/A	UAS SP	—	—	18	—	1967
Sao Tome & Principe	Direct	College	UAS SP	—	—	18	—	1982
Saudi Arabia	Absolute	—	—	—	—	—	—	—
Senegal	Direct	Direct	UAS AMS	—	—	21	—	1956
Seychelles	Direct	E/A	UAS SP	—	—	17	—	1979
Sierra Leone	Party	E/A	UAS SP	—	—	21	—	1961
Singapore	Assembly	Direct	UAS SP	—	—	21	Yes	1965
Solomon Isles	Assembly	Direct	UAS SP	—	—	21	—	1978
Somalia	Party	E/A	UAS SP	—	—	18	—	1958
South Africa	Assembly	E/A	UAS SP	Direct	UAS SB	18	—	1930
Soviet Union	Party	Direct	UAS SB	Direct	UAS LV	18	SD	1917
Spain	Assembly	Direct	UAS PLS	—	—	18	—	1977
Sri Lanka	Direct	Direct	UAS PLS	—	—	21	—	1934
Sudan	Military	Direct	UAS SP	—	—	18	—	1965
Suriname	Assembly	Direct	UAS SP	—	—	18	—	1975
Swaziland	Heredit	Coll/App	—	Coll/App	—	18	—	1968
Sweden	Assembly	Direct	UAS PLS	—	—	18	—	1919
Switzerland	Assembly	Direct	UAS PLS	Direct	UAS SP	20	—	1971
Syria	Direct	Direct	UAS SP	—	—	18	—	1949
Taiwan	College	College	UAS SP	—	—	20	—	1947
Tanzania	Party	El/App	UAS SP	—	—	18	—	1961
Thailand	Assembly	El/App	UAS SP	Appointed	—	21	—	1932
Togo	Party	Direct	UAS SP	—	—	18	—	1956
Tonga	Heredit	Direct	UAS SP	—	—	21	—	1960
Trinidad & Tobago	Assembly	E/A	UAS SP	Appointed	—	18	—	1946
Tunisia	Direct	Direct	UAS SP	—	—	20	—	1959
Turkey	Assembly	Direct	UAS PLS	—	—	21	—	1934

Table 32—World Election and Voting Patterns (contd)

	Executive Choice	Assembly Choice	Lower Chamber	Upper Chamber	Minimum Voting Age	Voting Compulsory	Date of 1st Female Franchise
Tuvalu	Assembly	Direct	UAS SP	—	18	—	1978
Uganda	Assembly	Direct	UAS SP	—	18	—	1962
United Arab Emirates	Absolute	—	—	—		—	—
United Kingdom	Assembly	Direct	UAS SP	Heredit/Appointed	18	—	1928
United States	College	Direct	UAS SP	UAS SP	18	—	1920
Uruguay	Direct	Direct	UAS PLS	UAS PLS	18	CD	1932
Vanuatu	Assembly	Direct	UAS SB	—	18	—	1980
Venezuela	Direct	Direct	UAS PLS	UAS PLS	18	Yes	1947
Vietnam	Party	Direct	UAS SP	—	18	SD	1956
Western Samoa	Assembly	College	—	—		—	1962
Yemen Republic	Direct	Direct	UAS SP	—	18	—	1970/1979
Yugoslavia	Party	College	UAS SP	UAS SP	18	—	1946
Zaire	Party	Direct	UAS SP	—	18	—	1960
Zambia	Party	E/A	UAS SP	—	18	—	1964
Zimbabwe	Party	Coll/App	UAS SP	—	18	—	1980

KEY:

Direct	—Direct election by the electorate	El/Coll	—Part elected direct and part indirectly elected by college
College	—Indirect election by an electoral college	LV	—Limited Vote
Assembly	—Indirect election by the assembly	SP	—Simple plurality vote
Party	—Indirect de-facto election by the party	AV	—Alternative Vote
Absolute	—Absolute executive	SB	—Second Ballot
Military	—Military executive or sole nominee of the military	PLS	—Party List System
Heredit	—Hereditary	AMS	—Additional Member System
UAS	—Universal adult suffrage	STV	—Single Transferable Vote
E/A	—Part elected and part appointed	CD	—'Civic Duty' or 'Obligation'
Coll/App	—Part elected by college and part appointed	SD	—'Socialist Duty'

TABLE 33   WORLD ELECTION SYSTEMS: SUMMARY TABLE DIRECT VOTING SYSTEMS FOR LOWER CHAMBERS

Voting System	All States	
	Number of States	As % of Total States
Simple Plurality	94	64
Party List PR	32	22
Second Ballot	11	8
Additional Member PR	5	3
Single Transferable Vote	2	1
Alternative Vote	1	1
Limited Vote	1	1
Total	146*	100

*The assemblies in eight other states are elected indirectly by other assemblies below them or by electoral colleges.

Voting System	Liberal-Democratic and Emergent-Democratic States	
	Number of States	As % of Total States
Simple Plurality	57	57
Party List PR	31	31
Second Ballot	4	4
Additional Member PR	4	4
Single Transferable Vote	2	2
Alternative Vote	1	1
Limited Vote	1	1
Total	100*	100

*The assembly of the remaining state, Western Samoa, is indirectly elected.

Minimum Voting Age	Minimum Voting Ages	
	Number of States	As % of Total States
15 Years	1	1
16 Years	4	3
17 Years	2	1
18 Years	106	74
19 Years	1	1
20 Years	8	5
21 Years	21	14
Total	143*	100

*In two states, Bhutan and Western Samoa, voting is restricted to extended family heads.

6.5 Election Rigging: Methods and Extent

One hundred and forty-seven countries currently hold regular national assembly elections. However, the great majority of these polls are either uncompetitive, involving no candidate or party choice, or of a 'façade' character, involving outward shows of open debate and candidate pluralism but with outcomes that are ultimately rigged by the incumbent regime.

To be truly free and democratic, election contests need to satisfy seven basic criteria:

1 Voting rights: all adults, regardless of race or religion, should enjoy the right to vote.
2 Voting practices: the ballot should be cast freely and secretly, without intimidation or subsequent redress.
3 Election timetable: elections should be held regularly, within prescribed time-limits and in accordance with constitutional rules.
4 Candidature rules: all sections of the community should be free to put forward candidates, form political parties and campaign openly.
5 Campaign: the campaign period should be of sufficient length to enable all parties and candidates to get their messages across. There should be reasonable equity in media access and coverage. Voter bribery by candidates and parties should be disallowed and maximum limits placed on campaign spending.
6 Election supervision: the campaign and vote counting should be supervised by an impartial administration, with an independent body being available to adjudicate in electoral disputes.
7 Power transfer: all parties and candidates should accept the adjudged results, handing over power to the successful party(ies) within a prescribed timetable.

At present, these conditions are approached only by the 102 countries which we have designated in Chapter 3 as liberal democracies or emergent democracies, and of these, 19 have embarked on pluralist politics during the past two years and are, therefore, operating virtually untested democratic systems. Communist and other one-party states fall short of the important pluralism condition 4 above, while authoritarian regimes, which allow semblances of candidature pluralism, invariably breach conditions 2, 5, and 6. Even many virtually well-established liberal and emergent democracies, totalling up to half, fall substantially short of meeting these conditions and can thus be viewed as holding only partially democratic elections.

This is true of the two liberal democratic states of Mexico and Singapore which hold what have been termed 'dominant-party elections'. In these contests, restrictions are placed on the free operation of opposition parties, media coverage is slanted in the ruling party's favour and state resources are employed both to bribe and intimidate voters.

In Mexico, the ruling Institutional Revolutionary Party (PRI), which has monopolised power at both federal and state levels for six decades since its inception in 1929, has succeeded in winning elections through building up an extensive rural and urban corporate client network. In return for pledging electoral support, the party has ensured a steady flow of contracts, pay rises and assured employment to its local political bosses (*caciques*). In recent years, however, as economic modernisation has progressively weakened the links binding together this traditionalist patronage-system, the PRI has been forced to resort to cruder ballot-rigging as a means of ensuring its continued electoral dominance. For example, in the 1986 Chihuahua governorship election, with the help of the government appointed Federal Election Commission, it set about falsifying the electoral rolls in areas of PRI strength and restricting polling station access elsewhere. The actual count was also rigged by impersonations and the crude stuffing of ballot boxes. In the July 1988 presidential and congressional elections, faced with a strong challenge by Cuauhtemoc Cardenas of the National Democratic Front (FDN), these practices continued. As counting got under way, the Electoral Commission's computer mysteriously broke down. It was a week later before official returns were published, giving the PRI's presidential candidate 50.7 per cent of the national vote. Condition 7 of a fully democratic electoral system had clearly been breached.

In Singapore, the dominant People's Action Party (PAP) has so far eschewed such crude methods of ballot-rigging. Instead, it has maintained its electoral dominance by infringing democratic election requirements 2 and 5. First, both prior to and during election campaigns, opposition candidates have been mercilessly hounded by the state, falling prey, for example, to trumped-up fraud and tax evasion charges. Second, and more generally, the electorate has been intimidated by fears that any votes cast against the government party might be traced, with adverse employment and financial consequences. By these means the PAP has invariably been able to secure well over 70 per cent of the popular vote in parliamentary elections. In elections in September 1988 the PAP's share of the national vote fell somewhat to 63 per cent; nevertheless, it succeeded in capturing all but one of the 82 available assembly seats.

For both Mexico and Singapore the striking feature of the past decade has been the marked and steady decline in dominant party support, even on the manipulated official returns. It remains an open question however whether official totals, particularly in Mexico where the psychological 50 per cent mark is being rapidly approached, will be permitted to fall much further in future contests. A peaceful change of regime, moreover, appears out of the question.

At least four other countries which have been classified in Chapter 3 as liberal democracies have only partially democratic elections. In three of these, Costa Rica, the Dominican Republic and Venezuela, election contests have been marred by civil violence which is such a prominent feature of this region. In the fourth, Western Samoa, vote buying, both with cash and goods, and impersonation have been past features of electoral contests. In the February 1982 elections the Human Rights Protection Party (HRPP), led by Prime Minister Va'ai Kolone, was removed from office by the Supreme Court on these grounds.

The remaining 44 liberal democracies listed in Table 4 substantially meet all seven of the above 'free-election' criteria. In addition, the majority of them have experienced electorally induced changes of government at some stage or other during the past two decades: a useful, though by no means essential, indicator of election fairness. These states can reasonably be said to hold democratic elections. Within the total, however, there exist gradations of openness in relation to condition 5: election campaign periods, media access and spending ceilings.

To these 44 liberal democracies which conduct substantially democratic elections can be added, from the evidence of recent polls, eight rapidly progressing emergent democracies: Argentina, Brazil, Cyprus, Fiji, Greece, Portugal, Spain and Turkey. South Korea and the Philippines could also tentatively be added to this list, although vote-buying and intimidation remained noticeable features of the recent 1987–88 presidential and assembly elections. In the remaining 23 emergent democracies election contests continue to be marred by combinations of vote-counting frauds, dominant party candidate list rigging and bribery, as well as voter intimidation by both government and opposition groups.

A recent prominent example of electoral fraud was the Bangladesh Jatiya Sangsad election of March 1988, which was boycotted by the opposition. It was reported that one villager, Shawkat Ali, from near Dhaka, complained, typically, 'I went to cast my vote, but found that someone else had already done it.'

Vote-buying has been a conspicuous feature of recent elections in Thailand. In the July 1988 assembly elections, despite the imposition of official spending limits of 350,000 baht (US\$ 15,000) per candidate, well over 3 billion baht (US\$ 120 million) were distributed to voters by the 3,606 candidates standing. In the poor north east 100 baht (US\$ 4.5) packages were openly on offer for each vote pledged, plus 10,000 baht bounties for entire villages which successfully elected candidates. Altogether, it has been estimated that this election resulted in an increase of expenditure equivalent to 0.5 per cent of Thailand's GDP.

Physical violence and intimidation, both during the campaign and on election day, have been a recurrent feature of contests in South and Central America. For example, the left-wing Farabundo Marti National Liberation Front (FMLN) seriously disrupted the March 1988 assembly elections in El Salvador by guerrilla terrorist tactics, reducing turnout levels to barely 50–60 per cent. The Colombian local election contest in the same month was marred by even more serious intimidation, by both right- and left-wing 'hit-squads', with more than 150 candidates and several hundred campaign activists being brutally assassinated.

Of the 60 liberal and emergent democracies which on the broadest count can be viewed as holding substantially democratic elections, 27 per cent are in Western Europe, 10 per cent in Eastern Europe, 17 per cent are in Oceania, another 17 per cent in the Caribbean and 8 per cent in Asia. Of the remaining 93 countries holding assembly elections, nine are communist states. Here, election contests are subject to rigid 'democratic-centralist' control although moves towards a new type of 'socialist pluralism' are under way in the Soviet Union. A further 26, the bulk of which are in Africa, are one-party socialist, nationalist or militarist states, in which non-party candidates are outlawed. Of the remaining 58 countries with some form of elected assembly, six are the recently 'liberalised' states of Eastern Europe and 13 have turned, or returned, to pluralist politics only since 1989. This leaves 39 countries, 26 per cent of the world total, in which elections are at present of a 'façade' nature. In these states, despite outward semblances of candidature pluralism, the results are effectively rigged to the incumbent regime's advantage. Control of the media, the electoral commission and the vote-counting process are the principal means of achieving this, following the cynical maxim, 'He who counts, elects'.

Also of importance is the imposition of severe constraints, and frequently outright bans, by the ruling regime on the candidature and campaign activity of opposition members. All such features were prominent in the February 1988 presidential and assembly elections in Paraguay, which returned General Alfredo Stroessner and his ruling Colorado Party with a 90 per cent share of the vote, the remaining 10 per cent being apportioned between legalised opposition candidates. A turnout of 93 per cent was officially claimed, but the opposition-formed Committee for Free Elections estimated the true figure to be below 50 per cent in many areas. The stuffing of ballot boxes and the impersonation of dead electors were practices which were frequently alleged.

Not surprisingly, such loaded contests are often succeeded by frustrated eruptions of opposition, leading to street violence. In Senegal, where the prepared result for the February 1988 presidential election was announced almost as soon as voting stopped, riots erupted in the streets of Dakar and Thies, prompting the government to arrest opposition leaders and declare a state of emergency which lasted for two months. In the Philippines, in February 1986, stronger and better co-ordinated public opposition to flagrant ballot rigging succeeded in bringing down the regime of Ferdinand Marcos. Even the long-established Stroessner regime in Paraguay was ousted by the military within a year of the disputed election result.

Recommended Reading

Bogdanor, V. and Butler, D. (eds), *Democracy and Elections: Electoral Systems and Their Consequences*, Cambridge University Press, 1983.

Bogdanor, V., *What is Proportional Representation?: A Guide to the Issues*, Martin Robertson, 1984.

Crewe, I. and Denver, D. (eds), *Electoral Change in Western Democracies: Campaign of 1983*, Croom Helm, 1985.

Dalton, R. L., Flanagan S. and Beck, P. A. (eds), *Electoral Change in Advanced Industrial Societies: Realignment or Dealignment*, Princeton University Press, 1984.

The Economist, *World Atlas of Elections*, Economist Publications, 1986.

Eisenstadt, S. N. and Lemarchand, R. (eds), *Political Clientelism, Patronage and Development*, Sage Publications, 1981.

Hague, R and Harrop, M., *Comparative Government and Politics: An Introduction*, 2nd edn., Macmillan, 1987, Ch. 6.

Harrop, M. and Miller, W., *Elections and Voters: A Comparative Introduction*, Macmillan, 1987.

Hermet, G., Rose, R. and Rouquie, A. (eds), *Elections Without Choice*, Macmillan, 1978.

Mackie, T. T. and Rose, R., *International Almanac of Electoral History*, Macmillan, 1982.

Roberts, G. K., *An Introduction to Comparative Government*, Edward Arnold, 1986, Ch. 4.

Chapter 7

POLITICAL PARTIES

7.1 The Mobilisation of Sectional Interests

Everyone has an interest in something, even if it amounts to little more than pure self-interest or self-preservation. Millions of people are regular television watchers and if someone sought to deprive them of this pleasure it is certain that they would be up in arms immediately. Some people attach great value to personal privacy and will resist any intrusion, particularly by a public body. Others are more concerned about what they see as the rights of others. Often they feel a duty to protect the seemingly defenceless, especially in the animal kingdom.

Whereas interests are shared by thousands, or even millions, of people, only a relative few will take the trouble to mobilise them into a source of influence and power. These are the organisers of interests: the active members of interest groups.

An interest group is therefore an association of people who come together, or are brought together, to represent, promote and defend a particular interest or set of interests. There are numerous examples to choose from.

Some are chiefly promotional, seeking to bring attention to the needs of particular people, such as the unmarried mother or the disabled. Others are mainly defensive, such as the environmental groups, anxious to protect natural conditions and phenomena. All are representational in one way or another but some, such as the labour unions and professional organisations, are particularly strong in this respect.

A distinction can be made between groups which are concerned with limited, specific interests and those which aim to promote and defend a much wider cross-section. These wider interest groups are often referred to as cause groups. They fight for a particular cause, irrespective of whether or not the people they seek to help have direct contact with them, or even know of their existence. They are usually impelled by higher motives than self-interest and could well be called conscience groups.

Cause groups usually ignore national boundaries and can be found throughout the world. Greenpeace, Amnesty International, Oxfam, Christian Aid are all well-known examples.

7.2 Pressure Groups

Sometimes interest groups are referred to as pressure groups as if the two terms are synonymous. This is not strictly the case.

A pressure group is a group representing an interest which seeks to achieve its aims by putting pressure on government. It will use a wide range of tactics to try to influence public opinion but it knows that ultimately the pressure must be on the government in whichever country it operates.

International cause groups will usually exert pressure on governments indirectly, knowing that they are unlikely to gain direct access to national seats of power. They make their case to the public at large, utilising the mass media, hoping that popular opinion in each country will apply the necessary pressure to produce action.

7.3 Monism, Pluralism and Corporatism

A monistic state may be said to be one in which interest group activity is frowned upon, discouraged or even banned. This contrasts with a pluralistic state where independently organised groups freely operate and act as intermediaries between the public and the government.

Communist regimes and most other one-party states are essentially monistic, mainly because they find it difficult to 'manage' an organisation which is outside the established political system. Because it is outside, its actions are unpredictable and unpredictability is seen as a threat to the settled order of things. A good example of this was the protracted opposition of the Polish government to the labour union, Solidarity.

Churches in one-party states produce similar problems. The activities of religious organisations extend beyond national interests, as defined by the ruling regime, and, again, tend to produce unpredictable behaviour. There are, however, states where a religion has been absorbed into the political system so as to become not only acceptable but its main driving force. Iran provides a striking example of this kind of theocratic state.

Some secular one-party states have accepted that interest activity cannot be ignored but can be managed if absorbed into the political system. Thus the pressures which in a pluralistic system express themselves in a wide variety of outlets are channelled into the state machine. As the state institutions are invariably controlled by party activists, interests become easily controllable too.

In stark contrast, pressure groups flourish in pluralistic systems, even though the most liberally inclined governments may find them an inconvenience. The United States is an example of a country where interest groups are particularly virile. Over the years their activities have become increasingly evident and their methods more sophisticated so that members of Congress, state governments, and even the presidency, ignore them at their peril.

In some parts of the world the pluralistic state has become the corporate state in which a limited number of powerful interest groups, industrial, financial and labour, dominate the political scene, the government choosing, or being forced, to negotiate with them before making a major policy decision.

In Austria, for example, political decisions are often arrived at, with the government's blessing, following discussions between strong chambers of commerce and labour unions. Once agreement between these powerful bodies has been reached the government takes over the task of legitimising and implementing what has been agreed.

The so-called 'social contract' in the United Kingdom in the mid-1970s, between the Labour governments of Harold Wilson and James Callaghan and the Trades Union Congress, whereby the unions accepted a policy of wage restraint in return for the government's promise to follow an agreed social welfare programme, was another strong example of corporatism in a liberal democratic state.

It can be argued that pluralism extends and enhances democracy, because it encourages people who would not normally involve themselves in politics to contribute to the policy-making process. Corporatism, on the other hand, can be said to be anti-democratic in that it increases the power of those sections of the community who organise themselves in the pursuit of self-interest.

Furthermore, corporatism is often associated with the fascist regimes of the 1930s when, in Italy in particular, the government incorporated interest groups representing capital and labour into the state machinery.

The dividing line between thriving pluralism and corporatism is not always easy to discern and sometimes, as in the United Kingdom in the 1970s, an essentially pluralistic state may become temporarily corporatist and then, with a change of government, revert. There is evidence of corporatism in some Central and South American countries. Here not only powerful groups representing capital and labour wield enormous power and influence, but both the Church and the military are involved in major policy decisions. Indeed, those states where the military have seized executive power may be said to have taken corporatism to its ultimate limits.

In economically undeveloped areas of the world it is probably misleading to discuss interest group activity in the form of monism, pluralism or corporatism. Here, groups are considerably less well organised and less sophisticated and sometimes represent little more than an updating and extension of old tribal allegiances.

7.4 Pressure Groups and Political Parties

A political party can best be described as an association of people who hold similar views about what should be a community's social and economic priorities and come together to establish these priorities by gaining control of the machinery of government. It is this wish to govern which distinguishes a party from an interest group but there are other important differences.

First, an interest group is concerned with a clearly defined range of interests whereas a political party is prepared to take on board a virtually unlimited number. Second, each interest group tends to play a distinctive and individualistic role while the agenda of one political party may be similar to that of another, the differences between them being based on alternative solutions to the same problems. The third difference has already been identified. An interest group aims to influence the government while a party is, or wants to be, the government.

Occasionally an interest group will step over the dividing line and become a party itself. Small political parties with narrowly defined aims, making them little removed from interest groups, have been organised in several countries. Some have been short-lived, some have survived for considerable periods with minimal memberships and funds and a few have achieved enough popular support to make them formidable political organisations.

In Denmark there is the Single Tax Party (Retsforbund) advocating the theories of the nineteenth-century US economist, Henry George (1839–97). Even on such a narrow base it has managed from time to time to win seats in the Folketing. The conservative, anti-bureaucracy Finnish Rural Party represents the interests of the lower middle class in Finland and, with a membership of about 25,000 has won assembly seats but not a position in government. In France the Ecology Political Movement (MEP) speaks for ecological and environmental interests and the National Restoration and New Royalist Action parties, although attracting little support, aim for the return of the monarchy. In West Germany the Five Per Cent Block was established in the mid-1970s, with a membership of barely 100, as a political movement to oppose the 5 per cent clause which denies parliamentary representation to parties failing to gain 5 per cent of the national vote. In contrast, the Green Party, with a large and growing membership, has emerged from among a number of ecology parties to become a significant political force. In the January 1987 election it captured 8.3 per cent of the national vote and 42 Bundestag seats.

Women's interests are being increasingly represented throughout the world by parties which have grown from non-political groups. In Belgium, for example, there is the Unified Feminist Party, in Iceland the Women's Alliance Movement and in West Germany the German Women's Movement. Parties based on specific religious aims are also found. In Israel the National Religious Party advocates the unity of people of the Jewish faith in Israel and throughout the world and the Netherlands Roman Catholic Party presses for adherence to Catholic principles on subjects such as abortion, euthanasia and sexuality.

Whereas interest groups in one form or another have existed since the beginnings of civilised life, political parties are relatively new, being products of the eighteenth century onwards. Their predecessors were cliques and factions, based usually on personal or family power. The modern party displays three essential features: a permanent structure and organisation; an authority to represent people, whether or not they are members of the party, based on open elections; and an intention to form a government or participate in government.

Table 34 lists the leading parties in the contemporary world and their political orientations. The number of active parties in each state, as shown, is something of an approximation in some cases because the emergence and disappearance of minor groupings is often a notable feature of some political systems.

TABLE 34   POLITICAL PARTIES OF THE WORLD

*See notes below

State	Number of Parties	Leading Parties	Orientation
Afghanistan	5*	People's Democratic Party of Afghanistan (PDPA)	Marxist-Leninist
Albania	1	Party of Labour of Albania (PLA)	Marxist-Leninist
Algeria	6	National Liberation Front (FLN)	Socialist-Islamic
		Front Islamique du Salut (FIS)	Islamic Fundamentalist
Angola	1	Popular Movement for the Liberation of Angola—Workers' Party (MLPA-PT)	Marxist-Leninist
Antigua & Barbuda	6	Antigua Labour Party (ALP)	Moderate left of centre
		Progressive Labour Movement (PLM)	Moderate left of centre
Argentina	26	Radical Civic Union Party (UCR)	Moderate centre
		Justicalist Party (PJ)	Right wing
Australia	11	Australian Labor Party	Moderate left of centre
		Liberal Party of Australia	Centre right
		National Party of Australia (National Country Party in Western Australia)	Centre with emphasis on non-metropolitan needs
Austria	12	Socialist Party of Austria (SPO)	Moderate left of centre
		Austrian People's Party (OVP)	Progressive centre
		Freedom Party of Austria (FPO)	Moderate left of centre
Bahamas	5	Progressive Liberal Party (PLP)	Moderate centre nationalist
		Free National Movement (FNM)	Centre left
Bahrain	0		
Bangladesh	17	Jatiya Dal (National Party)	Islamic nationalist (military-backed)
		Bangladesh Nationalist Party (BNP)	Right of centre, Islamic
		Awami League (AL)	Moderate socialist (socialist)
Barbados	2	Barbados Labour Party (BLP)	Moderate left of centre
		Democratic Labour Party (DLP)	Left of centre
Belgium	17	Christian People's Party (CVP)	Christian centre-left Dutch-speaking
		Christian Social Party (PSC)	Christian centre-left French-speaking
		Socialist Party (SP)	Left of centre, Dutch-speaking

Table 34—Political Parties of the World (contd)

State	Number of Parties	Leading Parties	Orientation
		Socialist Party (PS)	Left of centre, French-speaking
		Freedom and Progress Party (PVV)	Moderate centre, Dutch-speaking
		Liberal Reform Party (PRL)	Moderate centre, French-speaking
		People's Union's (VU)	Flemish nationalist
Belize	5	People's United Party (PUP)	Moderate left of centre
		United Democratic Party (UDP)	Right of centre
Benin	1	Benin People's Revolutionary Party (BRBP)	Marxist-Leninist
Bhutan	0		
Bolivia	13	National Revolutionary Movement Historic (MNRH)	Nationalist centre
		Nationalist Democratic Action Party (ADN)	Nationalist right wing
		Movement of the Revolutionary Left (MIR)	Nationalist Marxist
Botswana	7	Botswana Democratic Party (BDP)	Nationalist moderate centre
		Botswana National Front (BNF)	Left of centre
		Botswana People's Party (BPP)	Nationalist
Brazil	12	Social Democratic Party (PDS)	Moderate left of centre
		Party of the Brazilian Democratic Movement (PMDB)	Centre left
		Democratic Labour Party (PDT)	Moderate left of centre
		Brazilian Labour Party (PTB)	Moderate left of centre
		Liberal Front Party (PFL)	Moderate centre-right
Brunei	1*	Brunei National United Party (BNUP)	Businessmen loyal to the Sultan
		Brunei National Democratic Party	Moderate Islamic Nationalist
Bulgaria	4*	Bulgarian Socialist Party (BSP)	Left wing
		Union of Democratic Forces (UDF)	Left of centre
		Bulgarian Agrarian National Union (BANC)	Agricultural radical
		Movement for Rights and Freedoms	Left of centre
Burkina Faso	3*	Organisation for Popular Democracy—Workers' Movement (ODP-MT)	Nationalist communist
Burundi	1	Union for National Progress (UPRONA)	African socialist
Cambodia	1*	Kampuchean People's Revolutionary Party (KPRP)	Marxist-Leninist

Table 34—Political Parties of the World (contd)

State	Number of Parties	Leading Parties	Orientation
Cameroon	1	Cameroon People's Democratic Movement (RDPC)	Nationalist centre left
Canada	1*	Progressive Conservative Party Liberal Party New Democratic Party	Centre right Nationalist centre left Moderate left of centre
Cape Verde	1	African Party for the Independence of Cape Verde (PAICV)	African nationalist
Central African Republic	1*	Central African Democratic Rally (MDC)	African nationalist
Chad	15*	National Union for Independence and the Revolution (UNIR)	Nationalist
Chile	17*	Christian Democratic Party (PDC) League For Democracy and Peace (LDP)	Centre-right Left wing
China	9	Chinese Communist Party (CCP)	Marxist-Maoist-Dengist
Colombia	10*	Liberal Party (PL) Conservative Party (PCC)	Centrist Right of centre
Comoros	1	Comorian Progress Union (UPC)	Nationalist Islamic
Congo	1	Congolese Labour Party (PCT)	Marxist-Leninist
Costa Rica	20	National Liberation Party (PLN) Unity Party (PUSC) People's United Coalition (PU)	Left of centre Christian centrist Left-wing coalition
Côte d'Ivoire	20*	Democratic Party of the Côte d'Ivoire (PDCI) Ivorian Popular Front	Free enterprise nationalist Centrist
Cuba	1	Cuban Communist Party (PCC)	Marxist-Leninist
Cyprus	7	Democratic Rally (DISY) Democratic Party (DIKO) Progressive Party of the Working People (AKEL) Progressive Party of the Working People (AKEL) United Democratic Union of Cyprus (EDK)	Centre Federalist centre left Communist Communist Socialist
Czecho-slovakia	8*	Civic Forum (Czech) Public Against Violence (Slovak) Christian Democratic Party Communist Party of Czechoslovakia (CPCZ)	Left-of centre Left-of-centre Centrist Marxist-Leninist

Table 34—Political Parties of the World (contd)

State	Number of Parties	Leading Parties	Orientation
Denmark	18	Social Democratic Party	Moderate left of centre
		Conservative People's Party	Free enterprise centrist
		Liberal Party	Centre left
		Socialist People's Party	Socialist
		Radical-Liberal Party	Radical centrist
Djibouti	1	Popular Rally for Progress (RPP)	Nationalist
Dominica	4	Dominica Freedom Party (DFP)	Centrist
		Labour Party of Dominica (LDP)	Moderate left of centre
Dominican Republic	9	Dominican Revolutionary Party (PRD)	Moderate left of centre
		Social Christian Revolutionary Party (PRSC)	Independent socialist
		Dominican Liberation Party (PLD)	Nationalist
Ecuador	16	Democratic Left (ID)	Moderate socialist
		Social Christian Party (PSC)	Christian socialist
		Concentration of Popular Forces (CFP)	Left of centre
		Radical Alfarist Front (FRA)	Radical centrist
		Radical Liberal Party (PLR)	Radical liberal
Egypt	7	National Democratic Party (NDP)	Moderate left of centre
		New Wafd Party	Nationalist
		Socialist Labour Party (SLP)	Right of centre
		Socialist Liberal Party (LSP)	Free enterprise centrist
El Salvador	13	Christian Democratic Party (PDC)	Moderate left of centre
		Nationalist Republican Alliance (ARENA)	Right wing
		National Conciliation Party (PCN)	Right of centre
Equatorial Guinea	1	Democratic Party of Equatorial Guinea (PDGE)	Nationalist military
Ethiopia	1*	Ethiopian Democratic Unity Party	African socialist
Fiji	6	Fiji Labour Party (FLP)	Left of centre
		National Federation Party (NFP)	Moderate left of centre
		Alliance Party (AP)	Moderate centrist
Finland	16	Finnish Social Democratic Party (SSDP)	Moderate left of centre
		National Coalition Party (KOK)	Moderate right of centre
		Centre Party (KP)	Moderate centrist
		Finnish People's Democratic League (SKDL)	Left-wing coalition
		Swedish People's Party of Finland (SFP)	Centre left
		Finnish Rural Party (SMP)	Moderate decentralist

Table 34—Political Parties of the World (contd)

State	Number of Parties	Leading Parties	Orientation
France	39†	Rally for the Republic (RPR)	Right of centre
		Socialist Party (PS)	Left of centre
		Union for French Democracy (UDF)	Centre right
		Communist Party (PCF)	Marxist-Leninist
		Republican Party (RP)	Centre right
		National Front (FN)	Extreme right wing
		Centre of Social Democrats (CDS)	Centrist
		Left Radical Movement (MRG)	Left of centre
Gabon	1	Gabonese Democratic Party (PDG)	Nationalist
Gambia	4	People's Progressive Party (PPP)	Moderate centrist
		National Convention Party (NCP)	Left of centre
Germany	73	Social Democratic Party (SPD)	Left of centre
		Free Democratic Party (FDP)	Centrist
		Christian Democratic Union (CDU)	Centre right
		Christian Social Union (CSU)	Right of centre (Bavarian based)
		The Greens	Environmentalist
		Socialist Unity Party of Germany (SED)	Marxist-Leninist
		German Social Union (DSU)	Centre-left
		Democratic Awakening (DA)	Centrist
		League of Free Democrats	Centrist
Ghana	0		
Greece	14	Pan-Hellenic Socialist Movement (PASOK)	Nationalist socialist
		New Democracy (ND)	Centre right
		Communist Party (KKE-Exterior)	Marxist-Leninist
		Communist Party (KKE-Interior)	Non-Soviet communist
Grenada	7	New National Party (NNP)	Centrist
		Grenada United Labour Party (GULP)	Nationalist left of centre
Guatemala	8	Guatemalian Christian Democratic Party (PDCG)	Christian centre left
		Union of the National Centre (UCN)	Centrist
		National Democratic Co-operation Party (PDCN)	Centre right
		Revolutionary Party (PR)	Radical
		National Liberation Movement (MLN)	Extreme right wing
		Democratic Institutional Party (PID)	Moderate right of centre

145

Table 34—Political Parties of the World (contd)

State	Number of Parties	Leading Parties	Orientation
Guinea	1	Democratic Party of Guinea (PDG)	Progressive socialist
Guinea Bissau	1	African Party for the Independence of Portuguese Guinea & Cape Verde (PAIGC)	Socialist
Guyana	4	People's National Congress (PNC)	National socialist
		People's Progressive Party (PPP)	Marxist-Leninist
Haiti	1*	National Progressive Party (PNP)	Right-wing military
Honduras	5	Liberal Party of Honduras (PLH)	Centre left
		National Party of Honduras (PN)	Traditional right wing
Hungary	8*	Hungarian Democratic Forum (HDF)	Centre right
		Independent Smallholders' Party	Centre right
		Christian Democratic People's Party (CDPP)	Centre right
		Alliance of Free Democrats (FZD)	Centrist
		Hungarian Socialist Workers' Party (HSWP)	Left wing
Iceland	11	Independence Party (IP)	Right of centre
		Progressive Party (PP)	Radical socialist
		Social Democratic Party (SDP)	Moderate left of centre
		People's Alliance (PA)	Socialist
		Citizens' Party	Centrist
		Women's Alliance	Women's & children's interests
India	34†	Indian National Congress (Indira)/Congress (I)	Broad based, secular, left of centre
		Janata Dal	Opposition umbrella coalition
		Jan Morcha	Centrist
		Janata (People's) Party	Socialist
		Bharatiya Janata Party (BJP)	Conservative Hindu
		Lok Dal (People's Movement)	Left of centre
		Communist Party of India	Marxist-Leninist (pro-Soviet)
		Communist Party of India (Marxist)-CPI (M)	Marxist-Leninist (independent)
		Telugu Desam (Land of Telugu)	Left of centre (Andhra Pradesh based)
		All-India Anna Dravidian Progress Movement (ADMK)	Left of centre decentralist (Tamil Nadu based)
Indonesia	3	Golkar	Right-wing military
		United Development Party (PPP)	Right-wing Islamic
		Indonesian Democratic Party (PDI)	Moderate non-Islamic

Table 34—*Political Parties of the World* (contd)

State	Number of Parties	Leading Parties	Orientation
Iran	5*	Islamic Republican Party	Fundamentalist Islamic
Iraq	3*	Baath Arab Socialist Party	National socialist
Ireland	14	Fianna Fail (FF)	Moderate centre right
		Fine Gael (FG)	Moderate centrist left
		Progressive Democrats (PD)	Radical centre left
		Labour Party	Moderate left of centre
Israel	20	Israel Labour Party	Left of centre
		Likud (Consolidation Party)	Nationalist right of centre
Italy	12	Christian Democratic Party (DC)	Christian centrist
		Italian Communist Party (PCI)	Eurocommunist
		Italian Socialist Party (PSI)	Moderate socialist
		Italian Social Movement—National Right (MSI-DN)	Extreme right wing
		Italian Republican Party (PRI)	Left of centre
		Italian Social Democratic Party (PSDI)	Moderate left of centre
		Italian Liberal Party (PLI)	Right of centre
Jamaica	3	Jamaica Labour Party (JLP)	Moderate centrist
		People's National Party (PNP)	Left of centre
Japan	20	Liberal-Democratic Party (LDP)	Right of centre
		Socialist Party of Japan (JSP)	Moderate socialist
		Clean Government Party (Komeito)	Left of centre
		Japan Communist Party (JCP)	Marxist-Leninist
		Democratic Socialist Party (DSP)	Left of centre
Jordan	0*		
Kenya	1*	Kenya African National Union (KANU)	Nationalist centrist
Kiribati	2	National Party	Pro-government assembly grouping
		Christian Democratic Party (CDP)	Anti-government assembly grouping
North Korea	1	Korean Workers' Party (KWP)	Nationalist communist
South Korea	9	Democratic Liberal Party (DLP)	Centre right
		Party for Peace and Democracy (PPD)	Left of centre
Kuwait	0		
Laos	1	Lao People's Revolutionary Party (LPRP)	Nationalist communist

Table 34—Political Parties of the World (contd)

State	Number of Parties	Leading Parties	Orientation
Lebanon	19	Phalangist Party	Christian radical nationalist
		Progressive Socialist Party (PSP)	Muslim moderate socialist
		National Liberal Party	Centre left
		Parliamentary Democratic Front	Sunni Muslim moderate centrist
		Lebanese Communist Party (PCL)	Nationalist communist
Lesotho	4	Basotho National Party (BNP)	Traditional nationalist
Liberia	5	National Democratic Party of Liberia (NDPL)	Nationalist military
Libya	0		
Luxembourg	7	Christian Social Party (PCS)	Christian moderate left of centre
		Luxembourg Socialist Workers' Party (POSL)	Moderate socialist
		Democratic Party (PD)	Centre left
		Communist Party of Luxembourg	Left wing
Madagascar	7*	National Front for the Defence of the Malagasy Socialist Revolution (FNDR)	Nationalist socialist
		Vanguard of the Malagasy Revolution (Arena)	Nationalist socialist
Malawi	1	Malawi Congress Party (MCP)	Right-wing multi-racial
Malaysia	36	New United Malays' National Organisation (UMNO Baru)	Malay nationalist unity
		Malaysian Chinese Association (MIC)	Right of centre (Chinese)
		Democratic Action Party (DAP)	Moderate left of centre (Chinese)
		Islamic Party of Malaysia (PAS)	Malay Islamic nationalist
		Communist Party of Malaysia (CPM)	Left wing (Chinese)
Maldives	0		
Mali	1	Malian People's Democratic Union (UDPM)	Nationalist
Malta	3	Malta Labour Party (MLP)	Moderate left of centre
		Nationalist Party	Christian centrist
Mauritania	0		

Table 34—Political Parties of the World (contd)

State	Number of Parties	Leading Parties	Orientation
Mauritius	12	Mauritius Labour Party (MLP)	Centre left
		Mauritius Socialist Movement (MSM)	Moderate socialist
		Mauritian Militant Movement (MMM)	Marxist
		Organisation du peuple rodriguais radriguail (OPR)	Centre left
Mexico	13	Institutional Revolutionary Party (PRI)	Moderate left wing
		National Action Party (PAN)	Christian socialist
		Socialist Workers' Party (PST)	Trotskyist
		Mexican Democratic Party (PCM)	Democratic socialist
		Popular Socialist Party (PPS)	Marxist-Leninist
		Authentic Party of the Mexican Revolution (PARM)	Right wing
		Democratic Revolutionary Party (PRD)	Nationalist left wing
Mongolia	5*	Mongolian People's Revolutionary Party (MPRP)	Marxist-Leninist
		Mongolian Democratic Party (MDP)	Left of centre
Morocco	14	Constitutional Union (UC)	Right wing
		National Rally of Independents (RNI)	Royalist
		Popular Movement (MP)	Moderate agrarian socialist
		Independence Party (Istiqlal)	Nationalist right of centre
		Socialist Union of Popular Forces (USFP)	Progressive socialist
		National Democratic Party (NDP)	Nationalist moderate
Mozambique	1	National Front for the Liberation of Mozambique (Frelimo)	Marxist-Leninist
Myanma (Burma)	117*	National Unity Party (NUP)	National communist
		National League for Democracy (NLD)	Left wing
Namibia	1*	South West African People's Organisation (SWAPO)	Left-wing African nationalist
Nauru	1	Democratic Party of Nauru (DPN)	Assembly opposition grouping
Nepal	0		

Table 34—Political Parties of the World (contd)

State	Number of Parties	Leading Parties	Orientation
Netherlands	17	Christian Democratic Appeal (CDA)	Christian right of centre
		Labour Party (PvdA)	Moderate left of centre
		People's Party for Freedom and Democracy (VVD)	Liberal centrist
		Democrats '66 (D'66)	Environmental centrist
		Radical Political Party (PPR)	Moderate socialist and ecological
		Communist Party of the Netherlands (CPN)	International communist
		Pacifist Socialist Party (PSP)	Left-wing pacifist
		State Political Reform Party (SGP)	Calvinist
		Reformational Political Federation (RPF)	Calvinist reformist
		Reformed Political Association (GPV)	Calvinist
New Zealand	6	Labour Party	Moderate left of centre
		New Zealand National Party	Centre right
		New Labour Party	Moderate left of centre
Nicaragua	14	Sandinista National Liberation Front (FSLN)	Marxist-Leninist
		Democratic Conservative Party (PCD)	Centrist
		Independent Liberal Party (PLI)	Moderate centre left
		Popular Social Christian Party (PPSC)	Christian socialist
Niger	0		
Nigeria	0		
Norway	10	Norwegian Labour Party (DNA)	Moderate left of centre
		Conservative Party	Progressive right of centre
		Christian People's Party (KrF)	Christian centre left
		Centre Party (SP)	Left of centre non-socialist
Oman	0		
Pakistan	18	Pakistan People's Party (PPP)	Left of centre
		Islamic Democratic Alliance (IDA)	Anti-Bhutto, right-wing Islamic coalition
		Pakistan Muslim League (PML)	Islamic right wing
		Mohajir Quami Movement (MQM)	Sind-based partition immigrants (*mohajir*) rights
		Jamiat-i-Ulema-i-Islam (JUI)	Islamic
		Awami National Party (ANP)	Socialist and federalist

Table 34—Political Parties of the World (contd)

State	Number of Parties	Leading Parties	Orientation
Panama	17	Labour Party (PALA)	Right wing
		Nationalist Republican Liberal Movement (MOLIRENA)	Right of centre
		Authentic Panamaninist Party (PPA)	Right wing
		Republican Party (PR)	Right wing
		Democratic Revolutionary Party (PRD)	Centre left
		Christian Democratic Party (PDC)	Christian moderate left of centre
Papua New Guinea	11	People's Progress Party (PPP)	Conservative centre right
		National Party	Right of centre
		People's Democratic Movement (PDM)	Centrist
		Melanesian Alliance (MA)	Left of centre
		People's Action Party (PAP)	Conservative centre right
		Papua Party (PP)	Centrist
Paraguay	9	National Republican Association-Colorado Party	Right of centre
		Radical Liberal Party (PLR)	Moderate right of centre
		Liberal Party (PL)	Right of centre
Peru	18	American Popular Revolutionary Alliance (APRA)	Moderate left wing
		United Left (IU)	Left wing
Philippines	25†	Kabisig ('shoulder to shoulder co-operation')	Left of centre pro-Aquino coalition
		Convenors' Group	Liberal left
		PDP-Laban Party	Centrist
		Liberal Party	Centrist
		Union for United Action	Right-wing anti-Aquino coalition
		New Society Movement	Right-wing pro-Marcos
		Grand Alliance for Democracy (GAD)	Right-wing anti-Aquino
Poland	5*	Polish United Workers' Party (PUWP)	Marxist-Leninist
		Centre Alliance	Centre right
		United Peasants' Party	Agrarian left wing
		Social Democratic Party (SD)	Centre left
Portugal	14	Social Democratic Party (PSD)	Moderate left of centre
		Socialist Party (PS)	Progressive socialist
		Democratic Renewal Party (PRD)	Centre left
		Party of the Democratic Social Centre (CDS)	Moderate left of centre
		Portuguese Communist Party (PCP)	Left wing

Table 34—Political Parties of the World (contd)

State	Number of Parties	Leading Parties	Orientation
Qatar	0		
Romania	22*	Romanian Communist Party (RCP)	Marxist-Leninist
		Romanian National Salvation Front (NSF)	Centre left
		Hungarian Democratic Union	Hungarian nationalist
		National Liberal Party	Centre right
		Ecological Movement	Ecological
		National Peasants' Party	Right wing
Rwanda	1	National Revolutionary Development Movement (MRND)	Socialist
St Kitts-Nevis	4	People's Action Movement (PAM)	Centre right
		Nevis Reformation Party (NRP)	Separationist
		Labour Party	Moderate left of centre
Saint Lucia	3	United Workers' Party (UWP)	
		St Lucia Labour Party (SLP)	Moderate left wing
		Progressive Labour Party (PLP)	
Saint Vincent and The Grenadines	9	New Democratic Party (NDP)	Moderate left of centre
		St Vincent Labour Party (SVLP)	Moderate left of centre
Sao Tome & Principe	1	Movement for the Liberation of Sao Tome and Principe (MLSTP)	Nationalist socialist
Saudi Arabia	0		
Senegal	18	Socialist Party of Sengal (PSS)	Democratic socialist
		Senegalise Democratic Party (PDS)	Socialist
Seychelles	1	Seychelles People's Progressive Front (SPPF)	Socialist
Sierra Leone	1	All People's Congress (APC)	Socialist
Singapore	21	People's Action Party (PAP)	Right of centre
		Workers' Party (WP)	Socialist
Solomon Islands	5	Solomon Islands United Party (SIUP)	Right of centre
		National Front for Progress (NFP)	Right of centre
		People's Alliance Party (PAP)	Centre left
Somalia	1	Somali Revolutionary Socialist Party (SRSP)	Socialist

Table 34—Political Parties of the World (contd)

State	Number of Parties	Leading Parties	Orientation
South Africa	13*	National Party of South Africa (NP)	(Whites) Right centre racialist
		Democratic Party (DP)	(Whites) Moderate non-racial
		New Republic Party (POB)	Whites) Left of centre multi-racial
		Conservative Party of South Africa (CPSA)	(Whites) Extreme right wing
		United Democratic Front (UDF)	Multi-racial Church orientated
		Afrikaner Resistance Movement (AWB)	Right wing
		Labour Party of South Africa (LP)	(Coloureds) Left of centre
		People's Congress Party (PCP)	(Coloureds) Right of centre
		National People's Party	(Indian) Right of centre
		Solidarity Party	(Indian) Left of centre
Soviet Union	1	Communist Party of the Soviet Union (CPSU)	Marxist-Leninist
Spain	21	Spanish Socialist Workers' Party (PSOE)	Democratic socialist
		Popular Coalition (CP)	Moderate centre right
Sri Lanka	15	United National Party (UNP)	Centre right
		Janata Vimukti Peramuna (JVP)	Left wing
		Sri Lanka Freedom Party (SLFP)	Nationalist socialist
Sudan	14*	New National Umma Party (NNUP)	} Islamic nationalist
		Democratic Unionist Party (DUP)	
		National Islamic Front	
		Sudanese National Nuba Party (SNNP)	Nationalist
Suriname	18	National Democratic Party (NDP)	Military-backed centrist
		Front for Democracy and Development (FDD)*	Left of centre, multi-racial coalition
Swaziland	1	Imbokodvo National Movement (INM)	Traditional nationalist
Sweden	12	Swedish Social Democratic Labour Party (SAP)	Moderate left of centre
		Moderate Party	Right of centre
		Liberal Party	Centre left
		Centre Party	Moderate centrist
		Christian Democratic Community Party (KdS)	Christian centrist
		Left Party—Communists (UPK)	European Marxist

Table 34—*Political Parties of the World* (contd)

State	Number of Parties	Leading Parties	Orientation
Switzerland	23	Christian Democratic People's Party of Switzerland (CVP)	Christian moderate centrist
		Radical Democratic Party of Switzerland (FDP)	Radical centre left
		Swiss Social Democratic Party (SPS)	Moderate left of centre
		Swiss People's Party (SVP)	Centre left
		Swiss Liberal Party (LPS)	Federalist centre left
		Green Party of Switzerland (GPS)	Ecological
Syria	1*	National Progressive Front	Arab socialist (Baath Arab Socialist Party) Arab Socialist Party (ASP) Arab Socialist Union (ASU) Socialist Unionist Movement (SUM) Syrian Communist Party (SCP))
Taiwan	7	Nationalist Party of China (Kuomintang: KMT)	Nationalist (Chinese)
		Democratic Progress Party (DPP)	Centre left
		Party of Workers of Labour	Left of centre
Tanzania	1	Revolutionary Party of Tanzania (CCM)	African socialist
Thailand	18	Thai Nation Party	Right wing
		Social Action Party (SAP)	Moderate right of centre
		Democratic Party	Moderate right of centre
		Thai Citizens' Party	Far right monarchist
		Citizens' Party	Right wing
Togo	1	Rally of the Togolese People (RPT)	Nationalist socialist
Tonga	0		
Trinidad and Tobago	8	National Alliance for Reconstruction (NAR)	Moderate left-wing coalition
		People's National Movement (PNM)	Moderate nationalist
Tunisia	4	Constitutional Democratic Rally (RDC)	Nationalist socialist
Turkey	7	Motherland Party (ANAP)	Nationalist Islamic right of centre
		Social Democratic Populist Party (SHP)	Moderate left of centre
		True Path Party (DVP)	Centre right

Table 34—Political Parties of the World (contd)

State	Number of Parties	Leading Parties	Orientation
Tuvalu	0		
Uganda	7	National Resistance Movement (NRM)	Centrist
		Democratic Party (DP)	Centre left
		Conservative Party (CP)	Centre right
		Uganda People's Congress (UPC)	Left of centre
		Uganda Freedom Movement (UFM)	Left of centre
United Arab Emirates	0		
United Kingdom	21*	Conservative and Unionist Party	Right of centre
		Labour Party	Moderate left of centre
		Liberal Democrats	Centre left
		Green Party	Environmentalist
		Scottish National Party (SNP)	Scottish nationalist
		Party of Wales (Plaid Cymru)	Welsh nationalist
		Official Unionist Party (OUP)	Northern Ireland Protestant right of centre
		Democratic Unionist Party (DUP)	Northern Ireland Protestant nationalist
		Social Democratic and Labour Party (SDLP)	Northern Ireland Catholic centre left
		Sinn Fein	Northern Ireland Catholic nationalist
United States	20	Republican Party	Right of centre
		Democratic Party	Centre left
Uruguay	6*	Colorado Party (PC)	Progressive centre left
		National (Blanco) Party (PN)	Traditional right of centre
		Bread Front	Moderate left wing
Vanuatu	10	Vanuaaku Pati (VP)	Melanesian socialist
		Union of Moderate Parties (UMP)	Centre left (Francophone)
Venezuela	10	Democratic Action (AD)	Moderate left of centre
		Christian Social Party (COPEI)	Christian centre right
		Movement to Socialism (MAS)	Left of centre
		Democratic Republican Union (URD)	Left of centre
Vietnam	1	Communist Party of Vietnam (CPV)	Marxist-Leninist
Western Samoa	4	Human Rights Protection Party (HRPP)	Centre right
		Christian Democratic Party (CDP)	Centre left
		Va'ai Kolone Group (VKG)	Centrist

155

Table 34—Political Parties of the World (contd)

State	Number of Parties	Leading Parties	Orientation
Yemeni Republic	2*	General People's Congress	Socialist
		Yemen Socialist Party	Socialist
Yugoslavia	9*	League of Communists of Yugoslavia (SKJ)	Marxist-Leninist
Zaire	1	Popular Movement of the Revolution (MPR)	African socialist
Zambia	1*	United National Independence Party (UNIP)	African socialist
Zimbabwe	1*	Zimbabwe African National Union-Patriotic Front (ZANU-PF)	African socialist

*NOTES

Afghanistan, Bulgaria, Chad, Chile, Côte d'Ivoire, Czechoslovakia, Ethiopia, Haiti, Hungary, Mongolia, Myanma (Burma), Poland, Romania, Sudan, Yemeni Republic and Yugoslavia	The political systems in these countries are currently in a particularly fluid state.
Brunei	Political groupings rather than parties.
Burkina Faso	Effectively one-party, controlled by the National Revolutionary Council.
Central African Republic	Political parties are currently banned but a number of passive opposition groups exist.
Colombia	The number of active parties is very variable.
Iran, Iraq, Kenya, Madagascar, Syria, Zimbabwe	These are all effectively, if not legally, one-party states.
South Africa	There are no legal political parties for blacks.
United Kingdom	The number of parties fighting general elections and by-elections fluctuates from year to year.
Uruguay	The two main parties, PC and PN, are both broad coalitions of a number of factions.

†In addition to those parties listed, there are three regional parties in France, 61 in India and 30 in the Philippines.

7.5 Parties in Liberal and Emergent Democracies

It is possible to distinguish five different bases of party formation and support in the states we have defined as liberal or emergent democracies. They are: social class, economic status, religion, regional differences and philosophical leanings. All parties are based on at least one of these factors, some on most, or all.

The United Kingdom provides a clear example of class-based parties, although the divisions are not as stark in contemporary society as they were earlier in the century. The creation of the Labour Party, known originally as the Labour Representation Committee, in 1900, to represent the working classes, provided a striking contrast to the Conservative Party, which sought to protect and promote the interests of the middle and upper classes. Before the advent of the Labour Party Britain's two-party political system had been based on a division between the Conservatives, representing landed interests, and the Liberals, representing urban industrialists.

Class-based parties are not as marked in most other countries. The Labor Party of Australia and the New Zealand Labour Party, although similar in origin to their counterpart in the United Kingdom, reflect the greater social openness in those two countries.

Ironically, communist parties in liberal democratic states have tended to be homes for left-wing, middle-class intellectuals rather than for the proletariat and have seldom won sufficient popular support to control the levers of political power. This is increasingly true of the two most significant of such bodies in Western Europe, the Italian Communist Party (PCI) and French Communist Party (PCF).

Economic status has largely replaced, or is replacing, class as an indicator of social position in most liberal democracies. In Italy, for example, class divisions are not clearly defined and economic status is becoming a dominant feature of party support. In West Germany the post-war rise of a non-unionised working class and a new middle class provide further evidence of the importance of economic, rather than social, factors as a basis for party allegiance.

Religion still provides a widely occurring foundation for political parties in contemporary liberal and emergent democracies. Parties in Italy, Israel, the Netherlands, Austria, West Germany, France and other Western European states display this

157

characteristic to varying degrees, having their roots in sides taken during earlier secular-clerical battles. In the United Kingdom economic disparities in Northern Ireland have been underlined by religious divisions.

Regional differences are, arguably, the most common foundation for party support. In the United States, for example, clearly distinguishable parties might well disappear if they were not supported on regional bases. In the Netherlands and Belgium regional variations, accentuated by linguistic differences, have multiplied the party groupings. In Belgium each of the four principal parties, Christian Democrat, Socialist, Liberal and Green, is currently divided into autonomous, and often antagonistic, Flemish and French wings.

Philosophy has not provided a reliable basis for mass party support in liberal democratic states in recent years. Indeed, surveys suggest that the great majority of contemporary electors not only care little for social and political theory but have no clear understanding of the philosophical stance of the parties for which they vote. The 'thinking elector' is certainly in a minority throughout the world and the chances of representation by a party which accurately mirrors the views of this kind of voter are very much determined by the vagaries of the electoral system, as we shall see later in this chapter. The new 'post-industrial' ecological parties, which have made notable progress in North-West European states, as a result of proportional representation, during the past decade, are examples of this process. They contrast significantly with the eclectic 'catch-all' nature of most major liberal democratic parties.

7.6 Parties in Communist States

The all-pervading influence of the party provides the sharpest contrast between communist one-party and multi-party states. It is the ultimate source of power and permeates all aspects of the political system and the state institutions.

In contrast to parties in most western democracies, membership of the party in communist states is a privileged and élitist acquisition. Whereas parties in liberal democracies actively compete with each other to increase their memberships, communist parties are highly cautious and selective about the people who are eventually admitted into full membership. Aspirants are initially inducted into the party's 'youth' wing for

14–28-year-olds, known in the Soviet Union as Komsomol. Years later, when old enough for consideration for full party membership, they must be nominated by three full party members of at least five years' standing. Then, if accepted, they are required to serve a year's probation under the title of 'candidate member'.

Despite these hurdles to be surmounted, party membership, with its associated economic and social advantages, is highly sought after in communist states. For this reason, party membership as a proportion of the total population is invariably at a higher level in communist than liberal democratic states, as Table 35 shows.

TABLE 35   POLITICAL PARTY MEMBERSHIP AS A PROPORTION
OF STATE POPULATIONS IN COMMUNIST AND
LIBERAL DEMOCRATIC STATES

| | Communist States | | | Liberal-Democratic States* | |
| | Ruling Party Membership (m) | % of Total Pop | | Combined Party Membership (m) | % of Total Pop |
State			State		
N. Korea	3.000	14.6	Austria	1.300	17.2
Soviet Union	19.038	6.8	Norway	0.500	12.0
Cuba	0.524	5.1	Barbados	0.025	9.9
Albania	0.147	4.8	Italy	4.500	7.9
Mongolia	0.088	4.6	Belgium	0.700	7.1
China	44.000	4.2	Belize	0.010	6.0
Vietnam	1.750	2.8	Denmark	0.300	5.9
Laos	0.042	1.0	Switzerland	0.370	5.7
Cambodia	0.008	0.1	Ireland	0.150	4.2
			Japan	4.350	3.6
			West Germany	2.030	3.3
			United Kingdom	1.800	3.2
			France	1.700	3.1
			Netherlands	0.400	2.8
			Australia	0.420	2.7
			Sri Lanka	0.200	1.3

*This is a selective sample as accurate data are lacking for other liberal-democratic states.

Parties in communist states have clear ideological bases. Indeed, one of the main purposes, if not the main purpose, of the party is to preserve and project the ideology. This is done by the presence of party representatives throughout the political and social systems, including the media and work places.

This all-pervasiveness must be clearly recognised if the political systems of communist states are to be properly understood. Using the Soviet Union as the salient example, it can be seen that any position of reasonable seniority within the state must be 'confirmed' by the party; the more important the post the higher the echelon of approval. The most senior posts of all, amounting to nearly a third of a million, are closely controlled by the secretariat of the Central Committee of the party. From its earliest, Leninist, days the Communist Party of the Soviet Union set out to be an élite 'vanguard' organisation, comprising the country's 'best citizens', and, although the membership net has been cast more widely since the Second World War, more than quadrupling between 1945 and 1985, it has never deviated from that original aim. The stress on quality, rather than crude numbers or social background, has, in recent years, been a prominent theme for the new Gorbachev administration.

Other communist states, and some nationalistic socialist states, have similarly developed and promoted the party as the custodian of the nation's political future and the 'vanguard of the proletariat'. As Table 35 reveals, however, there exist significant variations in membership 'densities' between the 'mass party' of North Korea and the élitist cadres of Vietnam, Laos and Cambodia.

7.7 The Party in Non-Communist, One-Party States

Most contemporary non-communist, one-party states are found in what has become fashionable to describe as the Third World, even though this description can be a little ambiguous.

In these states the party, in addition to acting as a political recruitment, socialisation and resource distribution agency, usually performs two main functions: the promotion of nationalism and patriotism and the maintenance of a certain stable economic and social order. Support for nationalism invariably receives a high priority, the dominant parties usually being those which had spearheaded the independence movement, and the economic and social order is that which is determined by the ruling élite within the party.

Additionally, the non-communist single party often tends to

support and sustain the strong, charismatic leader. Most of the black African states display this characteristic, although it should be noted that the dominance of a strong leader is not always confined to one-party states. The constitution of the French Fifth Republic was originally designed with Charles de Gaulle in mind and the party which supported him not only made his continuance in office its main aim but assumed his name as the popular description of the political movement. Other states, particularly in South America, have spawned strong, autocratic leaders within a highly factionalised, multi-party system.

Compared with parties in liberal and emergent democracies and communist states, those in non-communist one-party countries are, with notable exceptions in black Africa, such as Mozambique, Tanzania, Zambia and Zimbabwe, relatively weak organisations and very much the instruments of those nations' political leaders. Some countries, although in theory one-party states, might better be regarded as having no parties at all. The reason for the comparative docility of party politics in these states stems mainly from history and social organisation. Modern political parties are not a 'natural' development in most so-called Third World states and many years may elapse before the economic and social environments can sustain a 'sophisticated' multi-party system. Social organisation, sometimes based on tribal loyalties or strong regional differences, has also favoured allegiance to the strong, personal leader rather than the 'anonymous' party.

7.8 Parties in Militaristic and Absolutist States

In states controlled by the military or absolute rulers political parties either do not exist or, if they do, are puppets of the ruling élite and façades for what is little more than autocratic, personal government.

Absolutist states such as those in the Arab world have never experienced what might be described as popular political activity, with representative institutions. Most of the countries which are today under the sway of military rulers have, in contrast, previously enjoyed some form of democratic government so that their present condition may be a temporary aberration. There is evidence that military rulers find it difficult to sustain their leadership for protracted periods without creating a single party and building it into the framework of the state or reverting to a multi-party political system.

161

In Bangladesh, the Jana Dal (People's Party) was formed in 1983 by Lieutenant-General Hossain Mohammad Ershad to support his presidential candidature. Now known as the Jatiya (National) Front, the party has subsequently established itself as a civilian governing front for what still remains a military-dependent regime. Similarly in Indonesia, the Joint Secretariat of Functional Groups (Golkar Party), which had been created in 1964 as a loose alliance of anti-communist sectional interest groups, was transformed into a civilian ruling front for the military when, in 1968, it was brought under government control by General Suharto.

7.9 Political Parties and Electoral Systems

Is there a direct connection between a country's electoral system and the structure and numbers of its political parties? Writers tend to be ambivalent, suggesting a 'chicken and egg' situation. Some argue that the kinds of parties in a particular country simply reflect its social and economic structure while others attribute much greater influence to the methods of voting available to electors. What is the evidence?

Of the 50 countries identified in Table 4 as liberal democracies 29 employ majoritarian voting systems of an alternative vote, simple plurality or second ballot type. The remaining 21 have some variety of proportional representation. An analysis of of the respective party systems reveals the pattern set out in Table 36 on pages 162–4.

TABLE 36   VOTING AND PARTY SYSTEMS IN LIBERAL DEMOCRACIES

States with Majoritarian Voting Systems	States with Some Form of Proportional Representation	Party Systems
Antigua and Barbuda (SP)		Two-party
Australia (AV)		Two-party
	Austria (PL)	Multi-party*
Bahamas (SP)		Two-party
Barbados (SP)		Two-party
	Belgium (PL)	Multi-party
Belize (SP)		Two-party

Table 36—Voting and Party Systems in Liberal Democracies (contd)

States with Majoritarian Voting Systems	States with Some Form of Proportional Representation	Party Systems
Botswana (SP)		Two-party
Canada (SP)		Multi-party*
	Costa Rica (PL)	Two-party
	Denmark (PL)	Multi-party
Dominica (SP)		Two-party
	Dominican Republic (PL)	Multi-party*
	Finland (PL)	Multi-party
France (SB)		Multi-party*
Gambia (SP)		Two-party
	Germany (AM)	Multi-party*
	Iceland (PL)	Multi-party
India (SP)		Dominant party†
	Ireland (STV)	Multi-party*
	Israel (PL)	Multi-party*
	Italy (PL)	Multi-party
Jamaica (SP)		Two-party
	Japan (LV)	Dominant party†
Kiribati (SB)		Two-party‡
	Luxembourg (PL)	Multi-party
Malaysia (SP)		Multi-party§
	Malta (STV)	Two-party
Mauritius (SP)		Multi-party*
	Mexico (AM)	Dominant party†
Nauru (SP)		Two-party‡
	Netherlands (PL)	Multi-party
New Zealand (SP)		Two-party
	Norway (PL)	Multi-party
Papua New Guinea (SP)		Multi-party
St Kitts-Nevis (SP)		Two-party
St Lucia (SP)		Two-party
St Vincent & the Grenadines (SP)		Two-party
Singapore (SP)		Dominant party†
Solomon Islands (SP)		Two-party
	Sri Lanka (PL)	Two-party
	Sweden (PL)	Multi-party
	Switzerland (PL)	Multi-party

163

Table 36—Voting and Party Systems in Liberal Democracies (contd)

States with Majoritarian Voting Systems	States with Some Form of Proportional Representation	Party Systems
Trinidad and Tobago (SP)		Two-party
Tuvalu (SP)		No parties
United Kingdom (SP)		Two-party
United States (SP)		Two-party
Vanuatu (SB)		Two-party
	Venezuela (PL)	Multi-party*
Western Samoa (Coll)		Two-party

ABBREVIATIONS:

AM—Additional Member
AV—Alternative Vote
Coll—College
LV—Limited Vote
PL—Party List
SB—Second Ballot
SP—Simple Plurality
STV—Single Transferable Vote

*Within these multi-party systems two major parties or alliances exist alongside one or two minor parties, which frequently hold the balance of power.

†One major party dominates in what is otherwise a multi-party system.

‡Formal party structures are weak, with candidates being elected substantially as independents. Within the assembly, however, a division between majority and minority members has emerged.

§Dominated by one party within a ruling multi-party coalition.

Of the 29 countries with majoritarian voting methods 21 have effectively a two-party system operating, two have a 'dominant party system', in which one party usually dominates electoral contests, and one has a system in which parties as such do not operate, candidates fighting assembly seats as independents. Only five majoritarian voting countries have political systems of a multi-party nature, with three or more parties regularly exchanging or sharing power. Conversely, of the 21 states employing some kind of proportional representation 16 have multi-party systems and only three have effectively two parties operating. In the remaining two countries 'dominant party systems' are in force. Although the evidence is not conclusive, a link between electoral systems and party systems seems more than a possibility.

The classic examples of two-party competition, in which minor parties are virtually non-existent, are to be found in the small island states of the Caribbean and Oceania. In these regions 18 (86%) of the 21 liberal democratic systems, excluding mainland Mexico, operate in this way. The smallness of their populations, which in the majority of cases average around 100,000–200,000, and of their assemblies, varying between 11 and 49 elected members, are important explanatory factors. The personalised style of politics and party formation in these regions has had the effect of creating polarisation, as have their simple plurality voting systems.

The textbook example of a two-party system is, however, the United Kingdom. Here the simple plurality voting system has played, arguably, a paramount role in fostering polarisation. The two major parties, Conservative and Labour, have shared power exclusively for more than 40 years because the electoral system has made it extremely difficult for third or fourth parties to secure enough parliamentary seats to break the monopoly. The advent of a strong challenge from 1981 onwards, first in the form of the Liberal-SDP Alliance and then the Democrats, on the centre-left of the political spectrum, has benefited the centre-right Conservatives, giving them clear majorities in three successive general elections.

Canada is only a partial exception to the rule of simple plurality voting producing a two-party system because, although the seats in the House of Commons have been shared in recent years by three parties, for most of the present century the Liberals and Progressive Conservatives have dominated Canadian politics. Similarly, in France and Mauritius, two other majoritarian electoral states which currently have multi-party systems, the assemblies are invariably dominated by two principal party groupings, with minor 'half-parties' holding a much smaller number of seats, though sometimes the balance of power. Only in one majoritarian state, Papua New Guinea, does a full-blown multi-party system operate.

The tendency for majoritarian voting systems to foster restricted party systems thus appears to be strong. In the cases of Canada, the United States and the United Kingdom the size, social complexity and regional differentiation of the countries are such that it seems almost certain that if proportional voting systems were in place a multiplicity of party groupings would emerge, although a core of three or four major parties would still

165

be likely to predominate. In the case of France firm evidence exists from the Fourth Republic period and, briefly, from the National Assembly election of 1986, when party list systems were in operation, that the second ballot majoritarian method has served to restrict party development.

The evidence presented in Table 36 also shows, however, that proportional voting systems do not always result in a multiplicity of parties vying for, or sharing, power. The fact that small parties are not disadvantaged by the voting system will not necessarily guarantee them better access to government, as the experiences of Costa Rica and Malta reveal. Historical and social factors can sometimes result in domination by two parties, however open the political system might be. In many other states with proportional representation systems, although a multiplicity of parties may have assembly representation, it is usual for three or four major parties to hold a majority of seats.

7.10 Parties and the Legal Environment

The majority of one-party states have the party's monopoly enshrined within the constitution. In some ostensibly multi-party states legal controls will sometimes favour the dominant government party, making life for opposition groups difficult. Singapore and Paraguay provide evidence of this. In genuine multi-party states the legal environment can range from positive encouragement at one extreme to minimum restraints on fraudulent practices at the other.

Austria provides probably the clearest example of positive support for political parties, the Party Law stating: '. . . the existence and diversity of political parties is an essential component of the democratic order of the Republic of Austria.' Here the state gives generous financial support. Each party with at least five members in the National Council receives a lump sum and then additional finance is provided on the basis of the number of votes won in the previous federal election. Parties which did not win seats but obtained at least 1 per cent of the popular vote are not overlooked, receiving *pro rata* support according to votes obtained.

Similarly in Germany, under the law of July 1967, parties are described as a 'constitutionally necessary element of a free democratic order', with state subsidies of DM 5 (US$3) per vote being provided to all political parties which secure 0.5 per cent or more of the popular poll.

Several other states give finance to help cover election expenses in varying degrees. They include Costa Rica, Denmark, Ecuador, Israel, Italy, Netherlands, Norway, Portugal, Spain, Sweden and Turkey, and the United States for presidential elections only. The amount of the grant usually depends on the size of the vote obtained at the last election but in Denmark on the size of the party. In many countries free time is made available to parties on the state radio and television networks. In the United Kingdom, although there are no state funds for elections, the official opposition party, once elected, is given finance, its leader and a limited number of its parliamentary managers receiving state salaries.

Many states require parties to register and sometimes the conditions of registration can be severe, making it difficult for small or new parties to obtain a foothold on the political slope. Argentina, Brazil, India (where strict regulations were introduced in 1985 to discourage inter-election changes of allegiance by deputies: 'floor-crossing'), Malaysia, Mexico, Philippines, Thailand and Venezuela are among the countries requiring evidence of popular support as a condition of registration. In Indonesia the number of parties permitted to operate has been restricted to three since 1975.

At the other extreme, there are states where control is at a very minimum. They include Belgium, where one party fought an election under the banner of 'Snow White and the Seven Dwarfs', Bolivia, whose elections are generally subject to widespread fraud, France, where restrictions are minimal, Honduras, New Zealand, Sri Lanka, Switzerland and the United Kingdom, where 'oddball parties' are allowed to contest elections provided they are prepared to sacrifice a deposit of £500 if their vote count falls below 5 per cent.

Recommended Reading

Ball, A. and Millward, F., *Pressure Politics in Industrial Societies: A Comparative Introduction*, Macmillan,1986.

Bell, D.S. (ed), *Contemporary French Political Parties*, Croom Helm, 1982.

Cammack, P., Pool, D. and Tordoff, W., *Third World Politics: A Comparative Introduction*, Macmillan, 1988, Ch. 3.

Charlton, R., *Comparative Government*, Longman, 1986, Chs. 5 & 6.

Daalder, H and Mair, P. (eds), *Western European Party Systems*, Sage Publications, 1983.

Day, A.J. and Degenhardt, H.W. (eds), *Political Parties of the World: A Keesings Reference Publication*, Longman, 2nd edn., 1984.

Epstein, L., *Political Parties in the American Mold*, University of Wisconsin Press, 1986.

Hague, R. and Harrop, M., *Comparative Government and Politics: An Introduction*, Macmillan, 2nd edn., 1987, Chs. 7 & 8.

Hill, R.J. and Frank, P., *The Soviet Communist Party*, George Allen & Unwin, 2nd edn., 1983.

Lawson, K., *The Comparative Study of Political Parties*, St Martin's Press, 1976.

Merkl, P.H. (ed), *Western European Party Systems*, Free Press, 1980.

Roberts, G.K., *An Introduction to Comparative Politics*, Edward Arnold, 1986, Chs. 5 & 6.

Sartori, G., *Parties and Party Systems: A Framework for Analysis*, Cambridge University Press, 1976.

Solomon, S.G. (ed), *Pluralism in the Soviet Union*, Macmillan, 1983).

Stammen, T., *Political Parties in Europe*, John Martin Publishing, 1980

Thomas, A. and Paterson, W. (eds), *The Future of Social Democracy*, Oxford University Press, 1986.

Von Beyme, K., *Political Parties in Western Democracies*, Gower, 1985.

Ware, A. (ed), *Political Parties: Electoral Change and Structural Response*, Basil Blackwell, 1987.

Wattenberg, M.P., *The Decline of American Political Parties, 1952-1980*, Harvard University Press, 1984.

Wilson. G.K., *Interest Groups in the United States*, Clarendon Press, 1981.

Chapter 8

THE RELICS OF EMPIRE—COLONIES, DEPENDENCIES AND SEMI-SOVEREIGN STATES

8.1 The Building of the Colonial Empires: 1492–1919

Nine-tenths of the contemporary sovereign states outside Western Europe have, at one time or another during the two centuries before 1945, been subject to external rule by the 'great' colonial powers of Europe, the United States or Japan. The notable exceptions have been Japan itself, China apart from Manchuria and the coastal 'treaty port' enclaves, Afghanistan until 1979, Iran, Saudi Arabia, North Yemen, Liberia since 1847, Thailand, Bhutan and Nepal. 'Informal' external influence was, however, strong in many of these states, Nepal and Bhutan, for example, being bound by strict treaty obligations to Britain until 1947.

The process of modern colonisation occurred in a series of distinct phases. It began in the late fifteenth and early sixteenth centuries, with the conquest of Southern and Central America, including the Caribbean, by Spain and Portugal, the indigenous Amerindian civilisation being destroyed and replaced by a new mixed, white-creole-black, plantation and mining economy. This was followed, during the seventeenth century, by the Netherlands' assertion of supremacy over the East Indies' 'spice islands', and the creation of British and French settlements in coastal North America.

The majority of the early colonies on the mainland of the Americas were, following revolts by the settlers, to secure their independence during the late eighteenth and early nineteenth centuries, as Table 37 shows. Elsewhere in the world, however, European interests multiplied, an extensive new chain of dependencies being established across South and South-East Asia, Australasia, Africa and the Caribbean during what was the dominant era of imperial expansion, between the 1770s and the 1920s. The lead in this second phase of colonialism was taken by Britain and France. Also involved in the process were the rising nations of central, eastern and southern Europe, notably Germany, Tsarist Russia and Italy, the ambitious small kingdom

169

of Belgium, the old imperial states of the Netherlands, Spain and Portugal and the emergent world powers of the United States and Japan.

Imperial expansion during this 'mature' phase usually took the form of the imposition of a ruling body, or person, on indigenous peoples, or even indirect control, rather than the emigration and settlement of white colonists. The exceptions were the settler colonies of Australia and New Zealand, upland parts of southern and eastern Africa and the tea and rubber planter belts of South-East Asia. The expansion was at its maximum, in areal terms, at the time of the Versailles Settlement of 1919, when nearly all of Africa, South and South-East Asia, Oceania and the Caribbean, as well as much of West Asia and the Middle East, had been politically incorporated into the imperial nexus.

**TABLE 37   THE INITIAL WAVE OF COLONIAL EXPANSION—
THE AMERICAS, 1496–1903 (22 STATES)**

Country	Date of Colonisation	Original Colonising Power	Date of Independence
Argentina	1516	Spain	1816
Bolivia	1530s	Spain	1825
Brazil	1532	Portugal	1822
Canada	1604	France & UK	1851–67*
Chile	1541	Spain	1818
Colombia	1538	Spain	1821/30†
Costa Rica	1563	Spain	1821
Cuba	1511	Spain	1899
Dominican Republic	1496	Spain	1844
Ecuador	1532	Spain	1821/30†
El Salvador	1525	Spain	1821/38‡
Guatemala	1524	Spain	1839
Haiti	1697	France	1804
Honduras	1523	Spain	1821/38‡
Mexico	1521	Spain	1821
Nicaragua	1552	Spain	1838
Panama	1513	Spain	1821/1903§
Paraguay	1537	Spain	1811
Peru	1533	Spain	1824
United States of America	1607	United Kingdom	1776
Uruguay	1624	Spain	1825
Venezuela	1567	Spain	1821/30†

*Canada was not fully freed from the supremacy of Acts of the United Kingdom parliament until 1931, while Newfoundland remained under British administration until 1949.

†These states formed part of a federation between 1821 and 1830.

‡Part of a federation of Central American States until 1838.

§Part of Colombia until 1903.

8.2 The Decolonisation Process: 1920–85

During the inter-war years, the first halting steps towards decolonisation were taken, beginning in the Middle East, where, in 1922, Britain, prompted by the outbreak of serious nationalist riots, transferred full sovereignty in Egypt. It continued to maintain, however, a strategic military presence to protect its Suez Canal interests. Then in 1932 and 1944 respectively, Britain and France, which had been administering the territories under League of Nations mandates since 1920, conceded independence to Iraq and Lebanon. During the same period the 'white settler' Dominions of Canada and South Africa, which had experienced a substantial measure of self-government from as early as the mid nineteenth century, became effectively fully independent with the passage of the Statute of Westminster, in 1931. Australia and New Zealand, the other two overseas Dominions, delayed accepting the terms of this legislation until 1942 and 1947 respectively. These cases were, however, the exceptions. Elsewhere, the 1920s and 1930s were a period of imperial consolidation, and even some further expansion by countries such as fascist Italy, militarist Japan and, finally, remotivated to imperial ambitions, Nazi Germany.

Matters changed dramatically after the Second World War, the process of decolonisation now gaining an unstoppable momentum. The initial factor behind this sea change was the strain imposed on ruler-colony relations by the war itself. For example, in the case of India, where a powerful nationalist movement had already won significant political concessions during the inter-war period, the British government was forced, in 1941, to offer the carrot of Dominion status as a means of securing civilian co-operation in the war effort. By the end of the war, however, the popular desire for full independence had become irresistible, with the result that full sovereignty, on a partitioned basis, was transferred in August 1947. The adjacent South Asian countries of Ceylon (later Sri Lanka) and Burma soon followed suit and were granted independence in 1948. The loss of the Indian sub-continent, the linchpin of the British imperial system, was to have far-reaching consequences, undermining its whole economic and strategic rationale.

Further to the east, in South-East Asia, the French and Dutch colonies in 'Indo-China' and the 'East Indies' had been even more seriously affected by the events of the Second World War.

Between 1942 and 1945 both had been occupied by Japan, which had sponsored new puppet nationalist governments. The re-imposition of European colonial rule proved highly unpopular and was fiercely resisted. Full autonomy was thus granted to the Dutch 'East Indies', now Indonesia, in 1949 and substantial semi-autonomy, within the 'French Union', to France's possessions in Indo-China: Vietnam, Cambodia and Laos. They achieved full independence some five years later after a prolonged military struggle.

During the later 1940s and mid 1950s, the British- and French-administered states of North Africa and the Middle East were also granted independence: Syria in 1946, Israel, formerly Palestine, in 1948, Libya in 1951, and Sudan, Morocco and Tunisia, all in 1956. In addition, the 'informal colony' of Oman regained full sovereignty in foreign and defence affairs in 1951. It was not, however, until the Suez and Algerian crises of 1956 and 1958 that the pace of decolonisation decisively quickened. Both events had profound repercussions on the internal political dynamics of the two leading imperial nations, and on their global outlooks, resulting in the accession to power of the realistic decolonisers, Macmillan, in the United Kingdom, and de Gaulle, in France. These crises also transformed public opinion, adding a new moral imperative to a decolonisation process which had now gained an irresistible momentum.

The first indication of this changed perspective was the granting of full independence to the British West African colony of Ghana, known as the Gold Coast, in March 1957, by the handing over of power to the popular radical socialist, Kwame Nkrumah. Ushering in what the British Prime Minister, Harold Macmillan, termed a 'wind of change' across black Africa, 33 African states secured independence during the next ten years. In one year alone, 1960, 17 new African states were proclaimed. Independence was also granted during this hectic decolonisation phase, between 1957 and 1968, to nine small island states in the Caribbean, Oceania and East Asia, as Tables 38 and 39 show.

The Relics of Empire

TABLE 38   THE CHANGING PACE OF DECOLONISATION BETWEEN 1920 AND 1985

(a) THE DISTRIBUTION OF FORMER COLONIAL POWERS IN RELATION TO THE COUNTRIES 'FREED' DURING THIS PERIOD

(Number of Countries 'Freed' per Year)*

Period	Under British Control	Under French Control	Under Dutch Control	Under Belgian Control	Under Portuguese Control	Under US Control	Under the Control of Other States	Total
1920–45	5	1	—	—	—	—	1	7
1946–50	6	1	1	—	—	2	2	12
1951–55	1.7	3.3	—	—	—	—	—	5
1956–60	7.5	16.5	—	1	—	—	—	25
1961–65	13	1	—	2	—	—	1	17
1966–70	9	—	—	—	—	—	2	11
1971–75	5	1	1	—	5	—	2	14
1976–80	7.5	1.5	—	—	—	—	—	9
1981–85	4	—	—	—	—	—	—	4
1920–85	58.7	25.3	2	3	5	2	8†	104
% Share of Total	56.4	24.3	1.9	2.9	4.8	1.9	7	100

*Where control was shared between two or more colonial powers, the number of 'freed' countries is shown proportionately.

†Australia 2, Spain 2, China 1, New Zealand 1, Soviet Union 1, Italy 1.

(b) REGIONAL DISTRIBUTION OF 'FREED' COUNTRIES, 1920–85

Period	Central & Southern Africa	Middle East & North Africa	Asia	Central America & the Caribbean	South America	North America	Oceania	Western Europe	Total
1920–45	2	3	—	—	—	1	1	—	7
1946–50	—	3	8	—	—	—	1	—	12
1951–55	—	2	3	—	—	—	—	—	5
1956–60	20	2	2	—	—	—	—	1	25
1961–65	10	2	1	2	—	—	1	1	17
1966–70	5	1	—	1	1	—	3	—	11
1971–75	6	4	—	2	1	—	1	—	14
1976–80	1	1	—	3	—	—	4	—	9
1981–85	—	—	1	3	—	—	—	—	4
1920–85	44	18	15	11	2	1	11	2	104
% Share of Total	42.3	17.3	14.4	10.6	1.9	1.0	10.6	1.9	100

173

By the early 1970s, Britain and France, playing the leading roles in the decolonisation process, as can be seen in Table 38, had divested themselves of their principal mainland-based colonial possessions. They were now left mainly in control of small island dependencies in the Caribbean and Oceania, as well as treaty protectorates in the Gulf region. These were slowly 'set free', at an average rate of two per annum, during the 1970s and early 1980s.

Ironically, the last substantial European overseas empire was maintained during this period by Portugal, the pioneer of European imperial expansion. Comprising Guinea-Bissau in West Africa, Angola in south-western Africa, Mozambique in south-eastern Africa and the off-shore islands of Cape Verde and Sao Tome and Principe, this empire covered more than 2,000 square kilometres and had been under Portuguese rule for almost 500 years. With its still untapped mineral wealth and energy reserves, it remained moreover of considerable economic value to the colonial power, attracting extensive white settlement during the 1960s. Portuguese rule and immigration were however becoming increasingly unpopular with the indigenous population, fuelling a powerful guerrilla resistance movement, which was supplied with modern arms by the Soviet Union's Cuban and East German proxies. This eventually had calamitous repercussions for the Lisbon regime, provoking a left-wing coup by disaffected army units which succeeded in bringing down the conservative dictatorship of Marcello Caetano, in April 1974. In the immediate wake of this power change Portugal's African dependencies pressed for independence. Unable and unwilling to resist, the new Lisbon regime hastily acceded to the requests, and within the space of 14 months, between October 1974 and November 1975, the empire was dissolved.

This left only one major land-based European overseas empire which dated back to the pre-1945 period, the one established by Tsarist Russia in Central Asia between 1846 and 1895. It was an empire inherited by the 'anti-colonial' Soviet Union, but which it had firmly consolidated and incorporated within its federal structure. Since the war the Soviet Union has also established an informal hegemony over its East European neighbours, although the economic relationship by no means corresponds to a classic imperial one in terms of the nature of the goods interchanged, the USSR exporting mineral and energy products westwards and importing manufactured items. Two other major contemporary communist powers, China, in the case of Tibet, and Vietnam, in relation to Laos and Cambodia, also maintain both formal and quasi-formal imperial control over neighbouring regions.

TABLE 39 THE DECOLONISATION PROCESS, 1922–85

Year of Decolonisation or Sovereignty Transfer	State	Last Colonising Power	Date of Establishment of Control
1922	Egypt	Britain	1882
1931	Canada*	Britain (France 1604–1763)	1713–63
1932	Iraq	Britain (M)	1920
1934	South Africa*	Britain (Netherlands 1652–1795)	1795–1824
1941	Ethiopia	Italy (MO)	1936
1942	Australia*	Britain	1788
1944	Lebanon	France (M)	1920
1946	Jordan	Britain (M)	1920
1946	Mongolia	China	1689
1946	Philippines	United States (Spain 1565–1898)	1899
1946	Syria	France (M)	1920
1947	India & Pakistan (incl E Pakistan, later Bangladesh)	Britain	late 18th–early 19th century
1947	New Zealand*	Britain	1840
1948	Burma	Britain (Japan 1942–45)	1824–86
1948	Israel (formerly W Palestine)	Britain (M)	1920
1948	North Korea	Soviet Union (OZ) (Japan 1910–45)	1945
1948	South Korea	United States (OZ) (Japan 1910–45)	1945
1948	Sri Lanka (Ceylon)	Britain	1798
1949	Indonesia	Netherlands (Japan 1942–45)	1595
1951	Libya	70% Britain & 30% France (Italy 1912–42)	1942
1951	Oman	Britain (MP)	1891
1954	Cambodia (Kampuchea)	France (Japan 1941–45)	1863
1954	Laos	France (Japan 1940–45)	1893
1954	Vietnam	France (Japan 1940–45)	1867–83
1956	Morocco	France	1912
1956	Sudan	Britain	1899
1956	Tunisia	France	1881
1957	Ghana	Britain	1901
1957	Malaysia	Britain (Portugal 1511–1641 Netherlands 1641–1795)	1795–1888
1957	Singapore	Britain	1819

Table 39—The Decolonisation Process, 1922–85 (contd)

Year of Decolonisation or Sovereignty Transfer	State	Last Colonising Power	Date of Establishment of Control
1958	Guinea	France	1898
1960	Benin	France	1892
1960	Burkina Faso (Upper Volta)	France	1896
1960	Cameroon	80% France & 20% Britain (M) (Germany 1884–1916)	1919
1960	Central African Republic	France	1901
1960	Chad	France	1900
1960	Congo	France	1910
1960	Cyprus	Britain	1914
1960	Gabon	France	1890
1960	Ivory Coast	France	1893
1960	Madagascar	France	1885
1960	Mali	France	1881–99
1960	Mauritania	France	1904–12
1960	Niger	France	1901
1960	Nigeria	Britain	1861–99
1960	Senegal	France	1659–1840
1960	Somalia	Britain (Italy 1908–41)	1884–86
1960	Togo	66% France & 34% Britain (M) (Germany 1884–1914)	1914
1960	Zaire	Belgium	1885–1908
1961	Kuwait	Britain (MP)	1899
1961	Sierra Leone	Britain	1808
1961	Tanzania	Britain (M) (Germany 1885–1914)	1914
1962	Algeria	France	1830
1962	Burundi	Belgium (M) (Germany 1895–1916)	1916
1962	Jamaica	Britain (Spain 1509–1655)	1655
1962	Rwanda	Belgium (M) (Germany 1894–1916)	1916
1962	Trinidad & Tobago	Britain (Spain 1552–1797)	1797–1820
1962	Uganda	Britain	1888
1962	Western Samoa	New Zealand (M) (Germany 1900–14)	1914
1963	Kenya	Britain (Portugal 1498–1699)	1888–95
1964	Malawi	Britain	1887–92
1964	Malta	Britain	1814

Table 39—The Decolonisation Process, 1922–85 (contd)

Year of Decolonisation or Sovereignty Transfer	State	Last Colonising Power	Date of Establishment of Control
1964	Zambia	Britain	1891–1923
1965	Gambia	Britain	1816
1965	Maldives	Britain	1887
1965	Rhodesia (later Zimbabwe: UDI)	Britain	1897–1923
1966	Barbados	Britain	1624
1966	Botswana	Britain	1885
1966	Guyana	Britain (Netherlands 1616–1796)	1796–1814
1966	Lesotho	Britain	1868
1967	South Yemen	Britain	1839
1968	Equatorial Guinea	Spain (Portugal 1494–1778 Spain 1778–81 Britain 1781–1843)	1858
1968	Mauritius	Britain (Netherlands 1598–1710 France 1715–1810)	1810
1968	Nauru	Australia (M) (Germany 1888–1914 Japan 1942–45)	1914
1968	Swaziland	Britain (South Africa 1894–1902)	1881
1970	Fiji	Britain	1874
1970	Tonga	Britain	1900
1971	Bahrain	Britain (MP)	1861
1971	Qatar	Britain (MP) (Also temp 1868–72)	1916
1971	United Arab Emirates	Britain (MP)	1892
1973	Bahamas	Britain	1629
1974	Grenada	Britain (France 1674–1762)	1762
1974	Guinea-Bissau	Portugal	late 15th C
1975	Angola	Portugal	1491
1975	Cape Verde	Portugal	late 15th C
1975	Comoros	France	1912
1975	Mozambique	Portugal	1505
1975	Papua New Guinea	Australia (50% German 1885–1914 50% Britain 1885–1901)	1901
1975	Sao Tome & Principe	Portugal	1471
1975	Spanish Sahara (Western Sahara)	Spain	1912
1975	Suriname	Netherlands (Britain 1651–67, 1779–1802 & 1804–16)	1816
1976	Seychelles	Britain (France 1768–1814)	1814
1977	Djibouti	France	1859

Table 39—The Decolonisation Process, 1922–85 (contd)

Year of Decolonisation or Sovereignty Transfer	State	Last Colonising Power	Date of Establishment of Control
1978	Dominica	Britain (France 1778–83)	1763
1978	Solomon Islands	Britain (50% Germany 1885–1900)	1885
1978	Tuvalu	Britain	1875
1979	Kiribati	Britain	1892
1979	St Lucia	Britain (France 1651–1803)	1803
1979	St Vincent & the Grenadines	Britain (France 1779–83)	1783
1980	Vanuatu	Britain & France (JT)	1887
1981	Antigua & Barbuda	Britain	1632
1981	Belize	Britain	17th C–1862
1983	St Kitts & Nevis	Britain	1623
1984	Brunei	Britain	1888

*The white-settler colonies of Australia, Canada, New Zealand and South Africa achieved 'de facto' independence from British control at earlier dates than those shown. The separate Australian states, for example, enjoyed a substantial measure of autonomy as early as 1855–68; the Canadian colonies between 1851 and 1867; and New Zealand and Cape Colony in South Africa as early as 1853. These powers were extended in 1907 when Dominion status was conferred. Not until the dates shown, however, following the passage of the Statute of Westminster, 1931, were these territories fully freed from the supremacy of Acts of the United Kingdom Parliament.

ABBREVIATIONS:
JT—Joint condominium
M—League of Nations 'mandate' territory
MO—Military Occupation
MP—Independent and fully internally self-governing, but dependent on British military protection, much in the same way as Bhutan and Nepal
OZ—Occupied Zone
UDI—Unilateral Declaration of Independence

8.3 Remaining Colonial Possessions and Dependencies in the World Today

There currently exist, on the broadest count, 50 regularly inhabited colonies or dependencies, controlled by twelve colonial powers. These territories and the controlling nations are set out, in an aggregated form, in Tables 40, 41 and 42 below. They total fewer than 21 million people, a number which corresponds to less than 0.5 per cent of the global population. This compares with the situation in 1945 when almost a third of the world's population lived in colonies or dependencies or with early 1960, when the proportion stood at 5 per cent.

Included in these figures are the four 'independent' Bantustans (black homelands) of South Africa, the occupied territories of Namibia and Western Sahara, the Chinese 'Autonomous Region' of Xizang (Tibet) and the French internal 'Collective Territory' of Corsica. These areas do not always feature in textbook dependency categories. They have, however, been included in this chapter so as to provide more detailed treatments of their political structures and histories. Taken together, they embrace 9 million people, a figure which is equivalent to 43 per cent of the colonies/dependencies total.

TABLE 40   CONTEMPORARY COLONIES, DEPENDENCIES AND
EXTERNAL TERRITORIES

Controlling State	Number of Inhabited Colonies, Dependencies & External Territories	Area ('000 km²)	Population (m) (1985)	% Share of Total Colonial Population
Australia	3	0.20	0.006	0.0
China	1	1221.60	1.970	9.4
Denmark	2	2177.00	0.099	0.5
France	10	128.27	1.958	9.4
Morocco	1	266.00	0.165	0.8
Netherlands	2	0.99	0.270	1.3
New Zealand	3	0.51	0.023	0.1
Norway	1	62.70	0.003	0.0
Portugal	1	0.02	0.300	1.4
South Africa	5	923.35	6.607	31.6
United Kingdom	13	15.69	5.814	27.8
United States of America	8	11.69	3.717	17.8
Total	50	4808.02	20.932	100.0

TABLE 41   REGIONAL DISTRIBUTION OF CONTEMPORARY
COLONIES, DEPENDENCIES AND
EXTERNAL TERRITORIES*

	Oceania	Central America & Caribbean	North America	South America	Asia	Middle East & North Africa	Western Europe	Central Southern Africa
Number	16	13	1	1	3	1	5	8
Area (km²)	26.74	104.28	0.24	12.17	1222.69	266.00	10.85	926.74
Population (m) 1985	0.677	4.526	0.006	0.002	7.726	0.165	0.522	7.240
% Share of Total Colonial Population	3.2	21.6	0.0	0.0	36.9	0.8	2.4	34.6

*Two dependencies, not shown, lie in the Arctic region.

TABLE 42   DISTRIBUTION OF CONTEMPORARY COLONIES,
DEPENDENCIES AND EXTERNAL TERRITORIES
BY POPULATION SIZE

Below 10,000	10,000– 50,000	50,000– 100,000	100,000– 500,000	500,000– 1,000,000	1,000,000– 6,000,000	Total
12	11	7	12	2	6	50

In the remaining colonial territories and dependencies, there
are fewer than 12 million people. Almost three-quarters of this
total is accounted for by the two British and United States
dependencies of Hong Kong and Puerto Rico, with, as Table 42
shows, the majority of the other 'colonial relics' being relatively
tiny communities, with populations below 100,000. The territories still held by six of the colonial powers, Australia, Denmark,
New Zealand, the Netherlands, Norway and Portugal, are
particularly small. Only two of them, controlled by the Netherlands and Portugal, are the residue of earlier, and greater,
empires. Instead, there are three powers, the United Kingdom,
the United States and France, which dominate any record of
contemporary colonial holdings, the territories still under their
control embracing, respectively, 48 per cent, 31 per cent and 16
per cent of the total colonial/dependency population. The
territories they administer are spread across the world. There is,
however, a notable numerical concentration in Oceania and the
Caribbean, many of the dependencies being island communities
too small to have an independent political and economic viability.
In a few cases, most notably in some of the French Oceania
dependencies, colonial control has been maintained against the
wishes of a significant proportion of the indigenous population.
In general, however, in the bulk of the other, still dependent,
territories no discernible independence movement is visible and
colony-coloniser cultural and economic ties remain strong.

8.4 Existing Colonies and Dependencies

The twelve countries which still have colonies or dependencies
are Australia, China, Denmark, France, Morocco, the Netherlands, New Zealand, Norway, Portugal, South Africa, the United
Kingdom and the United States of America. Most are overseas
from the 'mother country' but in the case of South Africa they

are within the territorial boundaries of the republic but, as part of the government's policy of racial segregation, deemed to be 'self-governing'.

8.4.1 Australia's Dependencies

Australia's dependencies are called External Territories, of which, as Table 43 shows, there are seven. Five of them are within the Oceania region, two of which are uninhabited. The other two, both uninhabited, are within Antarctica.

	TABLE 43	AUSTRALIA'S EXTERNAL TERRITORIES	
Name	Date of First Coming Under Australian Administration	Area (km²)	Population (1985)
The Ashmore & Cartier Islands	1931	3.0	Uninhabited
The Australian Antarctic Territory	1936	6,112.4	Uninhabited
Christmas Island	1958	155.4	3,000
Cocos (Keeling) Islands	1955	14.2	579
Coral Sea Islands	1969	2.0†	Uninhabited
Heard Island & McDonald Islands	1947	409.2	Uninhabited
Norfolk Island	1913	34.5	2,400
Total	—	6,730.7	5,979

†This figure is the area of land only. The islands cover 1 million km² of ocean.

8.4.2 China's Dependency

China's one dependency is Xizang, or Tibet. It is one of the country's five Autonomous Regions.

8.4.3 Denmark's Dependencies

Denmark has two dependencies, described as Outlying Territories. They are the Faroe Islands and Greenland.

TABLE 44   DANISH OUTLYING TERRITORIES

Name	Date of First Coming Under Danish Administration	Area (km²)	Population (1985)
Faroe Islands	1380	1,399	46,000
Greenland	985†	2,175,600‡	53,000
Total	—	2,176,999	99,000

†Formally in 1917.   ‡80 per cent covered by ice-cap.

8.4.4 France's Dependencies

The French dependencies consist of four Overseas Departments, two Overseas Collective Territories, four Overseas Territories and one Internal Collective Territory, as listed in Table 45.

TABLE 45   FRENCH OVERSEAS DEPARTMENTS, TERRITORIES AND COLLECTIVE TERRITORIES

Name	Date of First Coming Under French Administration	Area (km²)	Population (1985)	French National Assembly (NA) & Senate (S) Seats
OVERSEAS DEPARTMENTS				
French Guiana	1817	90,000	84,177	2 NA/1 S
Guadeloupe	1613	1,780	333,378	4 NA/2 S
Martinique	1635	1,100	328,281	4 NA/2 S
Réunion	1642	2,512	560,000	5 NA/3 S
OVERSEAS COLLECTIVE TERRITORIES				
Mayotte	1843	376	67,167	1 NA/1 S
Saint-Pierre et Miquelon	17thC/1816	242	6,041	1 NA/1 S
OVERSEAS TERRITORIES				
French Polynesia	1842	4,200	176,543	2 NA/1 S
French Southern & Antarctic Territories	—	7,567*	210†	—
New Caledonia	1853	19,103	145,368	2 NA/1 S
Wallis & Futuna Islands	1842	274	12,391	1 NA/1 S
Total	—	127,154	1,713,556	22 NA/13 S
INTERNAL COLLECTIVE TERRITORY				
Corsica	1768	8,600	244,600	—

*Excludes 500,000 km² of the uninhabited mainland of Antarctica.
†Scientific mission workers.

French Overseas Departments

Départements d'Outre-Mer

Overseas Departments, which form integral parts of the French Republic, have an administrative structure similar to that of the Departments of metropolitan France, although the former have their own Courts of Appeal. Prior to the decentralisation reforms of 1982, each Overseas Department was administered by a central government-appointed Prefect, assisted by a directly elected General Council and an indirectly elected Regional Council. After the reforms the Prefect was renamed Commissaire de la République (Government Commissioner), his formal executive power being transferred to the General Council, while the powers of the Regional Council, which was now directly elected, were considerably increased in the social, economic and cultural spheres. An earlier plan to merge the two councils into one was blocked by a decision of the French Constitutional Council in December 1982. French Overseas Departments also send representatives to the French national parliament and participate in French presidential elections.

French Overseas Collective Territories

Collectivités Territoriales

The status of a Collective Territory (CT) is intermediate between that of an Overseas Department and an Overseas Territory. CTs constitute integral parts of the French Republic. They are administered by an appointed government Commissioner (Commissaire de la République), who works with an elected General Council, and they send representatives to the French parliament and participate in French presidential elections.

French Overseas Territories

Territoires d'Outre-Mer

Overseas territories, which form integral parts of the French Republic, are administered by an appointed High Commissioner or Chief Administrator, who works with an elected Territorial Assembly or Congress. They send representatives to the French parliament and participate in French presidential elections.

183

French 'Internal' Collective Territory

This category is a special one, since Corsica is so close to France that it is not usually thought of as an 'overseas' dependency. Prior to the decentralisation reforms of 1982, it constituted the twenty-second region of metropolitan France. It was then, however, elevated to the status of a Collective Territory and given a parliament with substantive powers, thus distinguishing it from the other 21 regions of metropolitan France.

8.4.5 Morocco's Dependency

Western Sahara, which Morocco has controlled in one way or another since the early 1950s, is in strict legality an occupied territory, rather than a colony or dependency, and its future has yet to be finally determined.

8.4.6 Netherlands' Dependencies

The two dependencies of the Netherlands represent the residue of what was once a considerable colonial empire, dating back to the seventeenth century, which had been built up on the basis of trade and exploration.

8.4.7 New Zealand's Dependencies

New Zealand's four dependencies were acquired 'second hand', all having been British possessions but, after it had achieved full independence, being more sensibly administered by New Zealand than by the 'mother country'.

TABLE 46   NEW ZEALAND'S OVERSEAS (ASSOCIATED)
TERRITORIES

Name	Date of First Coming Under New Zealand Administration	Area (km²)	Population (1985)
Cook Islands	1901	238.0	17,754
Niue	1901	259.0	3,300
Ross Dependency	1923	414.4	Uninhabited
Tokelau	1925	10.0	1,600
Total	—	921.4	22,654

8.4.8 Norway's Dependencies

Norway has five dependencies, all situated in the Arctic or Antarctic regions, and most of them uninhabited. The one inhabited possession, Svalbard, was finally secured by an international treaty after its sovereignty had been contested by other European powers. It is now administered by a Norwegian governor (Sysselmann), resident in the capital, Longyearbyen (Long Year City).

TABLE 47   NORWEGIAN DEPENDENCIES

Name	Date of First Coming Under Norwegian Administration	Area (km²)	Population (1985)
Bouvet Island	1928	60	Uninhabited
Jan Mayen Island	1929	380	Uninhabited
Peter I Island	1931	180	Uninhabited
Queen Maud Land	1939	(Antarctic Territory)	Uninhabited
Svalbard	1920	62,700	3,480
Total	—	63,320	3,480

8.4.9 Portugal's Dependency

Portugal was once one of the world's leading colonial powers, and one of the last to concede sovereignty to the local communities. It now has only one possession, Macau, and that will pass to Chinese control at the end of the century.

8.4.10 South Africa's Dependencies

South Africa's dependencies consisted of four so-called 'independent' Bantu homelands and the state of Namibia. The homelands were created as part of the racial separatism policy (*apartheid*), and Namibia was, in international terms, illegally controlled by South Africa from 1946. Under the Angola peace accord, signed in 1988, Namibia achieved full independence in 1989.

TABLE 48   SOUTH AFRICAN DEPENDENCIES

Name	Date of Creation or of Coming Under South African Control	Area (km²)	Population (1985)
BANTU HOMELANDS			
Bophuthatswana	1977	44,000	1,736,000
Ciskei	1981	8,500	730,000
Transkei	1976	41,002	2,530,000
Venda	1979	6,677	460,000
Total	—	100,179	5,456,000

The Bantu Homelands

In accordance with the apartheid, or segregated development, policy adopted by the South African government since the late 1940s, separate 'homelands' (Bantustans) have been established for the black community. These are deemed by the government in Pretoria to be self-governing, the four 'homelands' of Bophuthatswana, Ciskei, Transkei and Venda being officially declared independent states, thus depriving their inhabitants of South African citizenship. However, since their economies remain heavily dependent on the white-dominated government of South Africa, in terms of both financial subsidies and employment opportunities, two-thirds of Bantustan adult males working outside the 'homelands', and their political structures restricted by the apartheid system, these territories have not been accorded international recognition. Each of the 'independent' Bantustans has a small armed force of its own, consisting of between 850 and 2,600 men. These forces have, however, been effectively penetrated and controlled by the South African military and secret services. More substantively, the Bantustans' constitutions include the provision for joint consultation and administration in both the defence and customs and excise spheres.

8.4.11 United Kingdom's Dependencies

The British Empire began when the first successful English colony was founded at Jamestown, Virginia, in 1607. At its peak, at the end of the nineteenth century, it covered a quarter of the world's land surface and included a quarter of its peoples. It had spread over every continent to every race. Now most of the greatest empire history ever recorded consists of separate, independently sovereign states, banded together as much by sentiment and history as other ties, within the Commonwealth. This global body is described, with other world and regional groupings, in Chapter 9. What is left of the British Empire today consists of a number of states which still enjoy the protection of the British Crown. They are set out in Table 49 below.

TABLE 49   UNITED KINGDOM CROWN DEPENDENCIES AND
BRITISH DEPENDENT TERRITORIES

Name	Date of First Coming Under British Administration	Area (km²)	Population (1985)
UK CROWN DEPENDENCIES			
Channel Islands	1066	196	138,144
Isle of Man	1765	572	64,282
BRITISH DEPENDENT TERRITORIES			
Anguilla	1650	96	7,109
Bermuda	1612	53	57,145
British Antarctic Territory	1908	1,710,000	Uninhabited*
British Indian Ocean Territory	1965	60	Uninhabited*
British Virgin Islands	1666	153	11,858
Cayman Islands	1670	259	22,000
Falkland Islands	1765/1833	12,173	1,919
Gibraltar	1704	6	29,166
Hong Kong	1841/1860	1,069	5,456,200
Montserrat	1632	102	12,000
Pitcairn Islands	1790	5	62
St Helena & Dependencies	1659	501	6,467
South Georgia & the South Sandwich Islands†	1775	3,903	Uninhabited*
Turks & Caicos Islands	1765	500	7,413
Total	—	1,729,648	5,813,765

*With the periodic exception of scientific or military personnel.

†Dependencies of the Falkland Islands between 1908 and 1985, with the Falklands' governor continuing to serve as their administrative Commissioner.

World Political Systems

United Kingdom Crown Dependencies
These islands, although lying offshore, do not form integral parts of the United Kingdom. Instead they are designated as Crown Dependencies, enjoying effective self-government in internal affairs.

British Dependent Territories
These are overseas territories enjoying a colonial status, with varying degrees of internal autonomy.

8.4.12 United States' Dependencies
The dependencies of the United States have been acquired in a variety of ways. Guam and Puerto Rico were ceded, as part of the spoils of victory after a war, the American Virgin Islands were purchased, others are held as Trust Territories, on behalf of the United Nations, and many, particularly in the Pacific, form part of what the US sees as its defensive shield. In total, including three military bases, there are eleven territories in the anti-imperialist United States' 'mini-empire'.

TABLE 50   UNITED STATES EXTERNAL TERRITORIES

Name	Date of First Coming Under United States Administration	Area (km²)	Population (1985)	Form of Government
FORMAL DEPENDENCIES				
American Samoa	1899/1922	199	35,000	NSGT
Guam	1899	541	125,000	SGT
Puerto Rico	1898	8,897	3,282,000	SGT
US Virgin Islands	1917	343	111,000	NSGT
FORMER UN PACIFIC TRUST TERRITORIES				
Marshall Islands	1947*	180	35,000	SIS
Federated States of Micronesia	1947	691	85,200	SIS
Northern Mariana Islands	1947*	471	19,635	CT
Republic of Palau	1947*	367	14,000	TT
MILITARY BASES				
Johnston Atoll	1898	3	327	MB
Midway Islands	1867	5	453	MB
Wake Islands	1898	8	302	MB
Total	—	11,705	3,707,917	—

KEY:
*	Held by US as trustees	SGT	Self-Governing Territory
CT	Commonwealth Territory	SIS	Semi-Independent State
MB	Military base	TT	United Nations Trust Territory
NSGT	Non-Self-Governing Territory		

8.5 Semi-Sovereign States

Within Western Europe there are five tiny principalities, city and theocratic states, Andorra, Liechtenstein, Monaco, San Marino, and the Vatican City. Although often listed as independent nations in general reference works, these 'micro-states' lack full and effective sovereignty, being both politically and militarily closely linked to, and heavily dependent on, much larger neighbours for their security. They have thus been termed semi-sovereign states and are treated separately, in a condensed format, below.

Survivors from an earlier era when continental Europe was composed of a patchwork quilt of small duchies, principalities and kingdoms, they have variously adapted to modern conditions by establishing themselves as picturesque and duty-free tourist centres or as prosperous tax havens. None of the states is formally a member of either the United Nations or European Community. Their current prosperity is, however, endangered by the shift towards a single European market in 1992. Table 51 sets out aggregated data for these five states.

TABLE 51   SEMI-SOVEREIGN STATES

State	Area (km²)	Population (m) (1985)	Date of State Establishment
Andorra	468	0.035	1278
Liechtenstein	160	0.027	1342
Monaco	2	0.027	1297
San Marino	61	0.022	c 301 AD
Vatican City State	0.4	0.001	1377/1929
Total	691.4	0.112	—

Recommended Reading

Cammack, P., Pool, D. and Tordoff, W., *Third World Politics: A Comparative Introduction*, Macmillan, 1988, Part 1.

Clapham, C., *Third World Politics: An Introduction*, Croom Helm, 1985, Ch 3.

Fieldhouse, D. K., *The Colonial Empires: A Comparative Study from the Eighteenth Century*, 2nd edn., Macmillan, 1982.

Holland, R. F., *European Decolonization, 1918–1981: An Introductory Survey*, Macmillan, 1985.

Taylor, P. J., *Political Geography: World Economy, Nation-State and Locality*, Longman, 1985, Ch 3.

Chapter 9

THE WORLD GROWS SMALLER: INTERNATIONAL CO-OPERATION

9.1 Competition or Co-operation?

Ever since the birth of the nation-state, its history has been one of competition, rather than co-operation. Nations have vied with each other in trade. One state has tried to impose its own religion on another. Empires have been created by strong countries dominating the weak. Where co-operation has occurred it has nearly always been on the basis of national self-interest and rarely in any altruistic, international sense.

International alliances have often been between major powers which have temporarily joined forces, in military terms, to attack, or defend themselves against, another opposing alliance. During the nineteenth and early twentieth centuries the political maps of the world were drawn and redrawn as a result of treaties and agreements reached by victors in international disputes, the provisions of which were then imposed on the vanquished.

The two most significant examples of such international decision-taking in the present century are the treaties signed at the end of the two World Wars, in 1918 and 1945. The terms of the Treaty of Versailles, of 1919, sowed the seeds of the Second World War, 20 years later, but its lessons were partially, but not entirely, learned by the statesmen who had the responsibility of trying to secure lasting world peace after 1945.

Since 1945 there has been a virtually unending succession of regional conflicts but a global war has so far been avoided and there are encouraging prospects of greater, rather than less, international co-operation. A number of factors have contributed to this new sense of urgency and optimism in international affairs.

First, improvements in the ease and speed of communication have made the world shrink in physical terms.

Second, the complexities of production and distribution have resulted in international co-operation on a scale hitherto unknown, resulting in the growth of multi-national, rather than national, corporations.

Third, there has been a growing realisation that the economies of the major nation-states cannot be seen as discrete, separate entities, but are so intermeshed that the success or failure of one has its impact on the others.

Fourth, there has been a recognition in the years since 1945 that it is in the interests of the advanced world to assist the economic and social progress of the underdeveloped world by financial and technical means.

Fifth, the possibility of a nuclear holocaust has persuaded the major powers to step back from the brink of another global war.

The sixth, and ultimately the most significant factor in the long term, is the increasing recognition of the fragility of the world's ecology, in other words, the 'green factor'.

Seventh, and last, have been the recent encouraging moves towards more pluralistic and democratic political systems in many states, including, of course, the major changes which are taking place within the Soviet bloc and the likely effects of these changes on its relations with other nations in the world.

There are encouraging signs, therefore, that in the years ahead, running into the twenty-first century, international co-operation, rather than competition, is likely to be the prevalent force. It would be unwise, however, to be over optimistic. Political attitudes can quickly change and a regime favouring positive co-operation can easily be replaced by one based on negative self-interest. Nevertheless, there is already a widespread, and sometimes complex, array of global and regional schemes of co-operation already in being, some more successful than others, and those which have already proved their worth might well provide the foundation for yet greater future collaboration.

9.2 Global Co-operation: the United Nations Organisation

The United Nations (UN) originated from a conference held at Dumbarton Oaks, Washington DC, between the Second World War allies, the Soviet Union, the United Kingdom and the United States, at the end of September and the beginning of October, 1944. The name United Nations was devised by Franklin Roosevelt and was first used in the Declaration by United Nations, on 1 January 1942, when representatives of 26 nations pledged their governments to continue fighting the Axis powers of Germany, Italy and Japan. Its forerunner was the League of Nations which had been established after the First World War but had failed to fulfil its early promise and had eventually been abandoned by the United States.

The Dumbarton Oaks conference produced a set of proposals which were put before a conference held at San Francisco on 25–26 June 1945 and, after certain amendments had been agreed, a Charter was signed by 50 of the 51 founder members, on 26 June 1945. Poland, although a founder member, did not sign it at the time but at a later date. The United Nations officially came into being on 24 October 1945, which is now celebrated annually as United Nations Day. Membership is open to all peace-loving nations and currently stands at 159. The names of member states and the dates of their admission are shown in Table 52 below.

TABLE 52   UNITED NATIONS MEMBERSHIP

Country	Year of Admission	% Contribution to UN Budget†	Country	Year of Admission	% Contribution to UN Budget†
Afghanistan	1946	0.01	Cape Verde	1975	0.01
Albania	1955	0.01	Central African	1960	0.01
Algeria	1962	0.14	Republic*		
Angola	1976	0.01	Chad	1960	0.01
Antigua &	1981	0.01	*Chile	1945	0.07
Barbuda			*China, People's	1945	0.79
*Argentina	1945	0.62	Republic§		
*Australia	1945	1.66	*Colombia	1945	0.13
Austria	1955	0.74	Comoros	1975	0.01
Bahamas	1973	0.01	Congo	1960	0.01
Bahrain	1971	0.02	*Costa Rica	1945	0.02
Bangladesh	1974	0.02	Côte d'Ivoire	1960	0.02
Barbados	1966	0.01	*Cuba	1945	0.09
*Belgium	1945	1.18	Cyprus	1960	0.02
Belize	1981	0.01	*Czechoslovakia	1945	0.70
Benin	1960	0.01	*Denmark	1945	0.72
Bhutan	1971	0.01	Djibouti	1977	0.01
*Bolivia	1945	0.01	Dominica	1978	0.01
Botswana	1966	0.01	*Dominican	1945	0.03
*Brazil	1945	1.40	Republic		
Brunei	1984	0.04	*Ecuador	1945	0.03
Bulgaria	1955	0.16	*Egypt	1945	0.07
Burkina Faso	1960	0.01	*El Salvador	1945	0.01
Burma	1948	0.01	Equatorial	1968	0.01
Burundi	1962	0.01	Guinea		
*Byelorussian	1945	0.34	*Ethiopia	1945	0.01
SSR‡			Fiji	1970	0.01
Cambodia	1955	0.01	Finland	1955	0.50
Cameroon	1960	0.01	*France	1945	6.37
*Canada	1945	3.06	Gabon	1960	0.03

Table 52—United Nations Membership (contd)

Country	Year of Admission	% Contribution to UN Budget†	Country	Year of Admission	% Contribution to UN Budget†
The Gambia	1965	0.01	*Nicaragua	1945	0.01
Germany	1973	9.59	Niger	1960	0.01
Ghana	1957	0.01	Nigeria	1960	0.19
*Greece	1945	0.44	*Norway	1945	0.54
Grenada	1974	0.01	Oman	1971	0.02
*Guatemala	1945	0.02	Pakistan	1947	0.06
Guinea	1958	0.01	*Panama	1945	0.02
Guinea-Bissau	1974	0.01	Papua New Guinea	1975	0.01
Guyana	1966	0.01			
*Haiti	1945	0.01	*Paraguay	1945	0.02
*Honduras	1945	0.01	*Peru	1945	0.07
Hungary	1955	0.22	*Philippines	1945	0.10
Iceland	1946	0.03	*Poland	1945	0.64
*India	1945	0.35	Portugal	1955	0.18
Indonesia	1950	0.14	Qatar	1971	0.04
*Iran	1945	0.63	Romania	1955	0.19
*Iraq	1945	0.12	Rwanda	1962	0.01
Ireland	1955	0.18	St Kitts-Nevis	1983	0.01
Israel	1949	0.22			
Italy	1955	3.79	St Lucia	1979	0.01
Jamaica	1962	0.02	St Vincent & the Grenadines	1980	0.01
Japan	1956	10.84			
Jordan	1955	0.01	Sao Tome & Principe	1975	0.01
Kenya	1963	0.01			
Kuwait	1963	0.29	*Saudi Arabia	1945	0.97
Laos	1955	0.01	Senegal	1960	0.01
*Lebanon	1945	0.01	Seychelles	1976	0.01
Lesotho	1966	0.01	Sierra Leone	1961	0.01
*Liberia	1945	0.01	Singapore	1965	0.10
Libya	1955	0.26	Solomon Islands	1978	0.01
*Luxembourg	1945	0.05	Somalia	1960	0.01
Madagascar	1960	0.01	*South Africa	1945	0.44
Malawi	1964	0.01	Spain	1955	2.03
Malaysia	1957	0.10	Sri Lanka	1955	0.01
Maldives	1965	0.01	Sudan	1956	0.01
Mali	1960	0.01	Suriname	1975	0.01
Malta	1964	0.01	Swaziland	1968	0.01
Mauritania	1961	0.01	Sweden	1946	1.25
Mauritius	1968	0.01	*Syria	1945	0.04
*Mexico	1945	0.89	Tanzania	1961	0.01
Mongolia	1961	0.01	Thailand	1946	0.09
Morocco	1956	0.05	Togo	1960	0.01
Mozambique	1975	0.01	Trinidad & Tobago	1962	0.04
Namibia	1990	—	Tunisia	1956	0.03
Nepal	1955	0.01	*Turkey	1945	0.34
*Netherlands	1945	1.74	Uganda	1962	0.01
*New Zealand	1945	0.24	*Ukrainian SSR‡	1945	1.28

Table 52—United Nations Membership (contd)

Country	Year of Admission	% Contribution to UN Budget†	Country	Year of Admission	% Contribution to UN Budget†
*USSR	1945	10.20	Vietnam	1977	0.01
United Arab Emirates	1971	0.18	Western Samoa	1976	0.01
			Yemeni Republic	1990	0.02
*United Kingdom	1945	4.86			
*USA	1945	25.00	*Yugoslavia	1945	0.46
*Uruguay	1945	0.04	Zaire	1960	0.01
Vanuatu	1981	0.01	Zambia	1964	0.01
*Venezuela	1945	0.60	Zimbabwe	1980	0.02

*Founder members.

†These are assessments of percentage contributions to the UN budget for the years 1986, 1987 and 1988.

‡Byelorussian SSR and Ukrainian SSR are integral parts of the Soviet Union, and not independent countries, but they have separate UN membership.

§From 1945 until 1971 China was represented by the Republic of China, now Taiwan. Since 1971 the member has been the People's Republic of China.

The sovereign countries which are not UN members are: Andorra, Kiribati, North Korea, South Korea, Liechtenstein, Monaco, Nauru, San Marino, Switzerland, Taiwan, Tonga, Tuvalu and Vatican City.

The major declared aims of the United Nations are to maintain international peace and security and to develop international co-operation in economic, social, cultural and humanitarian problems, and, in pursuit of these aims, it has erected an impressive institutional structure of councils, commissions, committees and agencies, as well as the International Court of Justice. Some institutions, such as the International Court, are developments of earlier bodies from the days of the League of Nations and before. Others are new creations.

9.2.1 Principal UN Institutions

The principal UN institutions are the General Assembly, the Security Council, the Economic and Social Council, the Trusteeship Council, the International Court of Justice and the Secretariat. The permanent headquarters of the UN are in the United Nations Plaza, Lower Manhattan, New York City, USA, and meetings of its main organisations are usually held there, but they can be, and sometimes are, arranged elsewhere. The International Court of Justice is based in the Hague, in the Netherlands, and several other UN bodies have their head-quarters in Geneva, Switzerland, though that country is not a member of the UN.

General Assembly

The General Assembly is the UN parliament of which all nations are members, each having one vote. It meets once a year at the UN headquarters in New York in a session beginning on the third Tuesday in September, running through to the end of the year, or into the following year if business demands it. It can be summoned to meet at any time in an emergency session and there have been over 25 such special sessions convened to date, covering such topics as peace-keeping in Lebanon, the Suez crisis, Afghanistan, Namibia and the economic situation in Africa. Below the main Assembly is a network of committees.

General Assembly decisions are made by simple majority voting but on certain important matters, such as the condemnation of an act by one of its members, a two-thirds majority is needed. If the Assembly feels that the Security Council is not fulfilling its chief responsibility of maintaining international peace satisfactorily it may take it upon itself to consider a special case, such as an act of aggression, or some other breach of the peace, and recommend action to be taken.

Security Council

The Security Council has a membership of 15. There are five permanent members, China, France, the Soviet Union, the United Kingdom and the United States, and the other ten are elected for two-year terms by a two-thirds vote of the General Assembly. Retiring members are not eligible for immediate re-election. Any UN member may be invited to participate in its discussions if they bear on its interests, but only the permanent or elected members are permitted to vote.

In pursuit of its responsibility for maintaining peace and security, the Council may call on armed forces, and other assistance, from member states. It has at its disposal a Military Staff Committee composed of the chiefs of staff of the countries of the permanent members. The presidency of the Security Council is held for a month at a time by a representative of a member-state, in English language alphabetical order. The

Council has two standing committees: a Committee of Experts and a Committee on the Admission of New Members.

Economic and Social Council
The Economic and Social Council is responsible for economic, social, cultural, educational, health and related matters. It has 54 members, again elected by a two-thirds majority vote of the General Assembly. The Council has a large number of functional and regional commissions and committees working for it as well as hundreds of non-governmental agencies which have been granted consultative status.

Trusteeship Council
The Trusteeship Council is responsible for overseeing the administration of the UN Trust Territories. Its members are China, France, the Soviet Union, the United Kingdom and the United States. It holds one regular session per year but can meet in special sessions if required.

International Court of Justice
The International Court of Justice is composed of independent judges, elected by the Security Council and the General Assembly, sitting separately, and are chosen because of their competence in international law, irrespective of their nationalities. There are 15 judges, no two of whom can be nationals of the same state. Candidates for election are nominated by national groups, and once elected, serve for nine years, and may be immediately re-elected. Only states, not individuals, may be parties to cases before the Court.

The Court is based at the Hague, in the Netherlands, but may sit elsewhere if it chooses. It sits permanently, except for customary judicial vacations. Its official languages are English and French and it reaches its decisions by a majority of votes of the judges present. The President and Vice-President are elected by the Court itself and serve three-year terms. If the votes of judges are equal, the President has a casting vote. Judgements are final, and there is no appeal.

The Court's membership, until 1991, will include judges from the following countries: Algeria, Argentina, China, France, Guyana, India, Italy, Japan, Nigeria, Norway, Poland, Senegal, the Soviet Union, the United Kingdom and the United States.

Secretariat

The United Nations Secretariat consists of the Secretary-General, who is its chief administrator, Under and Assistant Secretaries-General and a large international staff. The Secretary-General is appointed by the General Assembly for a five-year term, which can be renewed. The present occupant, Javier Perez de Cuellar, of Peru, was originally appointed in 1981 and had his term renewed, until 1991, in 1986. The first holder of the post was Trygve Lie, of Norway (1946–53), and subsequent holders, before Javier Perez, were Dag Hammarskjöld, of Sweden (1953–61), U Thant, of Burma (1961–71) and Kurt Waldheim, of Austria (1972–81).

Being UN Secretary-General is clearly an important, and prestigious, job, but experience shows that its significance depends very much on what a particular holder makes of it. Trygve Lie and Dag Hammarskjöld, who was killed in an air crash while on UN business, became well known, even to ordinary people, as did U Thant, to a lesser degree. Hammarskjöld was awarded the Nobel Peace Prize for his efforts. Kurt Waldheim, on the other hand, made a less marked impression. The present Secretary-General, Perez de Cuellar, has not only become a popular, and even famous, international figure, but by the success of his practical efforts to secure peace in troubled parts of the world has done much to revive the standing of the United Nations, which had fallen to a low ebb during the 1970s.

9.2.2 UN Specialised Agencies

Working directly within the United Nations organisational structure are a number of specialised agencies, financed by the UN through contributions from the 159 member states. The scale of these contributions, which are based broadly on the principle of the 'ability to pay', are shown in Table 52. The specialised agencies operate mainly from the headquarters in New York or from Geneva, in Switzerland.

International Atomic Energy Agency (IAEA)

The IAEA was established in 1957 to accelerate and enlarge the contribution of atomic energy to peace, health and prosperity throughout the world and to prevent its diversion from peaceful purposes to military ends. It negotiates safeguard agreements with individual states, 164 of such agreements currently being in force. The Agency is based in Vienna, Austria.

International Labour Organisation (ILO)

The ILO pre-dates the United Nations itself, having been originally created in 1919 by the League of Nations. It is an inter-governmental agency with a tripartite membership of government, employer and worker representatives. It seeks to improve labour conditions, raise living standards and promote productive employment through international co-operation. It became part of the UN in 1946 and in 1969 was awarded the Nobel Peace Prize. It conducts research into industrial relations and publishes Conventions and Recommendations. If a member-state ratifies a Convention it automatically agrees to bring its national law into line with it. Recommendations are not binding but all member-states have a duty to consider them.

The ILO consists of the International Labour Conference, which is its supreme deliberative body and meets annually in Geneva, and the International Labour Office, which is also in Geneva. In 1960 it established the International Institute for Labour Studies and, in 1965, a training institution in Turin, Italy, particularly concerned with the needs of developing countries. Indeed, much of the ILO's work in recent years has been orientated towards the less developed parts of the world.

Food and Agriculture Organisation (FAO)

A conference in May 1943 at Hot Springs, Virginia, USA, provided the stimulus for the setting up of the FAO in October 1945. Its aims are to raise levels of nutrition and standards of living, to improve the production and distribution of food and agricultural products, to improve the living standards of rural populations and, by accomplishing all these things, to eliminate hunger. Like many other UN agencies, the FAO tends to concentrate its efforts on the less developed parts of the world. It provides guidance on food production and can sponsor relief in emergency situations. It operates from Rome, in Italy.

United Nations Educational, Scientific and Cultural Organisation (UNESCO)

UNESCO came into being in 1946 as a result of a conference held in London, in November 1945, under the auspices of the United Kingdom and French governments. Its main purpose is to promote peace by encouraging international collaboration in education, science and culture. It attempts to do this through teacher-training programmes, the promotion of research and the dissemination of information. Its headquarters are in Paris.

World Health Organisation (WHO)
The World Health Organisation was founded in April 1948. Its main purpose is to assist all peoples in attaining the highest possible levels of health. It does this by research, teaching and guidance through recommended standards of behaviour. For example, it has, in recent years, sponsored greater international co-operation in the prevention and treatment of AIDS and related infections. It has also made recommendations on the quality control of drugs. Its headquarters are in Geneva and it has regional offices in the Congo, Egypt, Denmark, the Philippines, India and the United States.

International Monetary Fund (IMF)
The inspiration for the IMF was the International Monetary Conference held at Bretton Woods, in New Hampshire, USA, in July 1944, under the chairmanship of the US Secretary to the Treasury, Henry Morgenthau. Conference delegates, including the British delegation led by the celebrated economist Lord Keynes, agreed to the creation of a Fund which would promote international monetary co-operation, establish a multilateral system of payments, and help remedy any serious disequilibrium in a country's balance of payments by allowing it to draw on the resources of the Fund while it took measures to correct the imbalance. The IMF was established on 27 December 1945, as an independent organisation, and began operating on 1 March 1947. It became associated with the UN, on the basis of mutual co-operation, on 15 November 1947.

IMF members subscribe to the Fund on a quota basis, determined by their ability to pay at the time of membership. The Fund itself can also borrow to supplement its resources. Most of the assistance given by the IMF is, naturally, to less developed countries but occasionally it is asked to provide temporary help to economically advanced nations. The United Kingdom, for example, had recourse to the Fund in 1976. When it is asked to assist, the IMF's representatives invariably impose conditions to ensure that the problem to be dealt with is only a temporary phenomenon. The headquarters of the IMF are in Washington, DC, and it also has offices in Paris and Geneva.

International Bank for Reconstruction and Development (IBRD)
The IBRD is often popularly known as the 'World Bank'. Like the IMF, it too, was conceived at the Bretton Woods Conference. Its

purpose is to provide funds and technical assistance to help the economies of the poorer nations of the world. It obtains its own funds from capital paid in by member countries, from loans, from repayments, from income from investments and from fees paid for the technical services it provides. Its headquarters are in Washington, DC, where it also has a staff college, called the Economic Development Institute.

International Development Association (IDA)
The IDA is an agency of the World Bank, concentrating on providing financial and technical help to the poorest nations. It came into existence in 1960.

International Finance Corporation (IFC)
The IFC is affiliated to the World Bank and was established in 1956. It makes investments in companies, to assist their development, or provides loans. It is particularly active in helping new ventures or providing finance for established companies which wish to expand or diversify.

International Civil Aviation Organisation (ICAO)
The idea for creating the ICAO came from a conference on international aviation held in Chicago at the end of 1944. The Organisation was formally set up on 4 April 1947. Its objects are to establish technical standards for safety and efficiency in air navigation, to develop regional plans for ground facilities and services for civil aviation, and generally to provide advice to airline operators. Its headquarters are in Montreal, Canada.

Universal Postal Union (UPU)
The UPU was established as long ago as 1875 when the Universal Postal Convention was adopted at a Congress in Berne, Switzerland. It was originally called the General Postal Union and changed its name in 1878. Currently, 158 countries are members. Its aim is to improve the standards of postal services and promote international co-operation. Its headquarters are in Berne.

International Telecommunication Union (ITU)
The aims of the ITU are to maintain and extend international co-operation in improving telecommunications of all kinds by promoting the development of technical skills and services and harmonising national activities. It originated in 1932 when, at a

conference in Madrid, it was decided to merge the Telegraph Convention of 1865 and the Radiotelegraph Convention of 1906 into a single Convention and functioning organisation. The ITU's headquarters are in Geneva.

World Meteorological Organisation (WMO)

The Directors of the International Meteorological Organisation, which had been set up in 1873, met in Washington, DC, in 1947 and adopted a convention establishing the WMO. Its main aim is to facilitate worldwide co-operation in the creation and maintenance of a network of stations for making meteorological observations and to ensure the rapid exchange of information. The headquarters of the WMO are in Geneva.

International Maritime Organisation (IMO)

Known until 1982 as the Inter-Governmental Maritime Consultative Organisation (IMCO), the IMO was established as a specialised agency of the UN in 1948. It began to operate effectively in 1959. Its aim is to promote co-operation between governments on technical matters affecting merchant shipping, with the object of improving safety at sea. It formulates and publishes conventions and regulations and has its headquarters in London.

General Agreement on Tariffs and Trade (GATT)

The GATT was negotiated in 1947 and came into force on 1 January 1948. It is a multilateral treaty which lays down a common code of conduct in international trade. It also provides a forum for discussion of trade problems, with the object of reducing trade barriers. Part of its purpose is to help less developed countries through its 'most-favoured-nation' treatment, which gives protection to 'infant economies'. The GATT is administered from Geneva.

World Intellectual Property Organisation (WIPO)

WIPO was established in 1967 as the successor to the United International Bureau for the Protection of Intellectual Property. It became a UN specialised agency in 1974. Its primary purpose is to protect intellectual property, which, in general, means patents and trade marks, throughout the world. It is based in Geneva.

International Fund for Agricultural Development (IFAD)
IFAD is the result of a recommendation of a World Food Conference which was held in 1974. The Fund began operating in 1977 with the prime object of mobilising funds for agricultural and rural development. IFAD has its headquarters in Rome.

Office of the United Nations Disaster Relief Co-ordinator (UNDRO)
UNDRO was established in 1972 to mobilise and co-ordinate international emergency relief for disaster-hit areas. It provides a 24-hour monitoring service for monitoring natural disasters and emergencies and has four main functions: relief co-ordination; disaster preparedness; disaster prevention and the provision of information and communications facilities. It operates from Geneva.

United Nations Centre for Human Settlements (UNCHS) (Habitat)
UNCHS was founded in 1978 to service the intergovernmental Commission on Human Settlements. It is particularly concerned with the shelter needs of disadvantaged people, and provides functional services in the areas of planning, construction, land and infrastructure development and finance. It is based at Nairobi, Kenya.

United Nations Children's Fund (UNICEF)
It was originally established, in 1946, as the UN International Children's Emergency Fund, to meet the emergency needs of children in post-war Europe and China. Four years later its mandate was changed to cater for children in developing countries and in 1953 it became a permanent part of the UN system. Its headquarters are in New York and it has major offices in Switzerland, Kenya, Jordan, the Ivory Coast, Colombia, Thailand, India, Australia and Japan.

United Nations Conference on Trade and Development (UNCTAD)
UNCTAD was established in 1964 to promote international trade, particularly in developing countries. It reports directly to the UN General Assembly and its headquarters are in Geneva.

United Nations Environment Programme (UNEP)
UNEP was set up in 1972 following a UN Conference on the Human Environment, which was held in Stockholm, Sweden. Its main functions are to monitor closely the state of the environment

and to promote environmentally sound developments throughout the world. As the public becomes increasingly concerned about threats to the environment so the role of UNEP is likely to be enhanced. Its headquarters are in Nairobi, Kenya.

United Nations Fund for Population Activities (UNFPA)
UNFPA was created in 1967 as the Trust Fund for Population Activities. It became a Fund of the General Assembly in 1972 and operates under the umbrella of UNDP. Its function is to provide finance for projects in the areas of family planning, education, and research into population trends and the needs of particular age groups. Its headquarters are in New York.

United Nations High Commissioner for Refugees (UNHCR)
The office of the High Commissioner was established in Geneva, Switzerland, in 1951 to provide international protection for refugees and to find solutions to their problems. The High Commissioner's services are available to anyone who has a well-founded fear of being persecuted for reason of race, religion, nationality or political opinion, and, being outside the country of his or her nationality, is fearful of returning to it. Its headquarters are in Geneva.

United Nations Institute for Training and Research (UNITAR)
UNITAR was established in 1965 to improve the effectiveness of the UN through training and research. It is based at UN headquarters in New York.

United Nations Research Institute for Social Development (UNRISD)
The Institute was founded in 1964, in Geneva, Switzerland, to conduct research, on behalf of the UN, into problems and policies of social and economic development.

World Food Council (WFC)
The WFC was established in 1974 on the recommendation of the World Food Conference, held earlier that year. Its purpose is to stimulate national and international policies and programmes for alleviating world hunger and to improve the global food system. Its headquarters are in Rome.

World Food Programme (WFP)
WFP was set up in 1963 as the food aid arm of the UN. It aims to

improve economic and social development through food aid and to provide emergency relief. Like the WFC, it, too, is based in Rome.

United Nations Industrial Development Organisation (UNIDO)
UNIDO assists developing countries with financial, technical and marketing advice and helps formulate development policies.

United Nations Relief and Works Agency for Palestinian Refugees in the Near East (UNRWA)
UNRWA provides health, education and training services for refugees displaced by the Arab-Israeli wars and carries out emergency relief programmes.

9.2.3 UN Development Programme (UNDP)

The UN Development Programme was begun in 1961 to promote higher standards of living in the poorer nations and to try to remedy the economic imbalance between industrialised and developing countries. The first part of the Programme was the UN Development Decade (1961-70) which aimed at achieving a 5 per cent growth rate in developing countries. It was not successful, however, growth rates of only 2 per cent being achieved. The UN General Assembly therefore decided to support another Development Decade, in the 1970s, this time with a growth target of 6 per cent. This was to be achieved mainly by the economically advanced countries providing financial and technical help and by adopting economic and commercial policies favouring the less advanced nations.

Currently UNDP has 48 members: 15 of them advanced industrial countries, including the United States; six of them communist states, including the Soviet Union and China; and the rest in varying stages of development. UNDP is headed by an administrator who is responsible to a Governing Council of the 48 member-states, and has its headquarters in New York. It operates through a number of regional commissions which are described later in this chapter.

9.3 Global Co-operation: the Commonwealth

The Commonwealth is the modern successor to the British

Empire. It is formally described as a free association of sovereign independent states. It has no charter, treaty or constitution, the association being based on a desire for co-operation, consultation and mutual assistance. The current membership of 48 countries is shown in Table 53.

It has been described as the world's most unusual 'club' and is a singularly British institution, still echoing the United Kingdom's imperial past. In recent years, however, the influence of the 'mother country' has shown signs of weakening and there are indications that the leadership might be taken up by states such as India, Canada or Australia. Nevertheless, it is inconceivable that the Commonwealth could survive in anything like its present form without Britain's active participation.

As the successor to the British Empire, the Commonwealth was initially based on allegiance to a common Crown. However, in 1949, India chose to become a republic and from that date the modern Commonwealth was born, based now on the concept of the British Monarch being a symbol, rather than a legal entity, and, as such, the 'Head of the Commonwealth'. At the moment 17 of the 48 members accept the British Queen as their head of state, 26 are republics and five have their own local monarchs.

Heads of government of Commonwealth countries meet every two years to discuss international affairs and areas of co-operation. Finance ministers meet annually and other ministers as and when the need arises. The Commonwealth is not a mutual defence organisation and most member countries are committed to regional treaties.

The Commonwealth is frequently criticised because it has little real power to influence world affairs. Its supporters would argue that its strength lies in its voluntary nature and that, should the need arise, its potentially immense resources could be put to considerable use. Britain's role as the originator of the Commonwealth would be crucial in this respect but as it is increasingly committed to its role in Europe its place within the wider organisation is put into some doubt.

The Commonwealth is serviced by a Secretariat which is based in Marlborough House, Pall Mall, London and headed by the Secretary-General, Chief Emeka Anyaoka of Nigeria. The Secretariat's staff come from a wide range of member countries which also pay its operating costs.

The World Grows Smaller: International Co-operation

TABLE 53   THE COMMONWEALTH

State	Date of Independence	Type	Head of state
Antigua & Barbuda	1981	Lib Dem	British Monarch
Australia	1901	Lib Dem	British Monarch
Bahamas	1973	Lib Dem	British Monarch
Bangladesh	1971	Emgt Dem	President
Barbados	1966	Lib Dem	British Monarch
Belize	1981	Lib Dem	British Monarch
Botswana	1966	Lib Dem	President
Brunei	1984	Absolutist	Local Monarch
Canada	1867	Lib Dem	British Monarch
Cyprus	1960	Emgt Dem	President
Dominica	1978	Lib Dem	President
Gambia	1965	Lib Dem	President
Ghana	1957	Mil Auth	President
Grenada	1974	Emgt Dem	British Monarch
Guyana	1966	Emgt Dem	President
India	1947	Lib Dem	President
Jamaica	1962	Lib Dem	British Monarch
Kenya	1963	Auth Nat	President
Kiribati	1979	Lib Dem	President
Lesotho	1966	Mil Auth	Local Monarch
Malawi	1964	Auth Nat	President
Malaysia	1957	Lib Dem	Local Monarch
Maldives	1965	Auth Nat	President
Malta	1964	Lib Dem	President
Mauritius	1968	Lib Dem	British Monarch
Nauru	1968	Lib Dem	President
New Zealand	1947	Lib Dem	British Monarch
Nigeria	1960	Mil Auth	President
Pakistan	1947	Emgt Dem	President
Papua New Guinea	1975	Lib Dem	British Monarch
St Kitts-Nevis	1983	Lib Dem	British Monarch
St Lucia	1979	Lib Dem	British Monarch
St Vincent and the Grenadines	1979	Lib Dem	British Monarch
Seychelles	1976	Nat Soc	President
Sierra Leone	1961	Auth Nat	President
Singapore	1963	Lib Dem	President
Solomon Islands	1978	Lib Dem	British Monarch
Sri Lanka	1948	Lib Dem	President
Swaziland	1968	Absolutist	Local Monarch
Tanzania	1961	Nat Soc	President
Tonga	1970	Absolutist	Local Monarch
Trinidad & Tobago	1962	Lib Dem	President
Tuvalu	1978	Lib Dem	British Monarch
Uganda	1962	Emgt Dem	President

Table 53—The Commonwealth (contd)

State	Date of Independence	Type	Head of state
United Kingdom	—	Lib Dem	British Monarch
Vanuatu	1980	Lib Dem	President
Western Samoa	1962	Lib Dem	President
Zambia	1964	Nat Soc	President
Zimbabwe	1980	Nat Soc	President

NOTE:

Fiji was a Commonwealth member, with the British Queen as head of state, until 1987 when a military coup overthrew the elected government and declared the country a republic. Its future within the Commonwealth has yet to be decided. South Africa withdrew from membership in 1961, following criticisms of its racial policies. Pakistan withdrew in 1972, after Bangladesh had been admitted, but reapplied for membership in 1989.

ABBREVIATIONS:

State type: Auth Nat—Authoritarian Nationalist
Emgt Dem—Emergent Democratic
Lib Dem—Liberal Democratic
Nat Soc—Nationalistic Socialist

9.4 Global Co-operation: the World Council of Churches (WCC)

The World Council of Churches was established on 23 August 1945 in Amsterdam by an assembly representing 147 Churches from 44 countries. By 1988 the number of member-Churches had risen to more than 300 and the number of countries to over 100. The Council's aim is to bring together diverse Christian movements. The Assembly, which is the supreme governing body, convenes every seven or eight years to frame policy. A 150-member central committee meets annually and a 22-member Executive Committee twice a year. The headquarters of the WCC is in Geneva.

9.5 Global Co-operation; the Helsinki Accord

The Helsinki Accord was signed by 35 countries, including the Soviet Union and the United States, at the end of a Conference on Security and Co-operation in Europe (CSCE), in 1985. The signatories consisted of the NATO and Warsaw Pact states plus 13 neutral and non-aligned nations. The Accord registered agreement on co-operation in a number of areas such as security, economics, science, technology and human rights, and is generally regarded as marking an end to the Cold War between the Eastern bloc and the West.

9.6 Global Co-operation: Organisation of the Islamic Conference (OIC)

The OIC was established in May 1971 following a conference of Muslim heads of state in Rabat, Morocco, in 1969, and meetings of Islamic foreign ministers in Jeddah and Karachi, in 1970. The main aim of the Organisation is to promote Islamic solidarity and its members include 45 countries in the Middle East and North Africa, Central and Southern Africa and Asia, plus the Palestine Liberation Organisation (PLO). The OIC has its headquarters and secretariat in Jeddah, Saudi Arabia.

9.7 Global Co-operation: the Antarctic Treaty

The Antarctic Treaty was signed in 1961 by 18 countries which conduct scientific research in Antarctica. They include five Western European states, two in East Europe, including the Soviet Union, and four in South America, plus Australia, China, India, Japan, New Zealand, South Africa, the United Kingdom and the United States. The main objective of the Treaty is to prevent military activity in the region.

9.8 Inter-regional Co-operation

there are several examples of mutual co-operation between countries which cut across the regions we have defined for the purposes of this book. Some are sponsored by the United Nations, some by the European Community, some are the products of Commonwealth membership, some have been inspired by the United States, on the basis of enlightened self-interest, and some are examples of self-help by states in different, but physically adjacent, regions. One is an example of co-operation between Eastern and Western Europe.

9.8.1 UN Inter-regional Groups

Within the United Nations organisation there are four Commissions intended to promote co-operation between under- or less-developed countries in various parts of the world.

Economic Commission for Africa (ECA)
ECA was founded by the UN in 1958. South Africa was originally a member but was suspended in 1963. The total current membership consists of 51 states, representing virtually the whole of north, central and southern Africa. The purpose of the Commission is to promote and facilitate concerted action for the economic and social development of Africa, and it seeks to achieve this through research and the co-ordination of national policies.

Some examples of ECA's work are the establishment of the African Development Bank, in 1964, the creation of the Association of African Central Banks, in 1969, and the setting up of the Centre for Mineral Resources Development at Dar es Salaam, Tanzania, in 1976. It is a regular publisher, largely of statistical material, and operates from Addis Ababa, in Ethiopia.

Economic and Social Commission for Asia and the Pacific (ESCAP)
ESCAP was founded in 1947 as the Economic Commission for Asia and the Far East and changed its name in 1974. It currently has 35 full members and 10 associate members. Most of the full members are states in Asia or Oceania but other countries with interests in the regions, such as the United States, the United Kingdom, the Soviet Union, France and the Netherlands also enjoy full membership. The associate members are the smaller countries of Asia and Oceania.

ESCAP performs a broadly similar role in Asia and Oceania to that of ECA in Africa. It, too, has had success in setting up a number of ventures and organisations, such as the Asian and Pacific Centre for Development Administration, the Asian Clearing Union and the Asian Development Bank. ESCAP has its headquarters in Bangkok, Thailand.

Economic Commission for Europe (ECE)
ECE was also founded in 1947 and includes all Western and Eastern European countries except East Germany and Switzerland, the latter participating in a consultative capacity. The United States is also a consultant. The Commission's role is similar to that of the other UN inter-regional commissions. It is based in Geneva, Switzerland.

Economic Commission for Latin America (ECLA)
ECLA was founded in 1948 with the object of raising the level of economic activity in Latin America, which, in the Commission's terms, includes what we have defined as Central America and the Caribbean and South America. It currently has 33 members. They include, in addition to the countries of the regions, Canada, France, the Netherlands, the United Kingdom and the United States. Its headquarters are in Santiago, Chile.

Economic Commission for Western Asia (ECWA)
ECWA was founded in 1973 and operates from the UN building in Amman, Jordan. It was set up to provide a better service for countries previously catered for by the UN Economic and Social Office in Beirut. Its objects are broadly similar to those of ECLA. The use of the term Western Asia in its title is a little misleading since its 14 members, which include 13 countries plus the Palestine Liberation Organisation (PLO), are all situated in the Middle East or North or Central Africa.

9.8.2 Commonwealth-inspired Inter-regional Co-operation

Colombo Plan for Co-operative Economic Development in South and South East Asia (CP)
The purpose of the Colombo Plan is to facilitate and co-ordinate economic and social development in the countries of South and South East Asia. It was set up in 1951 within the framework of the Commonwealth, on the initiative of the Commonwealth foreign ministers. Since that date it has lost much of its original Commonwealth character and most of its current members are not in the Commonwealth. They now total 26 and include, as well as the original Commonwealth states in the region, Cambodia, Canada, Iran, Japan, South Korea, the United Kingdom and the United States. The Plan's headquarters are in Colombo, Sri Lanka.

9.8.3 Western European-inspired Inter-regional Co-operation

The Lomé Convention
The Lomé Convention takes its name from Lomé, the capital of Togo, in Africa, where in 1975 the members of the European Community (EC) agreed to assist the less developed countries of

Africa, the Caribbean and the Pacific by establishing a 'special relationship' with them so that they would not suffer unduly from the tariff policies of the EC. The countries concerned include virtually all those in Central and Southern Africa, excluding South Africa, most of those in the Caribbean and the smaller states of Oceania. Under the terms of the Convention the EC guarantees the 66 states who benefit from it virtually unrestricted access for their agricultural products to Western European markets. The 66 ACP (Asia- Caribbean- Pacific) countries, as they are called, may, for their part, operate varying degrees of protection of their own economies. Aid to the ACP nations is also provided from the European Development Fund. The original Convention was renewed in 1979 and 1985.

Organisation for Economic Co-operation and Development (OECD)
OECD is the expanded successor to the Organisation for European Economic Co-operation (OEEC) which was set up in 1948, at the instigation of the United States, to promote economic recovery in post-war Europe. The OECD now has 24 members, including the twelve EC countries, the six EFTA nations plus Australia, Canada, Japan, New Zealand, Turkey and the United States. In its expanded form its object is to promote freer trade and to stimulate Western aid to undeveloped countries.

9.8.4 Eastern European-inspired Inter-regional Co-operation

Danube Commission
The Danube Commission is based on a Convention controlling navigation on the River Danube, which was signed in Belgrade in 1948. The Convention confirmed that navigation from Ulm, in West Germany, to the Black Sea was open and free to people, shipping and merchandise of all states. The Commission, which ensures the Convention's enforcement, is composed of representatives of all the seven states through which the Danube flows. The Commission represents an almost unique example of co-operation between Eastern and Western European countries. Its headquarters are in Budapest, Hungary.

Council for Mutual Economic Assistance (CMEA or COMECON)
CMEA was established in 1948 with the object of promoting improved co-operation and socialist economic integration, with particular emphasis on assistance to less industrialised countries.

Its founder members were the Soviet Union, Bulgaria, Czechoslovakia, Hungary, Poland and Romania. Albania joined in 1949, but ceased participating in 1961. Countries which later joined were East Germany, 1950, Mongolia, 1962, Cuba, 1972, and Vietnam, in 1978. Afghanistan, Angola, Ethiopia, Laos, Mexico, Mozambique, Nicaragua and North Yemen are observers, rather than full members. In March 1990 its members agreed to abandon the organisation's two most important functions, multilateral co-operation and the co-ordination of economic planning, future trade relations to be on a bilateral basis. This amounted to a significant reduction in COMECON's status as a co-operative body.

9.8.5 Middle East-inspired Inter-regional Co-operation

Organisation of the Petroleum Exporting Countries (OPEC)
OPEC was formed in Baghdad, Iraq, in 1960 with five founder members: Iran, Iraq, Kuwait, Saudi Arabia and Venezuela. Its membership later expanded to include, in addition to the founder members: Algeria, Ecuador, Gabon, Indonesia, Libya, Nigeria, Qatar, and the United Arab Emirates. Its primary object is to co-ordinate the production and pricing policies of the major oil producers so as to guarantee stable prices and stable incomes, based on what the Organisation would claim to be a fair return on capital invested. Despite its existence, oil prices on world markets have often been as much affected by changing economic conditions as by OPEC policies. Since coming into existence, however, it has done much to eliminate the worst examples of the exploitation of primary producing countries by the industrialised nations. The headquarters of OPEC are in Vienna, Austria.

9.8.6 Central and Southern African-inspired Inter-regional Co-operation

Organisation of African Unity (OAU)
The OAU was founded in Addis Ababa in 1963, on the initiative of Emperor Haile Selassie of Ethiopia. Its main aims are to further African unity and solidarity; to co-ordinate political, economic, cultural, health, scientific and defence policies; and to eliminate colonialism in Africa. There are 50 countries in membership, representing virtually the whole of Central and Southern Africa, excluding South Africa, plus Algeria, Egypt and Tunisia, in North

Africa and the Middle East. The Organisation is headed by an Assembly of Heads of State and Government which meets annually and a Council of Ministers which meets twice a year. It also has a secretariat which is based in Addis Ababa, Ethiopia. The elected post of OAU chairman is a highly prestigious position in Black Africa.

9.8.7 United States-inspired Inter-regional Co-operation

As a leading industrial and military power, and as part of a strategy of mutual defence and economic development, the United States has promoted or sponsored a number of inter-regional groups with Western European and North, Central and South American countries. Military groups are described later, in paragraph 9.10.

Organisation of American States (OAS)
The OAS was founded in 1948 by a charter signed at Bogota, Colombia by representatives of 30 states in Central and South America and the Caribbean, plus the United States. Its declared purpose is: 'To achieve an order of peace and justice, promoting solidarity among the American states; to defend their sovereignty, their territorial integrity and their independence; to establish new objectives and standards for the promotion of the economic, social and cultural development of the peoples of the Hemisphere, and to speed the process of economic integration.'

The origins of the OAS go back as far as 1826 when the First Congress of American States was convened by the Venezuelan revolutionary leader, Simon Bolivar. Since those early days the Organisation has become more formally institutionalised, with a General Assembly, a Permanent Council, consisting of one representative from each of the member states, and numerous other councils, commissions and committees. Although its objectives are clearly, and impressively, stated in its charter, and although its structure appears to be democratically representative of all the signatories, the OAS has become increasingly dominated by the United States, so that, in pursuit of the Monroe Doctrine, enunciated in 1823, which effectively warned off European powers from America's 'back yard', what is regarded as 'good' for the American continent is mostly what is seen as good in the eyes of the United States, and this is an attitude often resented by many of the OAS members. It is interesting to note that, although several signatories are Commonwealth members, Canada, which, of course, shares the American continent, is not one of them. The headquarters of the OAS are in Washington, DC.

Inter-American Development Bank (IADB)
The IADB was founded in 1959, at the instigation of the OAS, to finance economic and social development, particularly in the less wealthy regions of the Americas. Its membership is wider than that of the OAS and includes Austria, Belgium, Canada, Denmark, Finland, France, West Germany, Israel, Italy, Japan, the Netherlands, Spain, Sweden, Switzerland and the United Kingdom, as well as the states of Central and Southern America, the Caribbean and the United States. Its headquarters are in Washington, DC.

9.8.8 Latin American-inspired Inter-regional Co-operation

In an effort to avoid over-dependence on the United States, and to come out of the shadow of living in its 'back yard', some Latin American states have sought to pursue a more independent economic policy line.

Andean Group (AG)
The Andean Group, also known as the Andean Sub-Regional Group, or the Andean Common Market, was established under the Cartagena Agreement of 1969 to promote the balanced and harmonious development of member countries through economic integration. The members include Bolivia, Colombia, Ecuador, Peru and Venezuela, with Mexico as a working partner since 1972. Chile was originally a member but left in 1976. The Group aims to harmonise policies on tariffs, the protection of intellectual property, such as patents and trade marks, and industrial and commercial development. Its institutions include a parliament and an executive commission and its headquarters are in Lima, Peru.

Latin American Economic System (Sistema Economico Latinoamericana) (LAES/SELA)
LAES was founded by treaty in 1975 as the successor to the Latin American Economic Co-ordination Commission. The aim was to have a purely Latin American organisation, with neither of the

developed nations of North America involved. Its purpose is to create and promote multi-national enterprises in the region, to provide markets and to stimulate technological and scientific co-operation. LAES has 26 members, covering Central and South America and parts of the Caribbean, and its headquarters are in Caracas, Venezuela.

Latin American Integration Association (Asociacion Latino-Americana de Integration) (ALADI)
ALADI was formed in 1980 to replace the Latin American Free Trade Association (LAFTA). LAFTA encouraged trade by across-the-board tariff cuts while ALADI takes into account the different stages of economic development that individual countries have reached and so applies tariff reductions preferentially. The ultimate aim of the Association is to create a fully fledged common market. It has eleven member countries, all of them, except Mexico, in South America. ALADI is based in Montevideo, Uruguay.

9.8.9 Asian-inspired Inter-regional Co-operation

Asian Development Bank (ADB)
The idea of an Asian Development Bank, to foster economic growth by promoting investment and providing loan capital, was first mooted at a Conference of Asian Economic Planners in New Delhi in 1961. The ADB came into existence in 1966 and now has 28 regional members, representing most of the major countries in Asia and Oceania plus 14 non-regional members, including the United States, Canada and most of the states of Western Europe. The Bank's headquarters are in Manila, in the Philippines.

Association of South East Asian Nations (ASEAN)
ASEAN is an association of non-communist states in South East Asia which was formed in 1967 by the signing of the Bangkok Declaration. The declared aims of the Association are to foster economic and social progress and cultural development and to promote peace in the region. Its members include Indonesia, Malaysia, Philippines, Singapore and Thailand, and its headquarters are in Jakarta, Indonesia.

Asian and Pacific Council (ASPAC)
ASPAC was founded in 1966 to encourage cultural and economic

co-operation throughout the regions. Its members include Australia, Japan, South Korea, Malaysia, New Zealand, Philippines, Taiwan and Thailand.

9.8.10 Oceania-inspired inter-regional Co-operation

Rarotonga Treaty
The Rarotonga Treaty was signed in 1987 by Australia, Fiji, Indonesia, New Zealand and the Soviet Union. It formally declares the South Pacific a nuclear-free zone.

9.9 Intra-regional Co-operation

There are many examples of co-operation within our defined regions. Some are primarily political and cultural, such as the Arab League, many are essentially economic and at least one, the Palestine Liberation Organisation, is intended to be an instrument for creating a new, independent state. To try to include every intra-regional group currently operating would be a virtually impossible task but those which are described below are seen as the most significant as well as being representative of their respective regions.

9.9.1 Western Europe

The Second World War had a profound and lasting effect on the countries of Western Europe, whether they were the 'victors' or the 'vanquished'. Above all else, it convinced the leading politicians of the countries which had experienced the war at first hand, France, Belgium, Luxembourg, the Netherlands, West Germany and Italy, that they should take steps to set up institutions which would make another war in Europe virtually impossible. The first practical step towards this end, in 1951, was the establishment of the European Coal and Steel Community (ECSC), in the belief that if the leading nations shared coal and steel-making facilities, which were seen as the basic raw materials of war, future conflicts would be avoided. The ECSC was followed, in 1955, by the European Investment Fund and then, two years later, in 1957, by the momentous signing in Rome of the treaties which established the European Economic Community (EEC) and the European Atomic Energy Community (Euratom). The preamble to the treaty setting up the EEC declared its objectives as: the establishment of the foundations of an even closer union among European peoples; the improvement of their working and living conditions; the progressive abolition of restrictions on trade between them; and the development of the prosperity of overseas countries. The founder members of the EEC were France, West Germany, Italy, Netherlands, Belgium and Luxembourg. The United Kingdom, Ireland and Denmark were admitted into membership in 1973, Greece in 1981 and Spain and Portugal in 1985. The twelve countries of the ECSC, Euratom and EEC, now known collectively as the European Community (EC), have combined populations of more than 320 million, about 100 million more than the United States and 50 million more than the Soviet Union. Other forms of Western European co-operation are important but all are overshadowed by the sheer size, economic and political importance and the enormous potential of the Community.

European Community (EC)

The main EC institutions are the Commission, the Council of Ministers, the Committee of Permanent Representatives (COR-EPER), the Economic and Social Committee, the Court of Justice and the European Parliament.

The Commission is at the heart of the Community's decision-taking process. It consists of 17 members: two each from France, West Germany, Italy, Spain and the United Kingdom, and one each from Belgium, Denmark, Greece, Ireland, Luxembourg, Netherlands and Portugal. The members are nominated by each state for a four-year, renewable, term of office. One member is chosen as President for a two-year, renewable, term. The post of President is a mixture of head of government and head of the European civil service, and a highly respected appointment.

Although the commissioners are drawn proportionately from member-states, each takes an oath on appointment not to promote national interests. They head a comparatively large bureaucracy, with 20 directorates-general, each responsible for a particular department. Critics often complain about the size of the EC permanent machine but it is not unduly large in relation to the scope of its activities and its workload.

The Council of Ministers is the supreme decision-taking body and consists of one minister from each of the twelve member-countries. The actual representatives vary according to the subject matter under discussion. If it is economic policy it will be the finance ministers, if it is agricultural policy, the agriculture ministers. It is the foreign ministers, however, who tend to be the most active. The Presidency of the Council changes hands at six-monthly intervals, each member-state taking its turn.

The Committee of Permanent Representatives (COREPER) is a subsidiary body of officials, often called 'ambassadors', who act on behalf of the Council. The members of COREPER are senior civil servants who have been temporarily released by member-states to work for the Community.

The **Economic and Social Committee** is a consultative body consisting of representatives from member-countries and covering a wide range of interests. For example, they may include employers, members of labour unions, professional people, farmers and so on. The Committee advises the Council of Ministers and the Commission.

Membership of the **European Parliament** is determined by the populations of member-states. The total number of seats is 518, of which France, West Germany, Italy and the United Kingdom have 81 each, Spain has 60, the Netherlands 25, Belgium, Greece and Portugal 24 each, Denmark 16, Ireland 15 and Luxembourg six. Members are elected for five-year terms in large Euro-constituencies. Voting is by a system of proportional representation in all countries except the United Kingdom. The party composition of the European parliament, following the 1989 elections, is shown in Table 54.

Policy is made and carried out within the Community in the following way. The Commission makes a particular proposal which will have first been worked on by one of the 20 directorates. The proposal is sent to the Council of Ministers who will initially pass it to COREPER for further examination. At the same time it will be passed to the European Parliament for consideration. The Parliament's role is still mainly consultative, but it does have power to reject the Community budget and to dismiss the Commission if it has good grounds for doing so.

TABLE 54   PARTY COMPOSITION OF THE EUROPEAN PARLIAMENT: 1989

Belgium	24 seats:	Socialists	(8)
		Independent Socialist	(1)
		Christian Democrats	(7)
		Liberals	(4)
		Voksunie	(1)
		Ecology	(3)

Table 54—Party Composition of the European Parliament: 1989 (contd)

Denmark	16 seats:	Conservatives	(2)
		Anti-EC	(4)
		Social Democrats	(4)
		Liberals	(3)
		Socialist People's Party	(1)
		Centre	(2)
France	81 seats:	Socialists and Left Radicals	(22)
		Gaullists and Liberals (Combined Right)	(26)
		Communists	(7)
		National Front	(10)
		Centre	(7)
West Germany	81 seats:	Christian Democrats/CSU	(32)
		Social Democrats	(31)
		Greens	(8)
		Free Democrats	(4)
		Republicans	(6)
Greece	24 seats:	Socialists	(9)
		New Democracy	(10)
		Communist	(4)
		Democratic Renewal	(1)
Ireland	15 seats:	Fianna Fail	(6)
		Fine Gael	(4)
		Independents	(2)
		Other parties	(3)
Italy	81 seats:	Communists	(22)
		Christian Democrats	(27)
		Socialists	(12)
		Liberals/Republicans	(4)
		MSI	(4)
		Social Democrats	(2)
		Greens	(5)
		Other parties	(5)
Luxembourg	6 seats:	Christian Democrats	(3)
		Socialists	(2)
		Liberal	(1)
Netherlands	25 seats:	Labour	(8)
		Christian Democrats	(10)
		Liberals	(3)
		GPU	(1)
		Other parties	(3)
Portugal	24 seats:	Social Democrats	(9)
		Socialists	(8)
		Centre	(3)
		Communists	(4)
Spain	60 seats:	Socialists	(27)
		People's Party	(15)
		Centre	(5)
		Communists	(4)
		Regional Lists	(7)
		Other parties	(2)

Table 54—Party Composition of the European Parliament: 1989 (contd)

United Kingdom	81 seats:	Conservative	(32)
		Labour	(45)
		SNP	(1)
		DUP	(1)
		OUP	(1)
		SDLP	(1)
Main party groupings:	Left (260)	—Socialists	(180)
		Communists	(41)
		Rainbow (Greens)	(39)
	Centre (203)	—Christian Democrats	(123)
		Independents	(16)
		Liberals	(44)
		Gaullists (with Fianna Fail and SNP)	(20)
	Right (55)	—Conservatives	(34)
		Right	(21)

After examination by COREPER, with the addition of any views of the European Parliament, the proposal is formally considered by the Council of Ministers who decide whether or not action should be taken. Voting in the Council is weighted in favour of the larger member-states, but votes are taken only rarely. Either there is a unanimous decision or if one or more of the ministers argue that the policy would be against national interests the proposal is likely to be shelved. Once the Council has agreed a policy proposal it is passed back to the Commission for implementation.

A policy decision can take one of two forms. It can be a regulation or a directive. Both are legally binding but a regulation applies to all member-states whereas a directive relates only to one or more specific countries.

Decision-taking within the Community is only partially democratic and only marginally accountable to the electorates of the member-states but, as the European Parliament becomes more firmly established, on broad European party lines, its influence, and eventually its powers, will undoubtedly grow.

The European Court of Justice consists of judges and officials appointed by the member-states. Its task is to ensure that the Community treaties are fairly observed and that regulations and directives are followed. The Court can make rulings but it has no powers of its own to enforce them. This is the responsibility of the individual member-states in their own national courts.

The Commission, the Council of Ministers and COREPER are

based in Brussels, the European Parliament meets in Luxembourg or Strasbourg, France, and the European Court of Justice sits in Luxembourg.

The Community has not yet achieved its aim of creating a single European market, when all internal barriers to trade will be removed, but all member-states have agreed that this will happen at the end of 1992. The broader objective of agreeing common economic and foreign policies, eventually leading, as pro-Europeans would hope, to political union, is a much longer-term aim and some heads of government would clearly like to postpone its implementation indefinitely, or even summarily abandon it.

Council of Europe

The Council of Europe was established in Strasbourg, France, in 1949 to secure 'a greater measure of unity between the European countries', by the discussion of common interests and problems and the discovery of new methods and areas of co-operation. Its membership is wider than that of the EC, including Austria, Cyprus, Iceland, Malta, Norway, Sweden, Switzerland and Turkey, as well as ten of the twelve European Community members, the absentees being Spain and Portugal. It has a Consultative Assembly which meets annually and a Standing Committee to represent it when it is not in session.

The Council has been particularly active, and effective, in the field of human rights. Under the European Convention of Human Rights of 1950, it established the **European Commission of Human Rights**, also based in Strasbourg, to investigate complaints by states or individuals. The findings of the Commission are then considered by the **European Court of Human Rights**, in Strasbourg, which was formed in 1959. Many European states have recognised the jurisdiction of the Court by making its decisions binding nationally, and this has resulted in ordinary citizens who feel aggrieved by judgements in their own national courts taking their cases, over the heads of governments, to Strasbourg.

Benelux

A customs union, to encourage trade between the three countries, was established by Belgium, the Netherlands and Luxembourg in 1948 and was called Benelux. It was later overtaken by the creation of the European Economic Community, and the other bodies which now form part of the EC, but in 1960, by the Benelux

Treaty, the economic union of the three states was formalised. This made them, in economic terms, a single unit, while retaining their political independence and their obligations to the European Community. The organisation has a Committee of Ministers, comprising at least three ministers from each state, which meets every two months, and a Council of Economic Union which is an umbrella body with the task of co-ordinating the work of the many Benelux committees. The head of the permanent Secretariat, which is based in Brussels, is always Dutch and is assisted by two deputies from the other member-states.

European Free Trade Association (EFTA)

EFTA was originally established in 1960 as a free trade alternative to the European Economic Community. Its original members included Austria, Denmark, Norway, Portugal, Sweden and the United Kingdom. Finland became an associate member in 1961 and Iceland a full member in 1970. It soon became clear that EFTA could never supplant the EEC and several members began to apply for entry into the Community. Denmark and the United Kingdom left in 1972 and Portugal in 1985. EFTA now comprises Austria, Finland, Iceland, Norway, Sweden and Switzerland. It is essentially an economic association whereby import duties between the six member countries have been abolished. It has its headquarters in Geneva, Switzerland.

Nordic Council

The Nordic Council was founded in 1953 by Denmark, Iceland, Norway and Sweden as a consultative body to increase co-operation between them. They were joined in 1956 by Finland. Council members are elected by the parliaments of member-states, 16 each from Denmark, Finland, Norway and Sweden and five from Iceland. The Council does not have permanent headquarters.

European Space Agency (ESA)

ESA is an organisation to promote space research and technology for peaceful purposes. It was originally founded in 1975 and reorganised in 1980. Its members include Belgium, Denmark, France, West Germany, Ireland, Italy, the Netherlands, Spain, Sweden, Switzerland and the United Kingdom. ESA has developed a number of scientific and communication satellites, as well as the Ariane rocket.

223

European Organisation for Nuclear Research (Centre D'Etudes de Recherches Nucléaires) (CERN)
CERN was established in 1954 as a co-operative venture for research into nuclear energy for peaceful purposes. It members include twelve major West European countries who provide teams of scientists to work together at laboratories at Meyrin, near Geneva, Switzerland.

9.9.2 Middle East and North Africa

Co-operation within the Middle East and North Africa is generally founded on a strong, and proud, sense of a common identity among Arabs, even though the region contains many races and religions. Israel has been excluded from virtually all the co-operative groups and associations and this has undoubtedly contributed to its sense of isolation and suspicions about neighbouring states. Future harmony in the region depends greatly on whether the degree of mutual trust which has been established between Egypt and Israel can be extended to the wider Arab world.

The League of Arab States (Al Jamia al Arabiyyah or Arab League)
The Arab League was founded in 1945 largely on the initiative of Egypt. It now has 21 members, comprising all the states of the Middle East and North Africa except Israel. Its declared purpose is 'to strengthen the close ties linking sovereign Arab States and to co-ordinate their policies and activities and direct them to the common good of the Arab countries'. It also acts as a mediator in disputes between Arab nations. The main body in the League is the Council, which includes representatives of all the member-states and usually meets twice a year, in March and September. Attached to it are 16 specialist, functional committees. There are a large number of agencies and bureaux operating within the League. The headquarters, with its secretariat, used to be in Cairo but when Egypt signed a peace treaty, in 1979, with Israel it was suspended from membership and the headquarters moved to Tunis. Egypt has since been re-admitted.

Arab Common Market
The Arab Common Market, providing for the abolition of customs duties on agricultural products, and reductions on other items, came into effect in 1965. Membership was open to all Arab

League states but only Egypt, Iraq, Jordan and Syria have signed the treaty which set it up.

Arab Monetary Fund (AMF)

The AMF was established in 1976 by 20 Arab states plus the PLO to provide a mechanism for promoting greater stability in exchange rates and to co-ordinate Arab economic and monetary policies. The Fund's headquarters are in Abu Dhabi, in the United Arab Emirates. It operates mainly by regulating petro-dollars within the Arab community to make it less dependent on the West for the handling of its surplus funds.

Organisation of Arab Petroleum Exporting Countries (OAPEC)

OAPEC was established in 1968 to safeguard the interests of its members and to encourage co-operation in economic activity within the petroleum industry. It currently has ten members: Algeria, Bahrain, Egypt, Iraq, Kuwait, Libya, Qatar, Saudi Arabia, Syria and the United Arab Emirates. Its headquarters are in Kuwait.

Palestine Liberation Organisation (PLO)

The PLO was founded in 1964 with the objective of bringing about an independent state of Palestine. It contains a number of factions, the most important being al-Fatah, which is led by Yasser Arafat. To achieve its main aim it has pursued a mixed policy of diplomacy and guerrilla activity. Although it has been long recognised in the Arab world as a legitimate political body, its reputation among Western nations has not been good, some political leaders referring to it as a terrorist organisation. However, in 1988, when Jordan announced its decision to relinquish its responsibility for the Israeli-occupied West Bank, and Arafat later publicly accepted the right of Israel to exist as an independent state, world opinion changed and the PLO became an organisation which could be regarded as the legitimate representative of the Palestinians and, therefore, could provide the nucleus of an independent Palestine state.

Co-operative Council for the Arab States of the Gulf (CCASG)

The CCASG was established in 1981 as an exclusively Arab organisation for promoting peace in the Persian Gulf area. Its declared purpose is 'to bring about integration, co-ordination and co-operation in economic, social, defence and political affairs among Arab Gulf states'. Its members include Bahrain, Kuwait, Oman, Qatar, Saudi Arabia and the United Arab Emirates and its headquarters are at Riyadh, Saudi Arabia.

9.9.3 Central and Southern Africa

Co-operation in economic and social matters in Central and Southern Africa has been fragmentary and sometimes duplicated. Because of this, it has been less effective than in some other regions of the world. This lack of cohesion has arisen partly because of the sheer size of the continent and the poor communications within it, particularly between the east and west coasts, and partly because of tribal and language differences. Co-operation is, therefore, frequently sub-regional and often influenced by the colonial histories of particular countries. Thus those states which used to form part of the French empire co-operate more naturally with other French-speaking countries whereas former British colonies tend to link with countries where English is the principal language.

Southern African Development Co-ordination Conference (SADCC)
SADCC was formed at its first conference in Arusha, Tanzania, in July 1979, when representatives of Angola, Botswana, Lesotho, Malawi, Mozambique, Swaziland, Tanzania, Zambia and Zimbabwe agreed to work more closely together to reduce their economic dependence on South Africa. Since then an organisation has been formed with its headquarters in Gabarone, Botswana. Annual meetings of heads of state and heads of government are held and SADCC ministers meet at least twice a year to formulate plans. The main areas that the organisation has targeted as in need of particular attention are transport and communications, energy and mining and industrial production, and a number of sector units have been set up to implement proposals.

Organisation Commune Africaine et Mauricienne (OCAM)
OCAM was founded in 1965 as the Organisation Commune Africaine et Malgache. This was itself a successor to the Union Africaine et Malgache de Co-opération Economique, which had operated between 1961 and 1965. In 1970 the name of Organisation Commune Africaine Malgache et Mauricienne was adopted but when Madagascar withdrew from the Organisation

in 1975 the present name was adopted. The full membership now includes Benin, Burkina Faso, Central African Republic, Ivory Coast, Niger, Rwanda, Senegal and Togo. The declared purpose of OCAM is to strengthen the solidarity and close ties between member-states and to raise living standards and co-ordinate economic policies. Through the Organisation, members share an airline, a merchant fleet and a common postal and communications system. The headquarters of OCAM are at Bangui in the Central African Republic.

Council of the Entente (CE)
The CE was set up in 1959 by four states, Benin, Burkina Faso, Ivory Coast and Niger, to strengthen economic links and promote industrial development. Togo joined in 1966 when a Mutual Aid and Loan Guarantee Fund was established. The headquarters of the Council are in Abidjan, Côte d'Ivoire.

Economic Community of West African States (ECOWAS)
ECOWAS was established in 1975, by the Treaty of Lagos, to promote economic co-operation and development. Its members include Benin, Burkina Faso, Cape Verde, Gambia, Ghana, Guinea, Guinea-Bissau, Ivory Coast, Liberia, Mali, Mauritania, Niger, Nigeria, Senegal, Sierra Leone and Togo. Its headquarters are in Lagos, Nigeria.

Preferential Trade Area for East and Southern Africa (PTA)
The PTA was established in 1981 with the object of increasing economic and commercial co-operation between member-states, harmonising tariffs and reducing trade barriers, with the eventual aim of creating a common market. The current members include Burundi, Comoros, Djibouti, Ethiopia, Kenya, Lesotho, Malawi, Mauritius, Rwanda, Somalia, Swaziland, Tanzania, Uganda, Zambia and Zimbabwe. The headquarters of the PTA are in Lusaka, Zambia.

9.9.4 Central America and the Caribbean

Caribbean Community and Common Market (CARICOM)
CARICOM was founded in 1973 as a successor to the Caribbean Free Trade Association, as a vehicle for increasing economic co-operation and reducing trade barriers in the area. Its members include Antigua and Barbuda, Grenada, Guyana, Jamaica,

Montserrat, St Kitts-Nevis, St Lucia, St Vincent and the Grenadines and Trinidad and Tobago. The headquarters of CARICOM are at Georgetown, Guyana.

Central American Common Market (CACM)
The CACM is roughly the mainland equivalent of CARICOM. It was founded in 1961 with similar objectives and its members include Costa Rica, Guatemala, Honduras, Nicaragua and El Salvador. Its headquarters are in Guatemala City.

Organisation of Central American States (ODECA)
ODECA was founded in 1951 for the purpose of strengthening unity in Central America and fostering economic, political and social co-operation, with a view to avoiding overdependence on the United States and its dominance in the Organisation of American States (OAS). ODECA's membership includes Costa Rica, Guatemala, Honduras, El Salvador and Nicaragua. Its headquarters are in San Salvador.

9.9.5 South America

The Amazon Pact
The Amazon Pact is a treaty signed in 1978 by Bolivia, Brazil, Colombia, Ecuador, Guyana, Peru, Suriname and Venezuela to protect and control the development of the Amazon River.

9.9.6 Asia

South Asian Association for Regional Co-operation (SAARC)
Established in 1985 to foster co-operation between Bangladesh, Bhutan, India, Maldives, Nepal, Pakistan and Sri Lanka.

9.9.7 Oceania

South Pacific Commission (SPC)
The SPC was established by an agreement signed in Canberra, Australia, in 1947, with the object of encouraging economic and social co-operation in the region. Its members include most of the

states in Oceania, including the dependencies, plus France, the United Kingdom and the United States, who are involved because of their past and present interests in the region. The headquarters of the Commission are in Nouméa, New Caledonia.

South Pacific Forum (SPF)
The SPF was created in 1971, as an offshoot of the SPC, to provide an opportunity for member-states to discuss common interests and develop common policies. The membership includes Australia, Cook Islands, the Federated States of Micronesia, Fiji, Kiribati, the Marshall Islands, Nauru, New Zealand, Niue, Papua New Guinea, Solomon Islands, Tonga, Tuvalu, Vanuatu and Western Samoa. In 1985 the Forum adopted a treaty for creating a nuclear-free zone in the Pacific.

South Pacific Bureau for Economic Co-operation (SPEC)
SPEC was founded in 1973, following a meeting of the SPF, as a practical scheme for stimulating economic co-operation and the development of trade. The headquarters of SPEC are in Suva, Fiji.

9.10 Military Co-operation

The examples of global, inter-regional and intra-regional co-operation described above are generally positive and peaceful in character. However, the world is still filled with distrust and insecurity and, because of this, a number of military pacts and organisations have been established to provide what states and regions see as vital defences against possible aggression. The hopeful signs are that nations, and groups of nations, are beginning to talk more openly with one another, across the barriers that schemes of military co-operation inevitably create.

North Atlantic Treaty Organisation (NATO)
NATO was established under the North Atlantic Treaty of 1949, which was signed by Belgium, Canada, Denmark, France, Iceland, Italy, Luxembourg, the Netherlands, Norway, Portugal, the United Kingdom and the United States. It is a mutual defence treaty by which it was agreed that 'an armed attack against one or more in Europe or North America shall be considered an attack against all'. Greece and Turkey joined the organisation in 1952, West Germany was admitted in 1955 and Spain in 1982. France withdrew from the organisation, but not the alliance, in 1966,

Greece withdrew politically, but not militarily, in 1974, and its re-entry was opposed by Turkey in 1980.

NATO's supreme body is the Council of Foreign Ministers of all the participating nations and its secretariat is based in Brussels, where there is also a Military Committee composed of the chiefs of staff of the member countries. The military headquarters, Supreme Headquarters Allied Powers, Europe (SHAPE), is at Chièvres, near Mons, in Belgium. The two Supreme Allied Commanders, Europe and Atlantic are US military officers and the Allied Commander, Channel is a British Admiral. In 1960 it was agreed to form a permanent, multi-national unit, called the Allied Mobile Force (AMF), to move immediately to any NATO country which appeared to be under threat. This mobile unit is based in Heidelberg, in West Germany.

NATO was originally formed to oppose a threat from the Soviet Union and its Warsaw Pact satellites and, although it has remained the keystone of Western defence for more than 40 years, relations between its members have not always been harmonious. The main areas of contention have been the degree of US dominance, the presence of nuclear weapons on European soil and the respective levels of contribution by signatories to the organisation's upkeep. The changed climate created by the new Gorbachev regime in the Soviet Union has added another dimension to NATO's role and to future attitudes within the alliance.

Western European Union (WEU)
The WEU is based on the Brussels Treaty of 1948 and was established in 1955 as a forum for the discussion of defence issues by West European governments. Its members include Belgium, France, West Germany, Italy, Luxembourg, the Netherlands and the United Kingdom, and, since 1989, Portugal and Spain. There is an Assembly which meets twice yearly in Paris, and sometimes in the Hague, and a Council, consisting of the foreign ministers of the member-states, which normally meets quarterly. The Union is pledged, under its charter, to work closely with NATO. It has a permanent secretariat based in London, but there has been pressure from the British government to locate both the Assembly and the Secretariat in Brussels. Other EC members, who are not also in the WEU, are sometimes invited to attend Assembly meetings as observers.

Warsaw Treaty of Friendship, Co-operation and Mutual Assistance—The Warsaw Pact

On 14 May 1955 Albania, Bulgaria, Czechoslovakia, East Germany, Hungary, Poland, Romania and the Soviet Union signed a 20-year treaty of friendship and collaboration, in Warsaw, which became known as the Warsaw Pact. Under the terms of the treaty, the eight states are pledged to a policy of mutual defence, an attack on one being regarded as an attack on all. It was also agreed that there should be a joint command for their armed forces. Albania ceased to be an active member in 1962 and formally withdrew in 1968.

The Treaty's organisation includes a Political Consultative Committee (PCC), a Committee of Defence Ministers, a Military Council, a Technical Committee, a Committee of Foreign Ministers and a Joint Command. The headquarters are in Moscow.

With the end of the 'Cold War' between East and West, both NATO and the Warsaw Pact are likely to assume less military and more political roles and their eventual fusion into a full European mutual defence organisation is not inconceivable.

Recommended Reading

Commonwealth Year Book (annual), HMSO.

Europa World Year Book, Vol 1, Part 1 (annual), Europa Publications.

Bulmer, S. and Wessels, W., *European Council*, Macmillan, 1987.

International Year Book and Statesmen's Who's Who (annual), Reed Information Services Ltd.

Archer, C., *Organizing Western Europe*, Edward Arnold, 1990.

Daltrop, A., *Politics and the European Community*, Longman, 1986.

Crouch, C. and Marquand, D. (eds), *The Politics of 1992: Beyond the Single European Market*, Basil Blackwell, 1990.

Year Book of the United Nations (annual), United Nations.

Chapter 10

1989 . . . AND AFTER

10.1 The Year of Revolution: 1989

The year 1989 was one of political revolution unprecedented in its scale and repercussions and likely to be viewed in retrospect as more significant than the revolutionary years of 1789, 1848 and 1911.

Before 1989 the political systems of the countries of Eastern Europe seemed set in stone. By 1990 most had moved from monism to pluralism and the barrier between East and West, graphically described in 1946 by Winston Churchill as an 'iron curtain', had been lifted.

It is now evident that the apparently solid structure of the Soviet empire, which had been built up by Josef Stalin during and after the Second World War, was more fragile than many had supposed. Yet, behind the imposing façade of the Soviet Union, its satellite states and its advocates and imitators all over the world, this was the reality.

Bulgaria, Czechoslovakia, East Germany, Hungary, Poland were not as 'reluctantly content' with their lot within the Soviet empire as had been popularly thought. Albania and Yugoslavia had already displayed their independent natures in different ways but still subscribed to a form of one-party communism. Inside the Soviet Union itself there was simmering discontent by frustrated nations within a nation, the Baltic states, Byelorussia, the Ukraine and Moldavia.

All this potentially damaging discontent had for decades been kept in check by the use, or threat of the use, of the military might controlled from Moscow.

East Germany had shown its dissatisfaction as early as 1953, after the death of Stalin. The Poles voiced their opposition in 1956 and in the same year Soviet tanks put down an insurrection in Hungary. The quest for freedom by East Germans was frustrated in 1961 by the building of the Berlin Wall, and the possibility of some liberalisation within the Soviet Union itself was destroyed by the ousting of Nikita Khrushchev in 1964. And yet the discontent continued to simmer. The Spring uprising in Czechoslovakia in 1968 was squashed and the growth of the Polish industrial-political movement, Solidarity, was met, in 1981, by the imposition of martial law.

Meanwhile, subtle, but significant, changes were taking place in the Soviet Union itself. The 18-year reign of Khrushchev's successor, Leonid Brezhnev, had become progressively static and corrupt and when he died, in 1982, the leadership battle was won by a much more agile-minded politician, Yuri Andropov. Already in ailing health at the time of his accession, Andropov sought to build up a cadre of younger, like-minded, potential successors. One of these 'new men' was the 51-year-old Mikhail Gorbachev. Andropov died of his long-standing illness in 1984 and his successor, Konstantin Chernenko, enjoyed only marginally better health. He too died within a year and the new generation of Soviet leaders, in the person of Gorbachev, assumed power.

Gorbachev represented, as far as the West was concerned, the opening of a completely new chapter in superpower relations. He was a man whom even the arch enemies of communism, Ronald Reagan and Margaret Thatcher, thought they 'could do business with'.

When, soon after his accession to power in 1985, Gorbachev made it evident that he was seeking a new relationship between the Soviet Union and its satellites, a relationship built on the expression, rather than the suppression, of their differences, the message was clear for the advocates of pluralist democracy throughout Eastern Europe.

First Hungary, in May 1989, then Poland, East Germany, Czechoslovakia, Bulgaria and eventually Romania: the monolithic, and often despotic, regimes which had been tolerated for more than 40 years suddenly collapsed like a house of cards, while the rest of the world watched in fascinated bewilderment.

The seemingly impossible had happened and the ripples which these momentous changes had produced on the apparently placid lake of authoritarian politics continued to spread.

10.2 Why did 1989 Happen?

Mikhail Gorbachev was the fuse which set off the explosion. Why did he choose to assume this role? The reasons must have been partly philosophical but mainly economic.

He realised, as some of his predecessors and contemporaries also did, that the national economy was in a perilous state. Although the Soviet Union had the technology to compete with the United States in space exploration and arms acquisition, it was unable to provide a standard of living for its own people remotely equivalent to that enjoyed by most Western nations. The Brezhnev doctrine of supporting revolutions in the developing world, and underpinning communist regimes such as that in Cuba, was draining the country of vital resources which the centrally-planned economic system Gorbachev had inherited could not replenish.

He not only recognised the need for new relationships with the neighbours that the Soviets had formerly dominated, but also the necessity of loosening the planning straightjacket which was inhibiting efficiency and stifling enterprise within his own country.

At first he attempted a speeding-up process, *uskorenie*, but soon concluded that nothing short of a radical restructuring, *perestroika*, would be sufficient. As a means of creating greater individual enterprise and self-reliance to support *perestroika*, he also embarked on a policy of greater political openness, *glasnost*. These became the two keywords which were to epitomise the Gorbachev era.

The concept of *perestroika* raised popular expectations that the Soviet economy could not speedily fulfil and the policy of *glasnost* allowed people's disillusionment to be expressed in outbursts of disillusionment from politicians and citizens alike. However, it was a process which, once embarked upon, was virtually irreversible.

Dissatisfaction with the failure of the economy to meet expectations raised by *perestroika* was also expressed in individualistic sentiments among the mixed collection of nations which comprised the Union of Soviet Republics.

10.3 The Future of Communism

Probably the most striking outcome of the events of 1989 has been the casting of doubt on the whole philosophy on which communism was built. It is almost as if the Christian communities had suddenly come to the conclusion that Jesus Christ had never really existed and that the concept of a universal, all-powerful God was just a myth.

In Chapter 3 we set out the four distinguishing characteristics of communist states: the adoption of Marxist-Leninism, or a variant of it, as the official ideology; state ownership and central planning; the dominance of the Communist Party; and the all-pervasiveness of that party.

All these four tenets have now been abandoned by virtually all the former Soviet satellite states, while the Soviet Union itself, although wishing to end central planning, has been reluctant to discard formally Marxism-Leninism or the commanding role of the Communist Party. How long it can retain these features while seeking to acquire the benefits of a market economy remains to be seen.

Paradoxically, China has pursued its own brand of economic *perestroika* but, at the same time, maintained, and even tightened, the party's control of the political system. This has, however, been achieved at great cost in individual freedoms, as the victims of the repressive measures following the 1989 pro-democracy demonstrations have testified. Communism, then, can still be maintained in a more liberal economic environment, even in the face of opposition, if the political leaders are willing to use the full power of the state to enforce their will.

Of the other six states listed as communist in Table 6, only Cuba seems determined to abjure any form of liberalisation and is willing to face the resulting international isolation.

Whatever happens, it is unlikely that the speed of change in any of the currently classified communist countries will be of the order that was witnessed in Europe in 1989 and 1990.

10.4 The Future of the Nation State

Between 1989 and 1990 a new nation state, Namibia, was recognised while two formerly divided countries united: East and West Germany and North and South Yemen. It is possible that before this century is over the process of reunification will have proceeded further, North and South Korea being obvious candidates.

At the same time, there is also the likelihood of some federal systems breaking down, or becoming a much looser amalgam than at present. The Soviet Union is a prime example of this likely development, with the Baltic states being the first to achieve some form of independence and other republics possibly following. Of the federal states listed in Table 2, Yugoslavia seems the other nation which might eventually dissemble itself.

As people with diverse ethnic and cultural origins wish to express their independence as separate nations, there is evidence of others willing to surrender some national pride for the benefits of membership of a wider political grouping. Although a United States of Europe is, at present, not viewed as a credible proposition by most European political leaders, there are some who see it as a target to achieve. Whatever the pace of change, it is certain that primarily economic forces will push the current twelve members of the European Community ever closer together politically.

10.5 The Future for International Co-operation

In Chapter 9 we describe the principal areas and institutions of international co-operation. Changes in this direction can also be expected within the forthcoming decades.

Already a queue has formed for EC membership, with Austria, Cyprus, Malta, Sweden and Turkey waiting in line, and even Finland and Switzerland may possibly follow Sweden's lead and be prepared to relinquish their traditional stance of neutrality in exchange for the benefits of joining. Looking further afield, the six newly-liberalised nations of Eastern Europe seem anxious to follow East Germany's lead, but there would have to be drastic improvements in their economies before this dream could become a reality.

As we have already suggested in Chapter 9, the fate of the Warsaw Pact and NATO organisation seems also to be in the melting pot. When the end of the Cold War seems a permanent reality, then the proposition by Czech President, Vaclav Havel, that they should merge into a pan-European mutual defence system might be feasible.

During these recent years of momentous change the enhanced role of the United Nations Organisation is encouraging. Under its energetic and competent Secretary-General, Señor Perez de Cuellar, it has successfully intervened in long-standing disputes in Southern Africa and the Middle East, and its standing is higher now than it has been for many years. We should also note its role in the Gulf conflict.

10.6 The Future Pattern of Voting Systems

In Chapter 6 we examined different electoral patterns and noted that 93 states currently use the simple plurality (SP) voting system. However, it is probably fair to say that few, if any, countries adopting new constitutions would choose that method for electing their assemblies. The drawbacks to the system are apparent in UK elections, as Table 31 shows. Consequently, it is not just fortuitous that all the newly-pluralised states of Eastern Europe have adopted some form of proportional representation (PR).

In those countries where SP voting persists the demand for change varies. There is no strong PR lobby in the United States or India, the two largest democracies using SP, and in the United Kingdom only the minor parties have adopted electoral reform as part of their policy programmes. However, there is growing support within the British Labour Party and much will depend on the outcome of the next general election. Either of the major parties could, pragmatically see it as advantageous to make a change, or a 'hung parliament' could force PR on a minority or coalition government which might emerge from the elections.

10.7 The Future Pattern of Executives

Unless there is a sudden urge to resurrect the discarded monarchies of Europe and introduce forms of parliamentary government on the British model, it seems likely that the executives of future liberal and emergent democracies will be of the limited presidential form. Indeed, the 35 states which in 1989 were identified as having such an executive system had risen to 53 by 1990. All the former Soviet satellites, for example, have adopted it. The dual executives which currently operate arose out of conditions peculiar to a particular country's history and development, and the number of unlimited presidential executives will, of course, diminish as pluralist political systems grow.

10.8 The Growth of Liberal Democracy

As recently as 1989 it was possible to identify only 82 states in the world which displayed the basic characteristics of liberal democracy. By the end of 1990 that number had grown to 101 and the process seems likely to continue.

Does this mean that a liberal democratic political system, as we have defined it in Chapter 3, is the model which, eventually, the whole world will follow?

No political system is perfect and this is as true of liberal democracy as any other government based on an alternative ideology. Built on the concept of a pluralistic society, in economic terms it inevitably places greater emphasis on market forces than monistic systems do. But market forces can, in social and individual terms, work unfairly and it would be foolish to think that everyone would flourish in a fully capitalist economy.

The advantage of socialism, in its purest form, is that it recognises, and compensates for, natural, individual inequalities. Thus the Soviet system, for example, guaranteed state-provided housing, transport, health and education for all, albeit in the first two cases at lower levels than most people would tolerate in the West.

A market economy, on the other hand, at its extreme, is based on 'the survival of the fittest', with little account taken of individual frailties.

Despite these limitations, the march of liberal democracy now seems inexorable. The 26 military authoritarian and absolutist regimes, listed in Tables 9 and 10, will surely, in time, disappear. In the case of the Middle East and North Africa, the Gulf conflict may well be the trigger to set the process in motion.

Since man is imperfect, the political systems he invents are imperfect. Nevertheless we are now faced with a challenge which politicians all over the world should accept. How to combine the best elements of socialism with the best elements of liberal democracy? Some Western European nations are showing the way but none has yet achieved the perfect blend.

Recommended Reading

Brzezinski, Z., *The Grand Failure: the Birth and Death of Communism in the 20th Century*, Macdonald, 1989.

Fukuyama, F., 'The End of History' in *National Interest* (National Affairs Inc), Irving Kristol, 1990.

Hawkes, N. (ed), *Tearing Down the Curtain*, Hodder & Stoughton, 1990.

Sword, K. (ed), *The Times Guide to Eastern Europe*, Times Books, 1990.

APPENDIX

DATA SOURCES

Bogdanor, V. (ed), *The Blackwell Encyclopedia of Political Institutions*, Basil Blackwell, 1987.

Chambers World Gazetteer: An A-Z of Geographical Information, Chambers & Cambridge University Press, 1988.

Day, A. J. and Degenhardt, H. W., *Political Parties of the World: a Keesing's Reference Publication*, 2nd edn., Longman, 1987.

Delury, G. E. (ed), *World Encyclopedia of Political Systems*, Vols I-III, Facts on File, 1987.

The Economist (weekly), London

The Economist, *World Atlas of Elections*, The Economist Publications, 1987.

The Economist, *World Human Rights Guide*, The Economist Publications, 1986.

Europa Publications: *A World Survey* (annual).
Africa South of the Sahara Yearbook (annual).
Western Europe—A Political and Economic Survey.
The Far East and Australasia.
The Middle East and North Africa.
South America, Central America and the Caribbean.

Facts on File.

Financial Times (daily), London.

Guardian (daily), London.

The Hutchinson Encyclopedia, 9th edn., Hutchinson, 1990.

Independent (daily), London.

Information Please Almanac: Atlas and Yearbook, 1987, Houghton Mifflin, 1987.

ITN Factbook, Michael O'Mara Books Ltd, London (annual).

Keesing's Record of World Events (monthly), London.

Kidron, M. and Segal, R., *The New State of the World Atlas*, revised 1st edn., Pan Books, 1987.

Kurian, G. T., *Encyclopedia of the Third World*, Vols I-III, 3rd edn., Mansell Publishing Ltd., 1987.

Kurian, G. T., *The New Book of World Rankings*, Facts on File, 1985.

Mackie, T. T. and Rose, R., *International Almanac of Electoral History*, new edn., Macmillan, 1982.

Minority Rights Group Reports, MRG.

Newsweek (weekly).

Observer (weekly), London.

Segal, G. *Guide to the World Today*, Simon & Schuster, 1987.

South (monthly), South Publications.

Statesman's Yearbook (annual), Macmillan.

Sunday Times (weekly), London.

Taylor, C. L. and Jodice, D. A. A., *World Handbook of Political and Social Indicators*, Vols 1 and 2, 3rd edn., Yale University Press, 1983.

Time Magazine (weekly).

The Times (daily), London.

United Nations, *Statistical Yearbook* (annual).

The World Almanac and Book of Facts (annual).

The World Bank, *World Development Report*, Oxford University Press, 1987.

Yearbook of International Organisations, München.

INDEX

INDEX

European Court of Justice, 221, 222
European Parliament, 219–21
European Court of Human Rights, 222
European Economic Community (EEC), 217, 218, 222, 223
European Investment Fund, 217
European Organisation for Nuclear Research (CERN), 224
European Space Agency (ESA), 223
executives
  absolute, 76–9
  communist, 66–9
  dual, 61–5
  limited presidential, 56–61
  military, 73–6
  parliamentary, 52–6
  permanent, 52
  political, 52, 80–2
  relations with assemblies, 103–5
  unlimited presidential, 69–73
Eyadema, Gnassingbe, 70

F
Falkland Islands, 188
Faroe Islands, 182
federalism, 17–25
Federated States of Micronesia, 188
Finland
  dual executive in, 63–4
fixed list system *see* voting systems
flexible list system *see* voting systems
'Flick Scandal', 105
France
  Collectivités Territoriales, 183
  constitution of, 15
  dependencies, 182–4
  Départements d'Outre-Mer, 183
  dual executive in, 61–3
  election turnouts in, 120
  Internal Collective Territory, 184
  political parties, 166
  second ballot voting in, 114
  staggered assembly membership in, 98
  Territoires d'Outre-Mer, 183

G
Gabon
  judiciary in, 26
Gaddafi, Muammar *see* Kadhafi

Gadhafi, Muammar *see* Kadhafi
GATT *see* General Agreement on Tariffs and Trade
General Agreement on Tariffs and Trade (GATT), 202
General Postal Union, 201
Germany
  federalism in, 21
Gibraltar, 188
Gorbachev, Mikhail, 41
Greenland, 182
Guam, 189

H
Helsinki Accord, 208–9
Hobbes, Thomas, 48
Hong Kong, 188
Hot Springs Conference, 199

I
ideologies
  classification of, 33
  future of, 49–50
  nature of, 31–3
India
  federalism in, 21–2
  staggered assembly membership, 98
Inter-American Development Bank (IADB), 215
International Atomic Energy Agency (IAEA), 198
International Bank for Reconstruction and Development (World Bank) (IBRD), 200–1
International Civil Aviation Organisation (ICAO), 201
International Development Association (IDA), 201
International Finance Corporation (IFC), 201
International Fund for Agricultural Development (IFAD), 203
International Labour Organisation (ILO), 199
International Maritime Organisation (IMO), 202
International Meteorological Organisation, 202
International Monetary Fund (IMF), 200